THE OAKEN HEART

To the children of
St. Nicholas Primary School, Tolleshunt D'Arcy
and their ancestors.

St. Nicholas Primary School in the 1930s.
(Alan Smith)

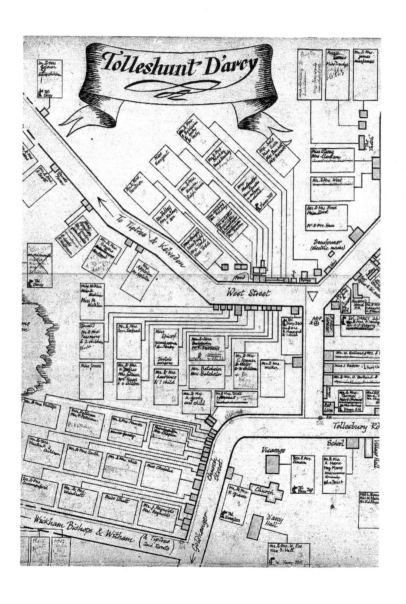

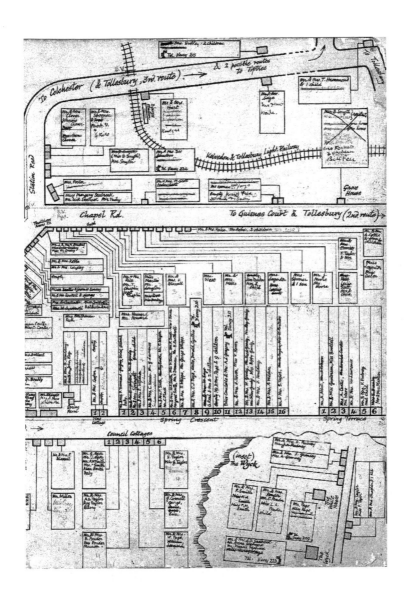

Notes on contributors:

RONALD BLYTHE is one of the country's leading rural observers and writers. His best-known book is *Akenfield: portrait of an English Village* (1969), which was made into a film by Peter Hall in 1974. *The Age of Illusion* (1963), *The View in Winter* (1979), *Divine Landscapes* (1986) and his Wormingford Diary in the *Church Times* are some of the highlights amongst the wealth of essays, short stories, poetry, novels, literary criticism and social history that has poured from his pen. In *Private Words* (1991) he edited a selection of letters and diaries from the Second World War. Ronald Blythe is a Fellow of the Royal Society of Literature and a Doctor of Letters from Anglia Ruskin University. He was educated in Sudbury, Suffolk and worked as a reference librarian in Colchester, Essex, just ten miles from Tolleshunt D'Arcy. He was in East Anglia throughout the Second World War. Ronald Blythe's most recent book, *Aftermath* (2010), is a selection from fifty years of his writing life.

JULIA JONES is the author of *The Adventures of Margery Allingham* and the editor of Philip Allingham's autobiography, *Cheapjack*. She plans to complete the series with *Fifty Years in the Fiction Factory: the working life of Herbert Allingham* (1867-1936).

LESLEY SIMPSON is the technical director of this project. Her skills in turning wartime paper from brown to white and making tiny, faded photos newly visible after seventy years may appear magical to the uninitiated. She is also the web mistress and membership secretary for the Margery Allingham Society (www.margeryallingham.org.uk).

Right: Master craftsmen Jack and Norry Emeny.
(Jack Birkin)

MARGERY ALLINGHAM

*

The Oaken Heart

Foreword by Ronald Blythe

Introduction by Julia Jones

GOLDEN DUCK

First published in 1941 by Michael Joseph Ltd.

This edition published in 2011 by
Golden Duck (UK) Ltd.,
Sokens,
Green Street,
Pleshey, near Chelmsford,
Essex
CM3 1HT

www.golden-duck.co.uk

Foreword © Ronald Blythe 2011

Introduction and Notes © Julia Jones 2011

Margery Allingham's diaries and letters © The Margery Allingham Society
http://www.margeryallingham.org.uk

ISBN 978-1-899262-03-8

Cover design by Roger Davies
rogerdaviesdesign@btinternet.com

Printed and bound in the UK by
Berforts Information Press Ltd.

Foreword

The fascination of *The Oaken Heart* lies in its immediacy. There are countless histories, official and local, of those strange months when these islands expected to be invaded after the fall of France, but most of them are retrospective. Many diaries give vivid day-by-day experiences nevertheless it was an American publisher who, seeing the unfolding of a vast drama, believed that a young novelist, whose stories were set in accurate descriptions of ordinary English village life, should describe these events as they occurred. Time was of the essence. Hitler was at the gates.

And so the thirty-six year old Margery Allingham put aside her latest Campion whodunit, placing it in a biscuit tin for safety, and wrote this astonishing book. It was published to great acclaim in 1941. In the writing of it she soon found that not only did she have to deal with the problem of revealing her rural neighbours as actual people, and not as 'characters', but also face up to the person she really was behind the comfortable privacy which class and literary success gave her. She emerges as what was then called a 'modern' young woman with Christian Socialist values, as well as a professional author. And *The Oaken Heart* reflects her truthfulness on every page. Her only fantasy, as it were, is to give her bit of Essex transparent names, calling her own village after Oliver Goldsmith's 'sweet Auburn'.

This play with Essex coastal geography apart, her eye is fixed on reality. Tremendous happenings such as the Battle of Britain, Dunkirk, the Blitz etc. are kept within the comprehension of a farming community as it was at the time. Her set pieces are the hugger-mugger situations of wartime, the uncomfortable throwing together of people of all backgrounds and ages, the drab days, the dreadful 'cheerfulness', the suppression of fear, the weariness and the sheer goodness of folk. Being young, she is often a bit wild and funny, and now and then almost out of a novel herself.

For us readers seventy years hence *The Oaken Heart* is more
delightfully readable as an often-enchanting autobiography than as
world war two history. Margery Allingham is, mercifully, no 'Mrs
Miniver', that paragon of British womanhood, and she saves the
conventional patriotism and morality of the period to the last
page. Her strengths are those of a professional storyteller and of
an honest soul. She sees, she watches, she misses nothing. Commissioned to write the kind of book which ordinarily would not
have crossed her mind, she does her very best. The result is
unusual and pleasurable, informative and surprising.

RONALD BLYTHE

The Street, Tolleshunt D'Arcy.

Contents

Left: Church Street.
(Alan Smith)

Right: The station.
(Alan Smith)

Left: The Thatcher's Arms.
(Footsteps Photographs)

Right: Cliff Otway's
cottage.
(Alan Smith)

List of Illustrations

Unless otherwise stated, all illustrations are reproduced by kind permission of The Margery Allingham Society. Their archive is held in the Albert Sloman Library, University of Essex. We are also very grateful to the families of the people of *The Oaken Heart* who lent their precious photos and to the various website owners for their assistance.

Introduction to the Fourth Edition

The first edition of Margery Allingham's *The Oaken Heart* was rushed out in the summer of 1941. It had been sent to the printers by its delighted publisher, Robert Lusty, almost as soon as it had been received. The official censor took out some detail about unexploded mines and the extent of bomb damage but otherwise it went to press as it was, proof-read but unedited, except by Allingham herself. In some respects this may have been a pity. At this stage in her career Allingham had developed a routine for the completion of her detective novels. She read sections to her husband, Pip Youngman Carter, as she wrote. They discussed plot twists and she noted his comments even if she didn't always act on them. (Pip was also the only person she would allow to correct her spelling.) When a novel was ready for its final draft it would be dictated aloud and at speed to their friend Grog (Joe Gregory). This ensured that sentences flowed easily and that anything that was not immediately clear could be amended. After the war Margery's practice changed but throughout the 1930s this had been the way she was used to working and it had been successful. When *The Oaken Heart*, her first and only non-fiction book, was finished in May 1941, Pip was away, waiting to be posted abroad, and even Grog was about to 'give himself up' to the recruiting officers. Margery had completed the first draft in three months, October to December 1940 – whilst simultaneously carrying out her local A.R.P. (Air Raid Precautions), billeting officer and First Aid duties. 'Queer stuff but very honest,' she commented in January 1941 when she pulled it out again for its final revision.

The unedited quality of *The Oaken Heart* is both its strength and its weakness. Margery conceived it, as she says in her preface, as a letter. A long letter to her American publishing friends, written partly to explain the British situation, partly also to assist the campaign to persuade America to abandon isolation and join the war. The book achieved only limited success, as far as America was concerned. The beauty of a letter is its immediacy, authenticity, its personal voice: its impediment can be obscurity, particularly when it is filled with local and family allusions. Margery was aware of this and laboured, sometimes too diligently, to explain herself to her potential U.S. readers. The unique value of *The Oaken Heart*, however, as Ronald Blythe points out, lies in the many passages where she records day-by-day happenings exactly as they occurred – emotions, reflections, family allusions and all. In Britain in 1941, when so many other people were sharing similar extraordinary experiences, *The Oaken Heart* was an immediate success. There were no problems with obscurity then.

In 1959, when Margery and Pip worked together on a new edition, a few explanations were added as well as a new cover design, some illustrations and the signatures of fifty-eight of the local people mentioned in the text. Otherwise *The Oaken Heart* stayed as it was, even down to the fictional names of the villages. As Margery explained, 'The names of the villages, which were altered originally for reasons of Security, have been left "disguised" to preserve their universal quality, for there was little about them that was different from thousands of others up and down the country in those tremendous times.' Once again the book sold well and this is the edition that is found in most Essex and older people's homes.

The third edition, published in 1987, and intended for that same generation – who might by then be in their eighties, as Margery and Pip would have been had they lived – was a well-meant mistake. I was running a small bookshop in an Essex village and was experimenting with publishing some local-interest titles in a larger-than-normal type size. This worked better for some books than others and, for *The Oaken Heart*, not well at all. The whole venture was run on a shoestring and the then technical requirements of small-scale publishing involved me sitting up late into the night after a day's work at the shop re-typing the text on a BBC

'B' computer to save on typesetting costs. There were no effective scanners then and the errors I introduced and the ugliness of my chosen 'clear type' make me shudder. The project was redeemed only by a delightful reading on BBC *Woman's Hour* by Joan Hickson (celebrated for her performances as Agatha Christie's Miss Marple) and by the friendship of Joyce Allingham, Margery's sister, who supplied a key to the village names.

This fourth edition is intended to do rather more than rectify the errors of the third. Margery Allingham was born in 1904. In 1939 she and her peers, those who had been children in the First World War, were in their early middle age, in the full flood of their careers, when their peaceable lives were shattered by the Second War. Those people have now gone. Men and women who were children and teenagers at that time can still tell us of their experiences and, for this edition, they have done so. The intended audience for this fourth edition, seventy years after first publication, is those of us who were not born then. It is a cliché to say that we need to remember the struggle and sacrifice of our parents, grand-parents, great-grandparents but it is nevertheless true. Particularly as we become more aware of all those who have suffered post-traumatic stress belatedly in the last years of their lives.

Nevertheless this does not entirely answer the question: why read *The Oaken Heart* now? There have been so many accounts and memoirs – some more searing, better-informed, more inspirational or extraordinary. What is it that makes *The Oaken Heart* 'astonishing' whilst also, admittedly, imperfect? There can be no one better qualified than the author of *Akenfield* to use this word. *The Oaken Heart* is the picture of a rural community deeply shaken by events completely beyond its control, which threaten its very existence and identity. 'We can't have they here, no, no.' The 1940 threat of invasion, as Allingham shrewdly points out, brought out many of the same parochial qualities that might cause people to band together to oppose the closure of a village school, for instance, or, more frequently nowadays to oppose some commercial or housing development. These are not necessarily admirable or attractive qualities. Nevertheless, 'A people who really will die for freedom, and have done so in vast numbers at intervals over a thousand years, must reasonably be supposed to struggle, quarrel, sulk and otherwise live for it also.' Not the most elegant sentence Allingham ever wrote and some readers today might feel uncomfortable with the momentary glorification of race. But the idea of 'sulking for freedom' is characteristically perceptive, humorous and un-sentimental.

Both national pride and sentiment find expression in *The Oaken Heart* but the strength of the book lies in the clarity and sense of surprise with which Allingham observes herself acquiring these qualities. There is a moment in the village hall, for instance, when the assembled villagers are being instructed how to gasproof a room. Allingham's mind is 'running over the suitability of various old curtains on the top shelf of the linen cupboard' when she suffers a moment of imaginative horror. 'I saw that they were talking about a corrosive poison to be sprayed over one civilised people by what was presumed to be another. I wondered if we were all insane and so nearly squeaked aloud, as one does in nightmares sometimes, that I felt the blood rushing into my face with embarrassment.' She glances round, furtively, and sees 'all the well-known faces turned gravely towards the stage. There was Bill who had been through the last war and knew something about it, and Charlotte, Albert's wife, with her fine shrewd face and wildish yellow hair, and everyone else, all intensely serious, as they certainly would not have been had they not seen the horror of the situation quite as vividly as I had.' Bill Cottis was a thatcher; Charlotte Smith the wife of a local builder. Allingham draws strength from her neighbours and learns from them. 'It seemed to me that the sooner I wrenched my mind out of its present super-sensitive gear and got it back onto curtains like a reasonable being, the better.' Her process of self-discovery and observation of the mental 'hardening-up' that became necessary for survival continues throughout the book. When, later, she says that she is 'proud' to belong to the same race as Bill, Charlotte, Albert and the 'grim, conserved' Londoners, we can understand such a feeling then, in the winter of 1940 and the early spring of '41.

The 'corrosive poison' did not come but the bombs did. They fell on London nightly as Allingham wrote *The Oaken Heart* and the sights and sounds of distant destruction and death were visible from Tolleshunt D'Arcy as from many other villages. For this edition we have included Allingham's diaries for 1940-1941 and the letters she wrote to her sister Joyce in 1942. These offer an additional glimpse of everyday life in 'Auburn', a.k.a. Tolleshunt D'Arcy, the Essex village where Margery and Pip had lived since 1935. On 30th April 1940, for instance, her diary records, 'Heard terrific explosion about 11.15 (German plane coming down over Clacton) with bombs'. A German Heinkel plane crashed into a house in Clacton-on-Sea and blew up, causing the first deaths of British civilians in World War Two. Years earlier, when she and her family had lived just a few miles away in the village of Layer Breton, many of her neighbours had witnessed the blazing end of the Zeppelin airship at Little Wigborough, on 23rd September 1916, which marked the only capture of Germans on British soil in World War One. Dr Salter, her predecessor in D'Arcy House had kept a lump of that Zeppelin in his garage. Some of the most convincing passages in *The Oaken Heart* come as Allingham puts the child's experience alongside the adult's and uses it to illustrate the sense of connectedness that was one of her personal wartime discoveries.

Civilian connectedness in World War Two needed to be a pragmatic working-together rather than a sentimental or prideful quality. One of the most educational moments for me was when I came across the thick piles of Incident Reports, which have been preserved in the Essex Record Office. I had seen both from the text of *The Oaken Heart* and from Allingham's diaries how much time, effort and passion went into A.R.P. but it was not until I began leafing through the heaps of pencilled messages that I really grasped the hours of conscientious vigilance that those civilian volunteers had mustered. Not only in watching but searching in the darkness and across the lonely fields. Not a water main burst, not a sheep was killed on the marshes without the event being checked, double-checked and recorded in triplicate. Among the Tolleshunt D'Arcy Wardens were Cliff Otway, a chauffeur/handyman, Johnny Reynolds, a builder, Driffield Smyth, a fruit-farmer, as well as Allingham's artist friend 'Grog'. The Wardens' Post was in D'Arcy House.

Meg Bunting, daughter of the then head teacher of Tolleshunt D'Arcy Primary School, was in her teens and working as the second matron at Endsleigh House, a Colchester boarding school. At night she took her turn at voluntary fire-watching duties and remembers the morning she woke to find lumps of shrapnel embedded in all the trees along the school drive. She described the work of her father, Arthur Moore, in the Observer Corps, another group of volunteers, on watch against hostile aeroplanes, day after day, night after night. Arthur had been gassed in World War One and still suffered breathing difficulties; his brother had been killed. One of his regular companions at the Observer Corps lookout point, Charlie Flack, the Tolleshunt D'Arcy postman, had a crippled arm from the same war.

Allingham writes eloquently, if only in passing, of the terrible legacy of loss and sadness left by the Great War. The memorial on the wall of Tolleshunt D'Arcy church records twice as many deaths from WW1 as from WW2. What the 1939-45 conflict brought to the village was immediate moments of shock and fear ('The Germans are here, madam.') and practical domestic disruption. The chaotic arrival of the evacuees, for example, jolted people out of their expected attitudes. 'It was extraordinary. People who had no room, who loathed the idea of strangers, and who had declared in all honesty that, while they were prepared if

necessary to die for their country, they could not and would not
stomach a child in their house for ten minutes, came up to the
sunny playground with unwilling, conscience-driven steps, paused
at the doorway of the big school aghast, and then went in and
collected some weeping young mother and her infants and carried
them home with tight lips and grim eyes.' This did not, always,
result in a joyful meeting of hearts and minds between host and
guests. The gap between urban and rural life in 1939 was very
much greater than it is now and there was wide scope for mutual
incomprehension and disillusion.

Most of the evacuees soon went home: one who did not was
Doreen Humphries (née Pearson) whose family lived in Barking
and who was taken in by members of the Houlding family.
Doreen was ten when she arrived in D'Arcy. She did not come as
part of a school party but privately with her mother and younger
brother. They returned to Barking but Doreen stayed. She remembers the darkness and emptiness of the village after life in
the docklands suburb but also the kindness of her hosts, the
wholesome country cooking and the uncomplicated acceptance of
the other children in the village school. Margery Allingham,
encountered in the big house, sweeping into the room in a long
dark dress to sign Doreen's official forms, made a lasting impression on the little girl for her warm kindness as well as for her
imposing presence. Allingham, for her part, noted Doreen in her
diary as the only child to stay long enough to fill an entire page of
the billeting record.

Doreen married locally and has lived in the neighbourhood
ever since, as has Dorothy Houlding (Blyth), whose family came
originally from Clacton. In the early years of the war they had
moved to Burton-on-Trent, where they experienced the bombing of the northern industrial areas, before returning to Essex. As
a teenager Dorothy's first job was counting sweet coupons in the
Tolleshunt D'Arcy village shop. She too married locally. Other
village girls found romance with the troops who were billeted in

the area. Ruby Houlding met her husband (serving with the King's Own Scottish Borderers) when he was billeted at Guisnes Court, just outside the village. They married before he was posted abroad and then she moved with him to his home in Manchester when the war ended. Clara Dickenson (Smith) was less lucky. She, too, met and married a passing soldier but had only her single week's honeymoon before he was posted to Eygpt and almost immediately killed.   Nora Curtis, from the neighbouring parish of Tolleshunt Knights, married at eighteen and volunteered to work in the NAAFI cooking for the troops when her Tolleshunt D'Arcy husband, Harold, was posted away. This meant she could stay near him while he was still in England. By the time he was posted abroad she was pregnant. She came home to the family smallholding but their daughter was over two years old before she first met her father.

All these are ordinary stories which could be replicated in villages all over the country. They are not included in *The Oaken Heart* for the simple reason that, when Allingham handed it to her publisher, nobody knew how this chapter in their lives would end. Allingham described herself as writing it 'in the only way such an account can be written, as if every day might be my last.' The book doesn't really have an ending. Allingham finished correcting the second draft on the night Rudolph Hess made his puzzling solo flight into Scotland to try and negotiate a separate peace. In these final pages she expresses intense love of her home, pride at belonging to the same people as the bombed Londoners and amazement at living in this particular historic time. Suddenly there is a note of haste and emotionalism in the writing: a note that is not in accord with the rest of the book, nor with Allingham's life as it developed subsequently. The reader is left poised.

For this edition I have been able to ask some of the people in Tolleshunt D'Arcy for their own memories of this period and for factual information about the dozens of people mentioned in the book who are now dead. Where did they live, what did they do,

who did they marry? As one of the main virtues promoted by *The
Oaken Heart* is steadfastness – rootedness to home as well as to
beliefs – it's been fascinating to discover how many of the same
families still live in the village. Interesting, satisfying, but, judging
as a long-term Essex country dweller myself, not entirely surprising.

This edition is published in association with the Margery Allingham Society. Lesley Simpson, Jo Hesslewood and I had a particularly enjoyable day visiting Tolleshunt D'Arcy and meeting some
of the people who had been young in 1940. This was in addition
to the hours of time local people had already given in phone calls,
emails and checking facts with one another. We are especially
grateful (roughly in order of appearance) to Jack Birkin, school
governor and member of the Emeny family, Mick Lawrence and
his parents-in-law, John and Dorothy Houlding (Blyth), Neil
Cooper and his godmother Doreen Humphries (Pearson), Julia
Seabrook, Pippa Golding, Pauline Smith, Alan Smith and other
members of the Smith family. Susie Powell, grand-daughter of
Mr and Mrs Parker from Tollesbury, told a funny anecdote of
her grandfather who was so embarrassed to discover that Margery
Allingham had included his somewhat exaggerated account of
being made a King's Corporal in World War One that he
removed the page from the edition she gave him in 1941. His
family had to buy another copy before they discovered the truth.
Jim Burmby told me about his father, Chief Petty Officer Jim
Burmby, Meg Bunting (Moore) talked about her mother, the
headmistress, as well as her father, stalwart of the Observer Corps.
Nora Curtis, who had sixty-five years of happy marriage with her
husband, Harold, gave a vivid account of being a young wife in
wartime. One of the stories she told, of an unexploded bomb on
her parents' small holding in Tolleshunt Knights, chimed in beau-
tifully with the cluster of incidents that the Censor cut out of
Margery Allingham's typescript in May 1941. We have included
these as an Appendix.

This really is a community edition. Among those who have helped are Sophie Massey (head teacher of St Nicholas Primary School), Geoff Bayliss (vicar of Tolleshunt D'Arcy), Gloria Greci (Margery Allingham's secretary), Seona Ford (Essex Advisory Service and Dorothy L. Sayers Society), Roger Pickett (Essex Fire Museum), June Turner (Essex Book Festival), Nigel Cochrane (Albert Sloman Library, Essex University), Bob Cross, Thelma Goodman, Ann Brown, Sally Bidmead, Angela Bunting, Fred & Yvonne Diggle and staff at the Essex Record Office. Many people have provided photographs and are acknowledged in the list of illustrations. We are very grateful to them and apologise to anyone whom we have not succeeded in contacting.

Thanks to Tamsen Harward representing Chorion (owner of *The Oaken Heart* copyright) for her sympathetic response and to Barry Pike and the committee of the Margery Allingham Society (custodians of letters, maps, photographs, diaries and manuscripts) for supporting the project. The book's production team were almost all volunteers: Lesley Simpson, Jo Hesslewood, Diane Cullen, Heidi Carhart, Roger Davies and Francis Wheen. Ronald Blythe has been my literary hero for years so his unforced praise for *The Oaken Heart* was, in its words, a 'king-wonder'.

JULIA JONES

Left: Grog, P.Y.C., Margery and Cooee before the war.

Preface, Explanation and Dedication

Auburn House,
Auburn,
England.

My dear Auburn,

  You will want an explanation of this book and to hear how I came to write it about you.

  Last November an American whom some of you know asked me to put it down so that he and his wife and his village in America could gather exactly what life has been like down here for us ordinary country people during the war.

  It was a business request, and I have made an ultra-careful job of it, as you will see, because I believed that he and his friends are sufficiently (but by no means exactly) like us for it to be possible for me to convey to him much more of the actual truth than is usual on these occasions if I only approached the task without unnecessary reticence and with many explanations. Also the war is getting very close to them over there, and they may have to go through the same sort of experience themselves should the worst (for us) happen and our island fall. It is not a private attempt at propaganda, nor yet a disinterested gesture on my part. I have been employed as a professional writer by the American to tell him what he wants to know. However, I am convinced that it will be a good thing for us should a small portion of this other great people, so like us in the main and so unlike us in the particular, acquire through this history a little clearer picture of at least one minute corner of a country in the throes of the difficulties which ours is experiencing now. If I did not think this I would not have written the book, because I am loath to publicise our personal affairs.

  I am telling you all this because I want to explain why I have put in anything whatever that I thought might possibly help to make the picture clearer. I have not given away any war secrets naturally, and I have disguised the names and positions of all places, but I have not disguised your nicknames nor those in my own family. I have quoted everybody as accurately as I could and I have done my utmost best, using whatever art I possess, to put down as vividly as possible what I myself believe on soul and conscience to be true.

Some of you may not agree with me in everything, of course, but I notice that we usually seem to think much the same things about affairs, and I lived down the road as a child and learnt first things from your relations and neighbours. Therefore I have set aside self-consciousness and have gone on writing, thinking of nothing but telling the American and his wife the truth as I see it here.

I hope you will approve of my behaviour in the matter and will not be embarrassed by a certain baldness, a sort of lack of covering of the heart, which you will notice in the letter—for the book is really no more and no less than a letter to the American and his family.

Lying, they say, is a new modern art of the enemy's, but telling the truth is not easy. In fact, telling the truth is the basis of all classic art, which has always been notoriously difficult. However, I have done the best I can. I have not dwelt on one thing more than another, and I have tried to put everything in.

With all my love, and God bless you and take care of you,

MARGERY CARTER
(*née* Allingham)

D'Arcy House,
Tolleshunt D'Arcy.
Scraperboard by Youngman Carter

> *Auburn House,*
> *Auburn,*
> *England.*

My dear T. and M.,
    Here at last is the letter.

The first thing to remember about it is that it is local. *This may or may not be Britain—that I cannot tell you because I do not know—but it is Auburn, I think.*

You will see from my note to Auburn how I feel about that part of it and why I have had the thundering impudence to write it.

The reference to you two not being exactly like us you will understand even better than we do! You are warm people; we are cold people who have been warm and still have warmth in places. Our heart is old and hard and true still, in spite of surface rot. Yours is seven hundred years younger, more tender, and as true as you care to make it to the point of pure perfection. You will not mind my saying this, I know, because you probably feel it as much as I do.

My love and all good wishes always, whatever happens.

> *Yours ever,*
>
> MARGERY ALLINGHAM

Top: The newsagent's shop. *(Alan Smith)*
Upper left: The butcher's shop. *(Alan Smith)*
Upper right: The baker's shop.

Lower left: Guisnes Court.
Lower right: A. J. Braddy, boot and shoe maker. *(Alan Smith)*
Bottom: Hammond's shop and the forge.

1

THIS village of Auburn might be so complacently picturesque if it weren't for the shop which Albert and his father built of public washroom brick slap in the middle of the Square, that we owe the two of them a debt of gratitude if only for that alone.

The building brings the whole place down to earth, sobers it up and takes it out of fancy dress, so to speak.

Albert still maintains that it is a lovely shop. He and his father have always liked it; in fact they built it twice with their own hands. They had just got it up once in all its nakedness directly in front of one of the only two genuine maypoles in England when the Council came along and wanted the road wider, so Albert and his father pulled the shop down again, all two storeys of it, carefully, brick by brick, and set it up again once more fifteen feet or so further back, where it stands (at least at the time of writing) a visible sign that the village is not an old-fashioned musical comedy backcloth.

The maypole is not used as a maypole now, of course. There is nothing arty about the place, which is still agricultural. The pole, which is only a pole, has a weathercock on top of it, and at its foot, where one waits for the bus, grow two may-trees, one red and one white, which the Old Doctor and Mrs. Graves put there forty years ago when they were uncrowned kings of the village.

Behind the maypole there is Norry's forge, which has not been altered in the last hundred years at least and which looks like one of those very neat and restrained advertisement plates in big American magazines, the kind beneath which the copy begins "*In olden days fine craftsmen worked under difficulties . . .*" You never saw such ordered clutteredness, and when the fire is in full blast and he and his second eldest brother Jack (the Mycroft of the family) are at work there in their goatskin aprons, clinking and clanking on the largest anvil, which rings like a firebell all over the village, the effect, if they will forgive me for saying so, is quite extraordinarily reminiscent of the diamond mine scene in *Snow White*. This is especially true on a dark and windy autumn day, when the black clouds pile up over the low roof of red pantiles and there seems to be no horizon.

Reg's grocer's shop, the Auburn Stores, is in the Square too, and so is the Queen's Head, which stands back in its own yard with a great sign swinging on a rather nice post which the brewers put up.

The Post Office is next door to the Queen's, and it does look a little as if it had come off a toffee tin. It has bow windows with small panes, one of which has been taken out to let in a red tin letterbox, and at one time it must have been a very important shop. Auburn is perhaps a little like that; not degenerate or decaying, but "retired." Most of the medium-sized houses used to be shops in the days when the ten miles to the town meant ten miles on foot or astride. Norry says that when he was "a little owd boy" the man who had Reg's shop had five assistants, each with a clean white tablecloth apron every Monday morning, and it was "Forward One, please" and "Two, are you serving?" which sounds mightily impressive and, considering the size of the building, astonishing.

As well as the Queen's there are two other pubs, which is plenty, since there are only six hundred odd of us counting the outlying farms, and a large percentage of the population is elderly and stays at home. One of these inns, the Thatcher's, is kept by Norry's brother Jack and their two sisters, Miss Vic and Miss Susie, and there they've got the ham in the glass case. This ham was cured for the christening of one of Norry's uncles, but never cooked or eaten because of a word or two over Church or Chapel which delayed the ceremony indefinitely. The ham has been there for ninety years and has shrunken till it is no bigger than a brown leathery hand, which it resembles.

The Lion lies up at the other end of the village, on the way to the church. That's a very popular house, and was even more so before Cis joined the W.A.A.F.'s. There used to be another house called the Wheatsheaf, but the village sold the licence a long while ago and invested the money, so that since then we have been one of the few parishes in England which possess a little capital of their own. In our case this is not a large sum. It represents three or four thousand pounds at the outside, but it means that we have our own row of council houses up past the school, and it also means that we're not quite so beholden to the Rural District Council or even to the County Council as we might be. Parochially, we have money in our purse.

Our other public possessions include a railway, composed of one derailed coach (which quite recently contained a poster which enquired fatuously, "Why not winter in Prague?") and a very small train indeed which goes there and back in the morning and there and back at night. This train, or rather the line upon which it runs, and which links us with the main track five miles away in one direction and Flinthammock-on-Estuary one and a half in the other, was the subject of a tremendous battle in the 'eighties. Since then, what with the petrol engine and one thing and another, the Auburn Flyer has not been quite so important; but it still runs twice a day, a memorial to the public spirit, enterprise and unconquerable obstinacy of our grandparents in the wars of the council rooms.

It is a nice little train, with a high-pitched tootle and a fearsome tendency to rock like a boat in the high winds from over the saltings; but it is very useful indeed for freight too bulky for the Osborne family's buses, which are our main means of transport.

At the other end of the village, on the main Auburn–Flinthammock road, is the school. It is my honest opinion (and certainly speaking for myself) that most of us were so busy fighting to keep the school open that we completely missed the first rumblings of the war. That is the worst of a Cause. The more parochial and intimate it is the more absorbing it becomes. I notice M. Maurois, in his heart-rending *What Happened to France,* accuses the English of thinking so much of their little green lawns that they did not see the danger until too late. That is terribly true, except that it was not our lawns but our little evergreen liberties which engrossed us then as ever. To be really free takes a lot of time and trouble.

I think probably the first occasion that most of us in Auburn ever seriously considered the possibility of another European war in our time was one night when Mr. Vernon Bartlett came out with a sudden note of alarm in that chatty voice of his on the radio. The wireless is odd like that. It seems to do the same thing to a voice as an overbright light does to a face. Anything genuine leaps out at one. Anything false grates on one's nerves. I cannot remember the exact date of the talk, but it was when Germany left the League. The family was listening attentively because Charles Ulm was flying to Australia at the time, and he had been to see us, and so everyone was anxious to know if he was going to be all right. That broadcast on foreign affairs was the first of all the radio talks to turn our hearts over suddenly, although I don't honestly think it was fear of fighting or even dying which gave us that sudden chill inside. It was rather the first of the misgivings, the first hint that this new world which we were knocking together so fast, and wherein time and distance were so happily vanishing, might not produce the universal brotherhood after all, or at least not overnight. There was even a sneaking presentiment, I remember, that to know all might not be to forgive anything, and to live in proximity to the other nations might not be to live in harmony.

Unfortunately that incident was only a flicker of an eyelid, only a turning over in our sleep. I seem to think there was some sort of fuss about that talk. Anyhow, there certainly was a general piping down on the subject of war altogether after that.

Meanwhile we in Auburn had our school to think about. I do not want to convey that the entire village became absorbed in the school to the exclusion of everything else. It did not. But the thing I can only call its public mind did

become rather preoccupied with the subject for the best
part of two years before the war.

In a very small village the public mind is apparent. What the
village thinks is clear, definite, and usually highly important.
In the ordinary way most of us do not think a great deal about
national affairs, except as they concern us directly, but I have
noticed over and over again that when a national question
does at last begin to worry us to the point of provoking
open speech about it, then Parliament settles the matter in
double-quick time and in our way, as if it realised its job
depended on it. This puzzled me for a long time, until it
occurred to me that the explanation was obvious and was
simply that we were not the unique group of individuals
that we see ourselves but merely an echo, a reflection, of
thousands of other little rural communities, all thinking and
feeling the same thing, sometimes the wrong thing, with an
instinctive unity which must be pretty impressive when seen
from the middle.

Auburn felt strongly about the school. To be honest the
school is not very big—in fact it's about as big as the train—
and it lolls by the side of the road under enormous elms
and is warm and sunny and just exactly as hygienic as the
law demands, but no fancy-work. It was built by public
subscription in Auburn, and generations of Auburn people
have learnt to read and write and add there. Moreover,
what is highly important, they have also had a little religious
instruction there, since it is a Church School and not one
of the new-fangled places who, in order to avoid inter-
denominational strife, have thrown away the baby with the
bath water and done away with the Catechism and the
Ten Commandments altogether.

In common with most of my generation I would blush to
call myself deeply religious, but I do find it odd that as a
nation we will fight and die for principles which we cannot
find time to teach in our free schools. However, that is as
may be, and, as I was saying, about the time when Hitler
was thinking of taking over Austria there was a minority
movement in Auburn which aimed to shut the school for ever.

The senior children—that is, those over eleven—were already bundled off to the town every morning and brought home at night in a special bus, and the argument was that since there were only twenty-odd babies left it seemed unnecessary to keep two schoolma'ams to look after them and that they might as well go into the town with their elders. The new arrangement was made somewhat perfunctorily, and the school was marked for closing.

Auburn's reaction was prompt and indignant. It was the same sort of reaction which you might get if you took a very old hat away from a dotard snoozing in the sun, with a brisk "You don't need that any more, do you, Grandpa? Here comes the salvage van."

It was in many ways a remarkable and even an epic struggle lasting the best part of two years. There was genuine bitterness in it, and real triumph; fear, exasperation, astounding endurance and tenacity of purpose, together with as much brains and leverage on both sides (as well as nearly as many distinguished people) as it takes to get a controversial bill through its second reading in Parliament.

Finally the closing order was rescinded at the eleventh hour and the school remains, if only to prove that the present generation of Auburn men is much the same as its predecessors. With the train the Church School is ours, small, obsolete, and remarkably if obscurely useful.

Yet all this time, according to even our kindliest critics, we ought to have been watching the Germans. But to be honest, I do not see what good that would have done. We hardly ever watch foreigners ourselves for the simple reason that, as old 'Anry said over in Suffolk, "we can't make head nor tail on 'em." Moreover, we have got our work cut out when it comes to watching, keeping an eye on Flinthammock in the east and Heath in the west. Flinthammock, in our possibly somewhat biased opinion, is "wuss nor *Paris*, if a b'y gets down there alone." They have a population of nearly two thousand people down there, and there, according to Auburn, everybody is fabulously rich and "nobody don't do no work, which is remarkably *strange*, so it is now." This rank libel has no foundation whatever in fact, but it goes to show that we have not by nature quite that broadminded imagination which would let us as individuals become citizens of the world without considerable mental and moral discipline.

Still, if we are very busy living our own lives and governing our own castles, we do keep an eye on our own politicians, noting carefully from their antics which way the wind blows. The relationship between the ordinary countryman and the politician is so seldom mentioned at home that it may be often misunderstood abroad. One sees frequent references to the fickleness of the public towards its leaders and to the short memory of the common man.

From childhood these observations have seemed to me to be wildly misleading. To begin with, the one thing we have obviously not got is a short memory. Some of our memories are so long that they embrace our fathers' and grand-fathers' as well, while that word "leader" is largely a politeness.

The ordinary English countryman, in Auburn at any rate, has a very clear idea of democratic government. I doubt if he thinks of it in the Greek, but to his eyes it seems fairly clear that the country is governed by the public in the end, call it by what name you like. We—me and thee and the parson and all the other lads of the village—constitute the public, and the politicians are our servants. They apply for the job (often rather obsequiously we notice with instant suspicion), we give it to them, we pay them in honours or cash, and we judge them solely by results. Sometimes we come to a bad patch when the men applying for this all-important work are not quite all we could have desired. There has been a patch like that these twenty years, and some of us cannot forget that lost generation in 1914-15. We lost too much good stuff there, stuff we could very well have done with now. Still, as we say so truly if inelegantly, "If you can't get fat bacon, you must do with bread and pull-it and take the best there is to give you."

The job of running the country is so important that only

the best men at their best are safe to be left with it, and
our anxiety about their capabilities before they get the
appointment is boundless. Once they are on the job, however, it is a rule, born out of long experience and so firmly
implanted that it has become a sort of instinct, that we
stand back and let them get on with it unmolested until
and unless things look really dangerous.

This does not mean that we lose interest, of course, or
that we have no other hand in the matter. On the contrary,
our part is often very arduous. In our experience, we have
to watch for the little indications they give us to show us
how they want us to play up. As many of these indications
have to be invisible to the foreigner, our joint performance
is not without merit.

Naturally I am not talking now about those politically
minded folk who form themselves into groups and do good
or bad work as the case may be, nor to the M.P. who will
never be a statesman and who thinks of us and treats us as
if we were always an election crowd, which is absurd. All
this only applies to the ordinary person, the chap who only
thinks of himself as British and East Anglian and as nothing
else, whose social class doesn't bother him either way, who
votes sometimes for one party and sometimes for another,
who plods along steadily towards what he hopes to God is
peace, freedom and that glorious economic state which is
always to have five bob to spare, and who corrects his
mistakes and reforms his judgments as he goes. His ideal
major-domo is the statesman who knows and loves his
country and who never makes the mistake of underestimating
his employer, either in intelligence or strength.

No one knows this arrangement better than the two
bodies concerned, and the great statesmen always seem to
have kept their place and their dignity, as good servants
should. In fact the greater the statesman the deeper and
closer is the understanding and co-operation between him
and the countryman. Theirs is a man-and-master relationship which is packed with sentiment on both sides but which
contains not one grain of sentimentality or false kindness.

The master knows his very life depends on the job being done well, and the statesman knows that any mistake he makes may be forgiven but for dear safety's sake will never be forgotten, neither in his own lifetime nor in his son's.

I can only explain this collaboration by saying that it is a sort of horse-and-rider arrangement, but seen from the point of view of the horse.

In Auburn we feel we are very reasonable (as no doubt others do elsewhere) about these riders of ours. We realise that to help us to negotiate different obstacles we need the ingenuities of different men. Earl Baldwin, who made some of us eye him very anxiously when we saw him over in Ipswich carrying a pipe so large that it must have been a sample or a theatrical prop, certainly underestimated Hitler (as well as us on that occasion), and that mistake might well have sent us hurtling over the precipice with our hooves flying. This vital lapse of his has destroyed our faith in his reliability as a Prime Minister, but on the other hand our long memory—which is like an animal's memory, without fancy intellectual thoughts to mutilate it—does not let us belittle his behaviour when he handled a very private and intimate disaster of ours with complete understanding, and did not let us put a foot wrong at a time when every step was an agony to us.

I have met clever people since that time who have solemnly accused Mr. Baldwin of deposing a King of England alone when the country was not looking. These people have simply forgotten. Now, when the bombers come every night to scatter careless death over our big cities and our little fields, when everybody's life is at stake and there is no telling every morning who of our lifelong friends may have died in the darkness, I am open to bet that not a tenth, not a twentieth of the tears are shed in any one week as were poured out all over the island on any day in that period of disillusion and bereavement in 1937.

Where the Government is concerned Auburn people have, I think, one other foible in common with many of their countrymen: they do not like to hear about dishonest politicians. In fact few things annoy them more than a tale of chicanery in Government circles, and they would far rather not know and put any shortcoming down to something else. In other countries, and among many of their compatriots, this peculiarity is often quite incomprehensible and usually passes for extreme stupidity or sentimentality. However, once one sees these men from our point of view— that is as grooms, so to speak, in charge of our most dignified and precious equine person—it is easy to realise the insult and the intolerable sense of shame which any perfidy on their part must produce in us. I do not say that most of us think this in so many words, but we feel it and react accordingly.

After the *Anschluss*, which startled us considerably, we cocked an anxious eye at the Government, but received no warning dig in the ribs from it. There was none of the time-honoured rumbling on the drums, no sudden and gratuitous reminder that the army was a man's life; nothing, only an insistence on social improvements at home, which as everybody knows, indicates an all-clear abroad.

The effect of this was to make us feel that, odd though it looked, there must be something in the inside story (which we never expect to know until afterwards) which made all the difference, and it was all right for us to go on putting the final touches to our recovery from the last war. What never occurred to us was the incredible fact that the men in charge at that time were mainly afraid of the *horse*.

The habit of confusing the strong urge towards a fairer chance for everybody with red revolution has been very common, but from a country point of view—which thinks in generations, or at least in decades—it still seems extraordinary that there should have been any real excitement anywhere about the country going anti-capitalist, when already we were the only state in Europe wherein by common consent money was taken regularly in cash from the rich and paid regularly in cash to the poor. We *are* anti-capitalist—in a Tory fashion—and have been so for some years.

I think had we realised then that the Government was nervous of us and was humouring us, as if we were an unbroken colt, while the road was growing wilder and wilder and the storm clouds were piling up like an illustration in the family Bible, we might have panicked badly. As it was, it set us back on our heels when we did see it, but by that time we had immediate danger to steady us and one of the last real statesmen in the nation to gather up the reins and jerk the bit tight in our mouths.

Even as late as July 1938, although no one in Auburn could help realising that something was going to happen, the general impression was that it could hardly be war because none of the signs were right. No one analysed it naturally, but it was as if one looked up at a sky flecked with peculiar coloured clouds and decided that whatever else it was going to do it would not rain ordinary rain.

We were all talking one evening out in the yard. It was very peaceful and a little too good to be true, as Auburn often is, with the leaves thick and luxurious overhead and the smell of dry grass pleasant in the air. The preparations for the August cricket party were in full swing, and Sam, who is Auburn's captain and who also sees to our garden, had come up with P.Y.C. and Grog from a long and earnest inspection of the pitch. Albert had wandered in to have another look at the big shed we used as a garage, to see if we could do anything with it as a dining-room if our luck didn't hold out and it should rain for the Feed.

Norry was there too. He had stepped over from the forge and was mucking about in the stables, talking to Cooee and having a busman's holiday at what he charmingly calls "horse pleasure." This may mean anything from plucking a tail or drenching a beast with the tin bottle to, as on this occasion, speculating on the chances of an unborn colt becoming a champion show-jumper, a point-to-pointer, or even, in wilder moments, the winner of the Newmarket

Town Plate. Cooee's mare, Struan, hung out of her box
and looked introspective. Her foal was due in May.

The talk was completely idle. Sam thought the sand P.Y.C.
had invested in and that Sam's Grandpa had thrown over
the pitch earlier in the year had been a mistake, and the
others were inclined to agree with him. The general feeling
was that we should see the benefit in 1939 or 1940, and that
meanwhile the important thing was to get the hay in from
the outfield.

Then someone mentioned the shadow which lay in the
back of all our minds and remarked that the wireless "was
dull," which was a direct reference to the Sudeten trouble
and typical of the national gift for understatement. No one
made any comment, and there was one of those very long
silences which punctuate, and sometimes take the place of,
most Auburn summer conversations.

Of all of us there just then only Norry had been adult
during the last war. He had been a vet's smith in the army,
and his martial reminiscences mainly concern food and
mules. But we others were all in the early or mid-thirties,
and our generation remembers the time when war was life,
when there seemed to have been no beginning and to be no
end to an intolerable condition of strain in which our elders
struggled irritably and which we appeared to be on the
point of inheriting.

Out in the yard that evening my own immediate reaction
to the sudden thought of war was much the same, I suppose,
as most of the others'. I was ten years old in 1914, and very
vivid impressions received at that age never alter but come
on one unexpectedly afterwards, bright and bald as they
were at the time. War simply meant death to me; a soldier
galloping up on a fat grey horse to kiss my tearful nurse
goodbye over the wall under the chestnut trees, and then
death.

It was not ordinary dying, either, nor even death in its
more horrible forms, but death final, empty and away
somewhere. I had a sudden recollection of women and old
people all in black, as country people were in those days on

a Sunday, standing about in the village street reading enormous casualty lists in a very small type which seemed to fill whole pages of the paper; a boy on a bike with not one telegram spelling tragedy but sometimes two or even three at a time; and long sad services in the small church which had been a barn and still smelt of hay.

It was a dreadful picture of annihilation, of ending off, of the hopeless destruction of practically all a whole human crop. I remembered names I had not thought of for twenty-five years: George Playle and a big cowman they used to call "Long 'un." I remembered the food shortage at the boarding school I went to later, and the miserable darkness too; but the principal thing was the hundreds and hundreds of far away deaths.

Then, of course, there had been the cleaning up as one grew and the effect that had had on us all.

When we of our generation were just preparing to break the earth over our heads we found that practically the whole batch of youngsters immediately in front of us had disappeared, and naturally that meant that most of us had heavy responsibilities from the first. This in itself is not very extraordinary, but added to it there was our very odd upbringing.

Those of us who were in our 'teens when the war ended came out early, even in Auburn, into a disillusioned world wherein everything, including God, was highly suspect.

To most of our elders—and they were considerably our elders—this was a passing phase, a temporary lack of faith in humanity, a time of exhaustion after great trial; but to those of us who were green and rather frightened, as all people are at that age, there was nothing but broken planks wherever we trod. Nobody knew anything at all for certain. The most elementary morals were in considerable doubt. Every formula for behaviour whose use was not instantly apparent had been thrown overboard. Our parents, school-teachers and clergy, sickened by a catastrophe which everybody said was the direct outcome of a world in which most of them had lived happily and innocently, turned from any

thought of instructing us with weary self-disgust. Having
lost their younger brothers and their elder sons, apparently
through some unspecified fault of their own or their fathers',
they had nothing they dared tell us. We were given doorkeys
and the freedom of a shambles. The pseudo-scientists and
the demolition merchants became the prophets of our more
sophisticated contemporaries and their doctrines filtered
through to us, showing us at least how we could get to work
for the time being, if it was only shovelling away more of
the debris.

Since then the whole generation has had to find out how
to live by trial and error, with the main result that it has
learnt what little it does know very thoroughly indeed. It
has found out from bitter personal experience the con-
sequences of most of the commoner sins and the value of
many conventions. Above all things it has learnt to watch,
to hesitate, and never to be surprised by the worst.

War reminiscences told on the sea-wall or on the benches
outside the pubs, or published in books and coming round
in the library vans, filled us with a horror of war which far
outstripped any evangelical horror of hell, and twenty years
of vigorous anti-war propaganda had given us an impression-
ist picture of modern warfare whose lack of detail could be
augmented by the vilest nightmare each individual mind
could conceive.

Moreover, from the beginning something had had to be
done about our material fortunes, for very few of us were
in the position in 1918 to go on with the programme for
which we had been prepared in '11 and '12. My own father,
for instance, gave up trying to keep up our big old house
down the road in late '17, and we all went to London to
live in a top flat in Bayswater, where we felt like pigeons in
a sealed dovecot. It was close on fifteen years before we
younger ones, by solid hard co-operative working, got back
again to home ground, and by that time someone had let
the house go to ruin and we had to come here, a little
further down the road, to the Old Doctor's house in Auburn.

We were not alone in this sort of experience by any

means, and it is an agonising business to be jerked out of one scheme into another when one is thirteen or so. Agony of that kind at that age generates power, and the present popular theory that it is a sin to be rich is due, I fancy, not only to the fundamental urge towards universal equality, but also to our passionate efforts at self-defence at that time when it was still a sin to be poor.

That evening in the yard the prospect of another war, of the generation after us going the same way as the one before us, was not only horrible but seemed hardly to be borne.

It was not as though we had made no progress. Looking round, it occurred to me that although none of us was rich we certainly had all recovered. We were all, after considerable effort, living something like the lives we wanted to live in the place we felt was our natural home.

Sam was the youngest of us, at thirty-one. He was born in Auburn, had never left it for long, and was married, with two remarkably fine children under five.

He was definitely not rich, but would have been very offended, and quite rightly, had anyone called him poor. As cricket captain, football secretary and collector for the Foresters he was a person of some small consequence, and as controller of a locally remarkable garden—the Old Doctor having made it a sort of legend in the district—he was well up in his profession and had done particularly well in the important annual flower shows.

He and I were still congratulating ourselves, not too privately, on our Finest Single Bloom award at the big town rose show, when a particularly lucky *President Hoover* had done the trick for us.

Sam had left the jam factory gardens at Heath some time before and had come to work in ours, where he was boss of his time, his acres, and incidentally his old grandfather, whom he refers to firmly as "my assistant." There was, and is, nothing whatever to stop him becoming Chairman of the Parish Council or local representative on either of the other Central Councils in time, if he is so minded.

His weekly earnings were then at the current rate, which

is to say that he received thirty-five shillings and sixpence plus insurance. He found them entirely satisfactory, and would have left us, albeit regretfully for we like each other, if he had not. To explain why these figures were possible— why, that is, we should be able to afford to have a garden, and he to undertake to manage it—perhaps I should mention something of the economics of life in Auburn just before the present war.

The first and most important factor was, as always in England, public opinion.

In Auburn everybody makes a point of knowing all about everybody else. Most people are related, and those who have no kin here have most of them known their neighbours as long as and as well as most cousins, so that the family atmosphere, with all its good and bad qualities, is present all the time. If you do not see what this has to do with domestic economy, perhaps you will cross off from your own outgoings every penny you are forced to spend because the people you mix with do not know every turn and twist in your affairs. Then imagine a public opinion which criticised you far more bitterly for spending too much for the size of your income than for excessive thrift; a public opinion, in fact, which cannot see why you should want a new coat this year when the one you had last still looks as good as new.

Rents were, and are, very cheap. Three shillings to as high as seven and six a week will hire a very good cottage complete with garden.

As well as their gardens most Auburn men have allotments, or "little estates," as Sam prefers to call them, and these not only provide their owners' households but often send fruit and vegetables by the train to the city.

The various clubs take care of the extra insurance, and the Government provides the children's education and sometimes their milk.

I do not suggest that there was any super-civilisation about this state of affairs, but it was by no means bad and, what was more, it was getting visibly better, save that there were still not enough children in the place to the older people's minds, and the young ones were coming round to agreeing with them.

The class question was pretty well settled, at least among we middle and younger folk. Roughly it had boiled down to this: you could still touch your hat to Money or Blood; but, if so, Money must subsequently breed money in your pocket and Blood must give you service, or you were making an ass of yourself. This reversion to the very root and beginning of the whole business in a free England was typical of our trial and error age and was at least logical.

In Auburn at the moment a gentleman is treated as a gentleman only so long as he remains gentle, and a rich man as a rich man only so long as his riches get around, so that it is what else either of them may be which really decides their friends (at least after the first year or two), which is as it should be.

Thus in twenty years the grass had begun to grow thick again, and yet now it had suddenly begun to look as if we might have made some terrible and mysterious mistake, as had our fathers before us, unless of course it could be that it was they who had done it again. Anyhow, the wireless certainly was dull about the Sudetenland.

Sam remarked that he couldn't seem to make much sense of that Herr Hitler, *he* couldn't, and we all echoed him privately. After all, it is only very recently that Charlie Chaplin has been said to resemble Hitler. In those days Hitler was said to resemble Charlie Chaplin. There was nothing whatever Napoleonic about him until he made Napoleonic strides.

Albert said that he didn't believe that the Germans wanted a war and made a reference to the ex-servicemen who had been over to our local town as guests of the Legion, who in turn had been royally entertained by them in Germany.

There was a lot in this, or so we thought at the time, and the reflection was comforting. Now, of course, most of us are convinced that those were mere spying expeditions on their part, and that if only our men had known the language better they would have been able to detect the fraud.

Grog observed that no sane person wanted a war ever and that the whole thing resolved into blasted greed, and meanwhile where was the bat oil?

This return to what honestly seemed then the more important, since more imminent, matters in life cheered everyone up, and the preparations for the party went forward earnestly.

Horses approaching the forge.
Scraperboards by
Youngman Carter

2

THE August party was terrific that year. It reached a zenith, achieved a ripeness, which lifted it out of the class of "Good Times" and planted it in the front row of "Life Experiences."

For some years then this annual jollification had constituted our only family holiday and was our one yearly reunion with all our hosts of old friends. We saved up for it like children, not only in money but in those precious odds-and-ends which one comes by in the country —a remarkable pot of jam, a vast marrow, new clothes, a picture one has painted or a dog kennel one has built, or even a lovely new joke. Sam coaxed his begonias to be at their best for it; Margaret and Chrissie saved their prize bottles of fruit for it; Mr. Doe the butcher kept a special look-out for just the right baron of beef for the Feed, and down the road at Marshling the hams were picked out early for the same occasion. Every one of these little things was of extreme importance to us all, and I think rightly, for the genuine pleasures of life are elusive and seem to lie in the special occasions of commonplace amenities. They are the highlights, so to speak, of the ordinarily good.

The proceedings had a traditional routine and lasted for the best part of a week. This routine had grown steadily from small beginnings and had finally flowered into a series of parties, all following closely on each other's heels.

It began on the Friday before the first Monday in August, and the house filled with people we had either known at school or as students. The only similarity between us all was in age and in the subsequent slight sameness of outlook. Younger brothers, wives, sisters and sweethearts crept in as the years went by, but there never seemed to be any older folk in the house-party.

When I say the house filled I mean it strained its seams. It is a largish rambling old place possessing endless store

and box rooms, which all came in very useful as spare
bedrooms at these times.

Out of this gathering P.Y.C. could always collect a full
cricket team, with certain augmentations from among the
neighbours. There was never any dearth of men, and in fact
they often had to play thirteen aside to get everybody in.
Friday evening was always taken leisurely, and also with the
various more important preparations which no one would
have liked to miss. Albert and Alec his assistant always
appeared on Friday, making an awful mess when everything
was tidy for the visitors. Every year he thought out something more ambitious and complicated in the way of garden
lighting, and the execution of his new masterpiece was
always well worth watching and assisting, for in the years
he had acquired as remarkable a collection of cables,
coloured bulbs and multi-way switches as ever delighted
human amateur. The assortment took rather a long time to
put up of course, and in the day-time the garden had a
tendency to look like a main overhead telephone section
after the storm, but, even allowing for fuses, by Monday
night the effect was always impressive and original.

Saturday began quietly and moved on, gathering momen-
tum, to the half-day match between P.Y.C.'s team and
Auburn Village. Immediately following the convivial
gathering after this match there was a scramble to dress up
for the Saturday night party, to which came many neighbours whom we did not know quite so intimately as our
house guests. This was always a set piece, the scheme of the
masquerade being carefully laid down beforehand.

The explanation of this rather unexpectedly precious
proceeding was prosaic. Even if childhood friends remain
one's friends they do not grow up like each other, and, like
the good people in the rhyme who had different opinions,
"some like apples and some like inions." Not to beat about
the bush, we had and have among our nearest and dearest
those who would not feel happy out of a boiled shirt at an
evening party and those who would not be seen dead in
one, proclaiming their own variety of costume the only

wear, so the natural thing to do was to arrange a function which everyone could attend in either or neither garment with complete propriety.

On that particular occasion Saturday night was to be Spy Night at the Embassy, and the effect aimed at a nice blend of Phillips Oppenheim and Limehouse Nights. Grog had been busy for days painting a brilliant collection of life-sized liveried flunkeys, unconventionally armed with revolvers and sub-machine-guns, which he pinned up about the house to give it the required tone. Our guests, arriving about nine, found us breathless but ready, and the noise and chatter, drinking and dancing and showing off went on until next morning.

Sunday usually passed in recuperation, for on Monday there was serious work to be done.

Among all the very good things there are in life I think I would put in the first flight the glorious bustle of the preparations for a country feast at which very old friends are to predominate. This is entertaining without worry or pretension, and if something goes wrong it is only an added excitement all can share.

There was never any question of hiring extra help on these occasions. Help started arriving at six in the morning and the weather was the only uncertain assistant.

On that day our luck held. At half-past five the sky was grey with the mist which means heat to come, and when Norry arrived with the trestles borrowed from the village hall and the baskets of crockery which Vic was lending us he assured me we were in for a scorcher, and we agreed that in view of this an extra firkin of beer ought to be set aside "in case."

At eleven the Pontisbright team arrived, and with them came their wives and children, mothers and fathers, uncles and aunts and everybody else who remembered us—sixty-odd of them.

We had once lived in Pontisbright, fifteen miles from Auburn, and had always had relations there; while Chrissie is Pontisbright born, so that this was another reunion, as important as the previous one on the Friday. Len was there, of course. He is the sexton and their slow bowler, and I have known the time at Pontisbright when half the team was helping to dig like fury all the morning so that he might be free to uphold the honour of the village on the green in the afternoon.

With him came the Ashby brothers from the Mill, and nearly all the Quinneys (who can make up a complete cricket team of brothers if need be), and Stan the parson and Mrs. Stan, and Mrs. Len and Doreen, and Laurie Smith and all the others.

Len was captain that year. His elder sister, Cissie, had worked for us in the last war, and it was she who had fled with we three children to London on that terrifying day when a mistaken order had started a false evacuation of our little corner of the East Coast. However, that was a long while ago, and no one was thinking about war that Monday morning in '38, although there had been a great deal of worried speculation about it on the day before.

It was a staggering morning. The sky was dizzily blue, and the heat haze hung over the bright green meadow and burnt on the trees round its borders. Sam and Len tossed, and the match began, with the regular Auburn team reinforced with the best of P.Y.C.'s to meet such serious opposition.

It is almost impossible to describe village cricket at its superb best. Those people who confuse it either with a game or a religion have given it a bad name in some quarters, but for those who enjoy its peculiar attributes there is no spectacle in the world to take its place. This kind of cricket is a country sport like fishing or making love. For those who do not know it well, perhaps I might venture to set down why I personally find it so good to watch.

Primarily, village cricket is a performance, and has something in common with the Lancers and much with the Harlequinade. It epitomises the very English secret of combining individualism with co-operative effort. Each player has his chance to shine alone, and yet his final success

or failure is the team's. Best of all, the day is never lost
until it is won. At any moment a thumping miracle may
happen, and usually it does. In fact there is a lot of magic
in it, and I do not use the word in any poetic sense. The
whole business has something of the elements of a rustic
charm, and on the right day, in the leafy privacy of the
meadow and conducted by the right country people, a very
potent sort of atmosphere indeed can be conjured up.

August Monday 1938 in Auburn was one of those occasions.
The lunch, or Feed, at which as many as could find places
sat down and the rest of us waited our turn after doing our
share with the serving, took place as usual under the ilex-tree
in the Lady Garden because no room in the house could
hold us.

Then there was more cricket, and tea with everybody's
name on the cake, and afterwards a finish to the game
which was so close that the score had to be checked over
before the winners were certain of their victory. Finally
came a gathering for more old-and-mild refreshment in all
the downstairs rooms at once, with last-minute bits of news
and a tremendous concerted ragging of a distinguished guest
(one of His Majesty's Recorders), who bore up magnificently
under the strain; while yet another four-and-a-half had to
be trundled down from the Thatcher's, bringing up the
score to the full thirty-six.

The exuberant hour lasted full and good and without
spoiling until the moon came up, and the bus drivers put
their feet down and carried a sleepy, happy Pontisbright
away to its deep green valley inland.

A cricket tea in the
garden of D'Arcy
House.

3

A FEW weeks later, when we were still clearing up and packing away things that might come in useful next year, the incredible descended upon us, and we were suddenly required to take instant precautions in case of an attack on our lives by poison gas.

In Auburn we don't care for drama very much. Certain of our good ladies have a flair for it, and generations of them presiding over illnesses and accidents have brought the whole thing into disrepute; so it happened that when real drama appeared it shocked and irritated us before it stimulated us.

The first thing that happened was the change in the wireless. It gave up being dull and became frankly hysterical, bursting into news bulletins every forty-five minutes or so, a phenomenon which reminded us of the death of the King and the Abdication. The painfully nervous light entertainment between the announcements was a change from the slow music of the other occasions, but if it was meant to be comfortingly normal it was a mistake, because we were inclined to be confused by it rather than soothed.

As I have said, few of us ordinary people in Auburn tended to be students of foreign affairs at that time, although most of us have done a little studying since; but, as Sam pointed out, we could at least read, and the bare facts, which we have a gift for seizing among the verbiage, suddenly resolved themselves into a path to disaster as clear as if we had suddenly seen it appearing across the marsh.

As far as we could find out—and this was not too easy, because the newspapers were very busy conjecturing—we were not pledged to help Czechoslovakia, but France was and we were pledged to help France. No one ever questioned that the Frenchies wanted a fight. In those days it was our convinced opinion that the Frenchies were always prepared to fight on any provocation, it being in their nature

32

as it were, and at that time the only military operations in Europe which we could imagine were those in which we painfully consolidated brilliant but dangerous French advances.

It was all very alarming, but, perilous though the situation looked, we still could not believe that it was actually war. We were still blinded by the absence of any hint whatever sent direct to us from the Government. It was that which kept us thinking that there must be a catch in it somewhere. The notion that for twenty years our politicians might have been inefficient, to put it mildly, and that our present man in an impossible position was backing his own theory without letting us in on it, never came into our heads for a moment

One evening we in Auburn got our first definite hint. Mr. Moore came up from the schoolhouse, where his wife is Headmistress, to ask P.Y.C. to take the chair at an Air Raid Precautions meeting on the following Tuesday. It was important, he said, and they were speeding it up all over the district.

Air Raid Precautions. This was more like it. This sounded more like business. We had had air raids before. A Zeppelin had come down in a village not far away in the last war, and there was a great chunk of it in the garage still. Also we had heard about Spain and had seen horrifying newsreels from China, and we had no illusions whatever about the value of the aeroplane as an offensive weapon.

Yet at that moment the wireless was giving us to understand that the crisis was upon us. Events were obviously moving fast. If one could believe one's ears and use one's head, air raids might begin that night. What in the name of sanity was this tale of a meeting next Tuesday?

"It won't come to nothin'." "There's something behind it." "He's a-playing for something." "He's frightening on 'em."

That was the general opinion, and it was not all wishful thinking. No one wanted a war. To some of us war seemed then to mean quite literally a sentence of death on everyone and everything we most loved, but no one felt war was impossible, whatever it meant. In Auburn death comes, war comes, night comes. There is no question of stopping any of them by a refusal to co-operate. In a country like England democracy has been fought for so many times, and won by so many battles small and large, that it has long ceased to become an ideal and is an instinct.

On the Monday of the Munich crisis it was a windy, showery day, and Auburn, I remember, seemed very old. In the spring the cut squares round the trees in the orchard are carpeted with aconites, and all through the year the memory of those blazing golden cushions hangs about it. There is a legend that aconites only flourish where Roman blood has been spilt, and if this is true there must have been a battle up there at the end of the Old Doctor's garden. There is a heap of old cannonballs up there too, much later in date, and only a mile or so away are the plains where Boadicea was captured. Remembering all this and the bit of Zepp in the garage, war seemed almost as natural to Auburn as peace.

That evening P.Y.C. and I drove into the county town to put a week-end guest on the London train. As we came out of the station we were held up by a procession of self-conscious-looking youths in tweeds walking along in formation. That stopped us talking, and we drove back in silence. When we got in we found "Me," the local bobby, and the Flinthammock policeman waiting for us.

I cannot remember how "Me" got his name, but he is a great ally of ours and is popular in the village. He is a Londoner and he served all through the last war. He opened the proceedings characteristically, his red hair standing on end as usual and his sepulchral voice lowered to a confidential bellow.

" 'Ere, do you know anything about poison gas?" he said. "You might like to read it up. You'll soon know why."

He lent us his book on the subject, and we all had a drink on it. Grog came down from the studio, and there was a conference about it. We knew nothing at all about gas naturally, except that it was loathsome, and I had seen a man with a horribly scarred face who had suffered from it twenty years before.

"Me" said that Lewisite was the Awful Stuff. "Smells of geraniums," he said. "One whiff, and you're a gonner."

It all seemed quite impossible, or rather it seemed as though time had gone out of gear. When I had seen "Me" only a few days before we had discussed dog licences and a certain matter of whether or not Cooee could ride a horse on a footpath. It seemed a long way from that to his tale about the place being threatened by Lewisite.

When the policemen had gone we looked at the handbook. Ten minutes made it clear that there was a lot to be learnt, and that if any sort of protection was to be achieved everybody in the country had got to swot it up thoroughly. The effects of the different stuffs were varied and sensational. Phosgene filled your lungs with water and produced gangrene of the extremities. Mustard had scarcely any odour, but blinded you and ate your flesh away. It did seem mad. One of Grog's flunkeys still leered from the wall of the breakfast-room. We had grown used to him and had forgotten to take him down. The whole business was so wildly melodramatic that all one's instinctive common sense said it could not be quite true. On one side there was that chap Hitler looking like Charlie Chaplin and behaving as far as one could gather like Captain Hook, and yet on the other there was this neat little police handbook of old "Me's" reading like useful hints for those about to be handed over to the Spanish Inquisition.

Because he thought it would amuse us, our week-end guest had brought us a frankly "scare" book which had just come out, and which contained very bald facts and figures purporting to be of use to the young soldier. One extract, I remember, ran something like this:

"Q. What do I do if an enemy infantryman thrusts a bayonet into my stomach?
A. You ask him to withdraw it gently, turning it very slightly to the left.
Q. What are my chances of survival?
A. Very small. Providing you have instant attention

from a skilled surgeon, your chance is 3·102 in the hundred."

And so on and so on.

P.Y.C. wanted to take this book to bed with him, and the rest of us became very abusive and quite unreasonably angry, I remember. We hung round the wireless until after the midnight news, not even caring to go down the village and meet the neighbours, and finally we went to bed, the sickening suspicion growing upon us that something might have gone wrong with the Government's calculations, and yet still feeling in our hearts that the God of simple people would not permit us to be caught quite so sound asleep.

However, at three o'clock the next morning (an unheard of, not respectable, secret hour in Auburn) P.Y.C. got a telegram by phone. The message was very much to the point and explained Me's unnaturally official visit and the loan of the handbook.

It said "Collect seven hundred gas-masks for your area and fit," and was signed "A.R.P., Fishling."

P.Y.C. got up dutifully and fetched out the car. Fishling is eight miles from Auburn and, although we come in its rural area, it is not very much used by us since it is not so large or so modern as Bastian, ten miles in the other direction. Fishling was practically unknown to us, therefore, as far as the townsfolk were concerned.

The next we heard of P.Y.C. was at noon, when he phoned in great haste to tell us to send a lorry, book the hall, and get a wireless loudspeaker down there. In a larger place none of these demands would present much labour, but in Auburn, where there is only one lorry available for odd jobs, the custodian of the hall is also the postman, and the only suitable wireless loudspeaker is owned by Albert, who may be absolutely anywhere doing any conceivable type of job for anybody, it represented a sort of minor mobilisation.

At last the difficulties were overcome, and Bill, who is an

ex-serviceman and lives by the pond, cut his afternoon's work and went off to Fishling with his lorry.

Late in the afternoon, when the entire village was fortunately aware that something definite and personal was afoot, P.Y.C. returned from Fishling a little dazed. He had with him a few notes on the back of an envelope and a sample gas-mask, one of the seven hundred which Bill and Charlie the postman were unloading at the hall.

Now that we are all so used to gas-masks all their visual horror has gone, but that one which P.Y.C. brought in was something new in Auburn then. The obscene elephant-foetus effect of the thing burst on us for the first time, and its obvious efficiency brought home the reality of the situation with a jolt like the kick of a mule. We all tried it on immediately. Most of us had seen the anti-war propaganda drawings of little children wearing them, and they had been unpleasant enough; but the sight of Chrissie in one, her starched apron and blue frock looking like fancy-dress under it, and her eyes, which I have known so long, looking out truculently at me (for, from the first, the mere mention of war had the unexpected effect of making her furious), turned my stomach over more sickeningly than anything else in that whole unbelievable day.

P.Y.C.'s story was simple, and his problem rather startling. In Fishling, he said, the A.R.P. Office was performing miracles. Thousands of gas-masks were being assembled by volunteer labour which included Albert's father among others, who had been working all night. Other volunteers were driving the things out to the villages and distribution centres in the town. The amount of work was tremendous and the strain terrific. One of their executives had fallen dead at his post at two in the morning. P.Y.C. had hung about getting all the information he could and had managed to get a short intensive course in gas from the A.R.P.O.'s assistant, who had given him the information between incessant telephone calls.

We all went over the notes he had made. The salient facts were these: the masks were a complete protection to the face and lungs if properly put on, everybody ought to have one in the next twenty-four hours, the area of our operations was roughly five square miles, and there was nothing yet for babies. P.Y.C. added that the thing they had impressed upon him most was that there was to be no panic.

At first the problem appeared to present great difficulties, and we all took a lesson in putting on the masks and adjusting the tapes. However, we were wrong. From the beginning the entire operation went with astonishing smoothness, and it was the first time I ever saw the unity of Auburn as a visible thing. It was almost as if the village was a big single gentle animal, rather startled and nervous but old and experienced and patient. I cannot describe this phenomenon, because it was apparent in such little things and was an impression which grew upon me very slowly. For instance, four hundred and fifty people out of six hundred of us turned up quietly to the village hall in the pouring rain at the appointed time, two hours after P.Y.C. came back, although the message was only passed round by word of mouth.

The hall, which is only a glorified army hut, has two main rooms, the smaller containing a billiard table. They put the masks on the table, and Albert's father and Charlie sorted them into the only two sizes we had—Large and Medium. Albert had got his big loudspeaker into position, and P.Y.C. and Sam, who had taken charge of the gathering, got everyone to listen to the Prime Minister's speech. Everyone was very quiet while the dry, harsh voice, which was so like a family solicitor's, put the situation to us so well and so honestly and with such courage. Even then, though, it did not sound like war. There was no trumpet, no inspiration to arms.

After it was over P.Y.C. began to explain the more personal aspect of the gathering. Certain English people become utterly unself-conscious and without any sense of the ridiculous at all when once their minds are fixed on a definite objective. He and Sam were on the stage together in the big room and were framed in an exceedingly dusty and shabby red curtain. Immediately behind them was a dilapidated forest glade with a tear in the sky and scraps of paint flecking off all over it, while a single electric light bulb with a prosaic green shade hung directly over their heads. Between them was a very shaky card table and one small creaking chair. Sam sat on the chair and put on the gas-mask, while P.Y.C. did the talking.

The line he took, I remember, was typical both of himself and of Auburn. He announced firmly, and as if he had had it personally from God, that the danger to us from poison gas in the village was not nearly so great as the one which every Londoner experienced every day from the perils of his city's traffic, but that we might as well take every precaution, as no doubt they did in their difficulty. The point about the absence of any protection whatever for babies gave him more trouble. It was obviously no good skating over the subject, because to thrust a very young child into an adult's mask would certainly be to suffocate it, so he plumped for a gasproof room.

None of us had any clear idea of the official method of proofing a room at that time, but it required only a very elementary intelligence to see that the main idea was to stop every conceivable draught. P.Y.C. pointed this out, and Auburn, who knows all there is to know about draughts when the wind skates over the marshes from the North Sea, grasped the situation instantly.

Meanwhile the rest of us were letting people into the inner room, fifteen at a time, and fitting their masks. As we were doing it, it occurred to me that if the main purpose of the distribution was really to allay panic, as P.Y.C. had told me he thought it must be, it might possibly be a highly mistaken policy.

You cannot attempt to frighten folk off war for twenty years without your efforts taking some effect upon them, and the sudden present of a gas-mask will hardly wipe out all that in ten minutes.

It is a curious fact that nearly everybody's eyes are nice,

and when you see them, startled and helpless, looking at you through a small mica window the effect is apt to be overwhelming. I obtained a lot of undeserved credit as a prophet by insisting in a burst of wishful thinking that there was not going to be any war for a bit.

All this time the rain was pouring down on the roof as if it had come from a hose, and there was the problem of how to take the things home through the lanes without getting them wet. People went hurrying away with them clasped to their bosoms like puppies under their coats. Everybody worked as fast as they could because of the shortage of time. There were a lot of us to help. Joan and Cynthia had come down from the Court, Mr. and Mrs. Carr Seabrook from beside the pond, and Chrissie, Margaret, Cooee, Olive and I helped Albert's father and Charlie, while Grog took down names and addresses.

We fitted four hundred and fifty before ten o'clock, when everyone went home.

The fact which seems so absurd now that we have experienced air attack, and yet was so painfully real then, was that we did expect air raids on a far more intense scale than any in the Spanish war, and we half expected them to begin without warning at almost any moment. No one in Auburn had been to the Spanish war, and we had therefore only written accounts to go by. One is apt to forget that written accounts only deal with the highlights, and naturally we had a somewhat distorted view.

We expected London to be razed in a week, and I know my own private fear was the idiotic notion that a terrorised city population would spread out like rings in a puddle all over the Home Counties, bringing fear and quarrels and chaos with it.

What we had no real idea about at all was the blessed limits to the powers of high explosives. What would have actually been the effect of one enormous persistent gas and high-explosive attack on London in that week in '38 I do not know. In two years we have all changed greatly, and I think for the better, but it was that threat which began the change. I do not suggest for a moment that at any time any single person whom I met ever hinted at surrender. They did not, and I do not think it was bravery, for nobody felt very brave at that time, nor was courage in fashion then (and fashion has much more say than most things) ; but the thought of surrender just never came up and never has since.

When we got home that night most of the helpers came with us, and presently Ronnie, our old friend the surgeon from Bastion, whom we have known since he was a student, with Mary his wife, and Jimmy, the young Irish doctor from Flinthammock, came in to see how we were going and what the verdict was. They too were our own age, responsible people all of them but no more experienced in war than we were. The dearth of folk ten to twenty years older had not seemed so apparent since we grew up.

Mary had sent my godchild and her sister away to Scotland, and Ronnie, so he said, had prepared for war by ordering two hams and thirty-six gallons of beer, not being able to think of anything more useful at the moment. It sounded very practical. Both he and Jimmy were naturally very full of the plans for emergency hospitals, and we remembered with a jolt from far back in our childhood that the wounded were coming through this village three days after the outbreak in 1914.

The Army was represented round the fire that night, too. The Captain and the Major from the Court had come in to collect their wives. They were both convinced that it was coming. In twenty-four hours, they said.

I woke the next morning to hear the talk in the street. Our house is right on the road just off the Square, and our high-pitched East Anglian voices carry a long way.

I could hear old Cliff, who has worked for Mr. Graves ever since he was ten, except for a brief period when he was Sir Edmund Ironside's batman in the last war. Bobby Graves used to be Vicar of Auburn until he retired a few years ago, and when he first came the village was still in smocks and gaiters and high silk hats on a Sunday. Cliff must have worked for him for close on forty years, and is

Auburn born. He always shouts the local news to anyone
he passes when he goes down for the paper, and if there is
anything one wants to know about local affairs he can
usually supply the information.

I lay listening to him with relief. Evidently we had not
gone to war in the night, or he would have referred to it;
but he was saying something which seemed almost more
important at the moment. As far as I could hear, someone
had not got his mask yet and was making a to-do about it.
There were two hundred people who had not got their
masks then, as I very well knew, and they all needed to
be found.

Meanwhile, however, some of the family had to get to
London; Grog to take care of his mother and P.Y.C. to
attend to business, while Cooee was busy with the animals,
who needed to eat even if the sky fell; so Albert's sister Olive
and Mr. and Mrs. Carr S. and I went down to the hall
and opened shop, as soon as we had sent word round that
we were going there. Sending word round Auburn consisted
of going into the shop where Albert's father was selling
newspapers and cigarettes and telling everyone who happened to be talking there. There was quite a crowd that
morning, and Albert's mother undertook to get the news
about.

There were several disconcerting factors that morning.
One of them was that the few ex-servicemen in the village
seemed more apprehensive than anyone else. It was cold
and sunny after the rain, but the sense of impending tragedy
was suffocating. Now, when sensational and sometimes
terrible things actually happen every day and no one takes
any of them too seriously, the peculiar quality of the
wretchedness of that morning is hard to recapture and
define, but the whole thing is analogous with the way one
feels when one first realises that someone one loves is going
to die and the way one feels when they do.

It was Cooee, my oldest student friend, who lived with
us, who raised the question of the animals, and that shook
everyone in the place. Norry was appalled, I remember.

We looked it up, but Me's handbook said nothing about animals.

Some English folk make too much fuss about their beasts, but there are degrees in these things, and the man who spends his whole life tending animals is a funny sort of chap if he is not fond of them. Norry's old pony Kit was over thirty at the time and not exactly valuable, but the idea of her being suffocated or burned and no drench of his brewing being able to save her shook him badly, while Cooee was very nearly demoralised altogether. It was not only the pet animals but all the stock. The cows might escape in the meadows, but what about the pigs in the backyards?

Of course, at that time we knew nothing about gas at all, and the notion of a concentration strong enough to envelop half the county did not then seem absurd. Fogs and sea-wracks are a commonplace with us, and it was only natural to assume that something like one of these, but possessing all the "injurious properties" mentioned in Me's book, was not really unlikely.

Meanwhile Albert's father suddenly remembered the Tye and Shadow Hill and Abbot's Dyke. These are outlying hamlets in the parish of Auburn, but separated from it by several miles of winding muddy lanes. The folks up there would not have heard about the masks yet, save in a general way from the wireless. Fortunately he knew of some first-rate people in each community, who came along at once and collected their own and their neighbours' masks.

All the morning the "shopkeeping" at the hall went on. Some of the more frail elderly ladies who had not felt up to joining the scrum the night before came in with embroidered shopping bags and bent their sleek little grey heads meekly for the rubber monstrosities and asked very gently for a good recipe for getting mustard gas off the skin.

It did all seem such wicked lunacy.

They were followed by a contingent from the fields, who had only just heard of the crisis. These men had fine Norman-French or purely agricultural names, like Clover or Cornell, and about as much kinship with chemical warfare as had the iron cannonballs in the aconite orchard.

Round about noon came the rumour. To this day I do not quite see how it arose, and it remains one of the few genuine mysteries I have ever known. Someone—I fancy it was Olive—came into the hall and remarked that a strange gentleman had passed through the village in a car and had stopped at the only petrol pump. While he was there he had told someone he saw standing by that everything was going to be quite all right, and that Signor Mussolini was going to intervene. It was the usual rumour, completely without any chance of verification at any given point, but it arose at least an hour and a half before the midday news, and we are a great many miles from the city.

The grace-note, I remember, was the additional information that the stranger had taken a road which was a cul-de-sac and never came down it again. It was a good story, but not unnaturally no one took much heart from it.

Not long after this Olive, who had been going round on a bicycle visiting every bedridden or infirm person (there seemed to be a pretty large percentage of these), came back to suggest we went down to Old Lady Fell, who "couldn't make her gas-mask work." The name did not convey much to me, except that I knew by the local courtesy title that she must be over seventy.

Olive led me down her garden path and mentioned as we turned the corner to the back garden, "She's ninety-four, you know."

I had never seen a hale and vigorous person of ninety-four before, and Old Lady Fell impressed me enormously. She was so old that her skull had flattened and the cartilage of her nose had shrunk, but she had a bright colour and was doing a bit of wringing in the wash-house of the cottage where she lived alone. Also she was very tall.

She said, "*Another* war?"

It was the first and last time I ever experienced any feelings of war-guilt, and I said hastily it was only might-be. She said she hoped I was right and went on to give me her opinion of wars and warmongers from the Crimea onwards.

"They've been a nuisance all my life, they Proosians and Rooshians," she said. "We ought to have done with they."

Olive and I agreed with her, and then went into the matter of the gas-mask. We found the trouble quite unsurmountable. Like the babies, she had not sufficient strength in her lungs to draw the air through the filter. She was not interested. It was the food question which was worrying her.

"Wars mean flat stomachs," she said.

I reassured her with honest conviction. "We learnt that lesson last time," I said. "The Government will have taken care of that."

She gave me a devastatingly shrewd glance and her boot-button eyes were as bright as a squirrel's.

"Think so?"

"Why yes," I said. "They're not barmy."

She sniffed. "Let's hope not," she said. "It 'on't be the first time if they are."

I gave up being silly after that and turned to something I did know a little about. I could see that the mask was dangerous and I was so frightened that she might put it on and suffocate if there was a scare, yet I felt I ought not to take it away. I began to explain this as tactfully as possible when I saw that she was laughing at me.

"I 'on't wear that, don't you worry," she said.

Finally we kissed and decided it wasn't going to happen anyway, but that should any warning reach her she would shut her door and her window and take a nap until the trouble was past. It seemed the only thing to do. She was quite as "wide" as I was.

Olive and I went back to the hall. We had missed the news and the Premier's decision to fly to Germany, but the story was all over the village. Even so the importance of the step did not quite register on us at once. Our country minds work slowly. But the grip on our vitals grew less and less intense and for the first time some of that secret invigoration, which we learnt so much about later, crept into the proceedings. It began to be possible to notice things with interest again and to appreciate the spontaneity of the service which came from all sides like a reflex action.

In the normal way, although we keep posted about everyone else's affairs, we do it very discreetly and modestly and have a tendency to live very much alone, but now suddenly all the ceremony had gone and people spoke to each other as if they at last realised that they really had known each other for years. More than that, it was a larger-than-life occasion and people became startlingly more like themselves. Bobby Graves at eighty-two was driving round among his ex-parishioners preaching decency and damn-the-enemy and the whole place was awake again in a night.

When P.Y.C. came home in the evening he had much the same story of London. He said it had been like going to the funeral of everybody's wife when he first arrived at Liverpool Street Station and that the streets and buses were silent as churches. Business had stopped and a pall of gloom which was almost a visible thing hung over the town. And then, just after lunch, he came out of an office building and saw someone laughing in the street. After that the good news spread before his eyes as he walked along, so that he knew something must have happened before he saw a placard.

For the more knowledgeable world I suppose that was the end of the crisis, although the second flight of Mr. Chamberlain was yet to come, but for the majority of us in Auburn, who think so much less fast and who I sometimes fancy scent so much more quickly, it was only a lull in the storm.

Before we had fully realised what was afoot we were being told the danger was over, but we were not deceived. We had had our batch of preliminary warnings and we were awake. What we had got into our heads at last was that, whatever Mr. Chamberlain might think, we had an enemy. What was more, it was an old enemy on his feet again and coming for us.

The full spate of the warnings was still to come, as it happened, for when someone presses a button in Whitehall the effects go rumbling on for days as the machinery makes a full revolution.

The following morning we were having a family row. I cannot remember what it was about at this distance, probably something infantile like P.Y.C. refusing to get up at a reasonable hour, but which must I think have been mainly weariness, for a mental, emotional and physical shake-up is very tiring. However, whatever it was, in the midst of it Mr. Doe stepped down from his butcher's shop (which is the only pretty butcher's shop I have ever seen, and looks as if it were composed, meat and all, of highly glazed china) and came in, bringing the latest bolt from the Government.

He said that the Sanitary Inspector had called upon him, dubbed him Billeting Officer, and told him eighteen thousand East Enders were due in the district. "Of course they won't all come here," he said.

We were all still standing in the studio discussing the ways and means of the project, sending round for Albert's father's advice and deciding that the somewhat ominous choice of a messenger presaged nothing more than that the scheme was being put over by the Ministry of Health, when the S.I. returned to say that one hundred and twenty children were arriving in Auburn the following day.

The effect of this news on the village as a whole was unexpected. Apart from certain qualms, because there are not very many houses in the place at all, the main reaction was excitement and a burst of remarkably practical energy.

This new mood was interesting because it lasted for such a very long time, was both spontaneous and efficient, and was rather as though everyone had slipped down into another gear. A committee came into being rather than was formed; that is to say certain people came and sat down at the dining-room table with old Doey at the head, and I for one began to enjoy it all enormously.

The local authorities had provided a vast quantity of cards, one for every household in the place, and based on the last census, then hopelessly out of date. Each card was divided into three columns. One contained a space for the number of rooms, the second for the number of people in the household, and the third for the answer to a subtraction sum, which was the number of evacuees to be received. From the warrant the Sanitary Inspector had given Doey he appeared to have dictatorial powers, and I suppose on paper the scheme looked almost easy.

Albert's father brought his morning newspaper lists from the shop and, with Olive and Clara, we went through them with the cards. Of course all sorts of things had happened since they had been prepared. People had moved, died and been born. Houses had been built, had fallen down or been split in two, and there were other snags.

"Poor Old Lady Rose," said Doey, pouncing on a card. "Four rooms, one in family, so three children. What would she do with three children? The house is no more than a barn. She's over eighty, practically bedridden, and Mrs. Rich next door goes in to look at her. Three children would kill her. Count her out. Someone else must take her lot. I wouldn't mind some little old boys."

Little old boys were in demand. The distribution of the children began to move with speed, with Doey as a sort of rubicund stork.

In the last twenty years an interest in children has too often been thought sentimental, but Auburn people are not particularly fashionable and the absence of young stock has got on many people's nerves, so that the prospect of a hundred and twenty young things bursting the school again and filling the streets was not altogether an unpleasant idea, even if they belonged to somebody else.

The actual organisation had the simplicity of the obvious and the new unity which we had so suddenly achieved carried the arrangement through with the beautiful ease of a conjuring trick.

There are five roads leading out of Auburn, and somewhere along each road there turned out to be someone who appeared to be not only the best but the proper person to help. This element of properness is always cropping up in Auburn, and, since it is based on personalities rather than on any material consideration, it is a very valuable thing.

In the ordinary way the gathering in the dining-room

might well have hesitated to ask so much of anybody, but
on that day it simply sent young Ralph down on a bicycle
to each of them and begged him or his wife to come at once
for the love of Mike. Although it was just after midday and
an awkward time, everybody came as naturally and as simply
as they had been approached and no one thought that part
of it at all odd. Doey and Albert's father took the cards
out of alphabetical order and put them into a sensible
geographical sequence, and as soon as each "proper" person
arrived they gave him the pack of cards for his own road
—miles long, some of them—and asked him to drop in at each
house, explain the situation, and see what could be done.

That was all. When everybody came back we went
through the cards again and marked them on the back with
honest opinions based on all the current circumstances.
Finally they were re-stacked into new groups, which are
worth mentioning if only because of their magnificent
optimism and as showing the way everyone felt about it
just then.

The main divisions were Good, Bad and Indifferent,
naturally, but these were sub-divided into "Very special
indeed (for grizzly or frightened kids)," "Special for little
kids," "Good for nice girls," "Good for tough boys," "Good
home for anybody," "Just good," "Good at a pinch,"
"Would, but not keen," "Could, but wouldn't without a
row," "Unsuitable," "Bad," "Impossible," and "Never on
your life."

By eight in the evening there were two hundred homes
waiting for children, all owned by people who really wanted
them. It was all very pleasant and intimate and simple.
There was a lot of bed borrowing and airing and messages
about taking two sisters, or two brothers, so they could sleep
together. Mrs. Golding sent up from the farm to say she
could manage six tough little boys, it didn't matter how
rough, and that did sound like a glorious offer for someone
because hers is a farm as live and vigorous as any of fifty
years ago.

In the midst of all this sentiment excitement, and rather

complacent (on my part) pride in our astounding efficiency, which was after all an unsuspected attribute and quite as surprising as discovering that we all had a mutual gift for part-singing or juggling, we suddenly remembered the cause of it all—the war, the gas-masks, the aerial bombardment which was "absolutely certain" to bring fifty thousand casualties a week to London the instant hostilities began. All these things bounced up again from the back of our minds where they had been thrust by the practical job in hand.

I think most of us found that we felt much better for it. The danger of a gas attack seemed far less likely and war itself more remote. However, to this day I marvel that anyone could ever question the ability of British morale to stand up to any sort of threat when it had swallowed the distribution of those gas-masks at such a moment and with no warning at all.

The children did not come that year and many people were disappointed. Little Miss Drudge, who lives down at *High View*, was very sad. She was cooking a meal for the two little girls we had promised her so blithely when we had to tell her it was all over and there wasn't going to be a war after all for a time.

Everyone admired Mr. Chamberlain's final effort, but his arrangement with Hitler that the two countries should never go to war with each other again sounded far too good to be true, which it was, of course.

Doey tabulated his billeting addresses, Olive and Clara made out the gas-mask lists, and the village settled down to quiet, leisurely preparation of mind. There was a lot of speculation. The discovery that the men from Ipswich who had been carting lime on to the Tye fields had spent the crisis carting empty coffins to London (private precautions taken by the undertakers, no doubt) set us back a bit, and every scrap of terror-talk from Spain was carefully discussed. But we were getting the idea; and this was important, everyone knew instinctively, for the one thing we country-folk—and I think it may be true of the nation as a whole—

are most afraid of is of being frightened, and nothing real, however ghastly, is liable to frighten one so much as the utterly unknown.

As the months went on, therefore, and we found out first of all what a vital and important part of Czecho-Slovakia had been taken by the enemy (no one had realised that at the time: geography is not our strong point) we got into the frame of mind for war, partly in resignation and partly in honest apprehension.

In some country places, according to the newspapers, the evacuation scheme was met with howls of execration, but it was not like that at first in Auburn. In the beginning Auburn rather liked the idea of having children—nice little girls and tough little old boys. In a way I think it almost mitigated some of the cold dread of the casualty lists which must lie behind the mind of everyone who has to stay at home.

This was partly sentimental, partly the idea of young stock in the place at last, and partly something else which I hesitate to mention but which ought to be put in. This is a peculiarity of temperament which I have not been able to help noticing in nearly all the ordinary unintellectual English people I have ever met, myself included.

In all nations the ordinary man likes to be thought something; that is to say he has to have an ideal, a picture of himself which he likes to present to his fellows with the idea, perhaps, of getting their admiration or interest. This is very human and natural and a truism, but whereas in some countries it is the national weakness to be thought smart, and in others worldly, or cynical, or whimsical, or even capricious, in England the very ordinary simple chap likes to be thought *good*.

That this is a mistaken idea if mere popularity is its aim is obvious, because virtue is not an instantly endearing quality in times of ease. Goodness, when it is assumed and not quite genuine, is an infuriating affectation and probably accounts for the exasperation which the English do arouse in so many foreign breasts. Yet most people fall short of their ideal. The smart folk are not always smart, but in their case the laughter at their expense has a kindly, forgiving quality, while the laughter provoked by the man who wants to be thought good, and muffs it, is not laughter at all.

I do not know how long the English have had this peculiar personal weakness, but as far as I can gather it is very old in us indeed, and the fact does remain that some of us achieve the ideal and are good in the classic rather than in the Christian sense; not charming, not even pleasant or entertaining, but just plain good, like a woollen vest or stout pair of shoes. In war, and other times of hardship, they come into their own with the virtues they pretend to or strive for or do actually achieve.

Taking care of a pack of other people's children seemed to demand just that peculiarity and not much else, and so that was another factor which made the child evacuee problem in Auburn something almost to look forward to amid the rest of the upheaval which was obviously coming our way.

When I remember what did happen when the war proper began I cannot help laughing at us a little and I fancy most of Auburn joins me.

Remains of the 1916 German Zeppelin at Little Wigborough.

4

OWN people often find the natural tenour of life in Auburn quite astoundingly slow, and so it is if one is not involved in getting something to grow, be it vegetable, animal, or a piece of private creative work. To be precise the pace of life here is exactly the same as the progress of the year, and is, like all questions of speed, purely relative, for it is difficult not to believe, if you watch her, that Nature herself is not under the impression that she is working at a breakneck lick. At any rate there never seems to be a hope of getting anything done in Auburn save at its proper season, so that in a way it was fortunate that the Munich crisis came when it did just after the harvest.

Late autumn is the time for change and preparations and beginnings, so it was natural that we should have settled down at once to get ready in our own way for whatever might be coming.

The attendance at the A.R.P. Officer's introductory lecture was good and serious. I have never forgotten that lecture myself because it was only then that I personally suddenly saw how war in Europe could ever possibly happen again. I *knew* how it could happen, of course; that is to say I knew what ingredients, if put together, would produce the explosion; but until that evening I could not see what on earth we in Auburn could ever be doing while the world was going up like a fire-balloon. Because of this inability the whole question had appeared unreal to me and about as difficult and profitless to consider as, say, the inside details of a fit of mania I might get at some future date.

The A.R.P.O. came over from Fishling to give the general lecture which had been so abruptly postponed by the gas-mask distribution. He turned out to be a retired Colonel with all the neatness and severity we expect in Colonels and we grew to like him. It was his proving to be a familiar and comprehendable figure in spite of his fantastic job (and

teaching people how best to minimise the risk of being
burned, maimed or clubbed in their own homes did seem
a fairly fantastic sort of occupation to us in Auburn then)
which began to put the whole thing on a credible basis.
The entire proceedings that night were conducted in
Auburn's most formal and normal manner and it dawned
on me that this war to end civilisation, this annihilating
stroke, or whatever it was that was coming to us, would
probably be received, at the outset at any rate, in exactly
the same way. It was the first time I ever saw the real virtue
of formality. One can even lose one's head for a minute
or two behind it and no harm done.

The Colonel came to dinner with us and we all walked
down to the hall together afterwards in the dark, carrying
his somewhat surrealist paraphernalia. The audience was
waiting in its usual formation, which is to say that the front
row is always left practically empty and the room gets
steadily more crowded towards the back. Even as late as
twenty years ago that front row was reserved, even in
church, for "the gentry," and now it always seems to be
avoided by nearly everybody. This is not because there are
no gentlefolk left but because very few of them want to
associate themselves with any society which ever took it for
granted that it should get the best view without paying
more at the door. It is a long time since *"When Adam delved
and Eve span, Who was then the gentleman?"* was first sung in
the lanes, but I don't think that as a countryside we have
ever entirely forgotten its biting humour, and so, whenever
there is a whiff of the old tune in the air, I rather think that
front row gets quietly empty again. It must have happened
several times in the long centuries since John Ball.

Everything was very solemn and very usual on this
occasion. Even the little clatter as P.Y.C. fell up the shaky
stairs on to the stage (with the forest glade still in position)
and handed the A.R.P.O. his singular "props" was accepted
without a smile, since it was a serious meeting and everyone
knew the steps of old.

The Colonel earned general approval in a way which I

suspect never occurred to him for his audience sat and
listened to him in inscrutable silence.

This condition of blank receptiveness is common in
Auburn and has been mistaken by the stranger for suspicion
or even pride. In fact it is nothing so active, but is an outward expression of a complete reservation of judgment. I
don't think any true East Coast man ever assumes a newcomer is either friendly or against him, or indeed that he
is anything save an object of interest, until he has absolutely
finished presenting himself and has been thinking of something else for some considerable time, say a day or so.

On this occasion the A.R.P.O., standing on the stage with
the glade behind him, a bright new dustbin full of imaginary
sand in front of him and a glistening zinc shovel on a pole
in his hand, satisfied 99 per cent of the room at once by
explaining that although this outfit was advised by the
Government for those about to deal with incendiary bombs
it was none of it necessary, and that any old pail of sand
and any long-handled fork, rake or spade would do equally
well. Afterwards he went over the official methods of gas-
proofing a room and advocated among other things a truss
of hay up the chimney and thick wet curtains over the doors.
It was all so alarmingly practical and simple, so obviously
meant for use. The audience was still with interest, if as
expressionless as so many Chinese.

Half-way through, when P.Y.C. (who was acting as a sort
of lecturer's stooge) was being shown exactly how to make
an air-lock entrance, and my mind was running over the
suitability of various old curtains on the top shelf of the
linen cupboard, I suddenly saw the abyss at our feet as
vividly as if I had looked over the side of a house. To realise
is one thing but to see is another and I saw that they were
talking about a corrosive poison to be sprayed over one
civilised people by what was presumed to be another. I
wondered if we were all insane and so nearly squeaked aloud,
as one does in nightmares sometimes, that I felt the blood
rushing into my face with embarrassment. This put me out
and I looked around me furtively to see if I had been

noticed and saw all the well-known faces turned gravely
towards the stage. There was Bill, who had been through
the last war and knew something about it, and Charlotte,
Albert's wife, with her fine shrewd face and wildish yellow
hair, and everyone else, all intensely serious, as they certainly would not have been had they not seen the horror
of the situation quite as vividly as I had. They had accepted
the danger and were busy finding out what was best to be
done about it and it seemed to me that the sooner I wrenched
my mind out of its present super-sensitive gear and got it
back on to curtains like a reasonable being the better.
Clearly whatever was going to happen to Auburn would
only be strange in fact. The lighting wasn't going to change
much.

One interesting sidelight on that lecture came from
Norry's brother Jack. I was in the forge the next day getting
some staples and I asked him what he thought of it. He
said that the Colonel had been wonderfully reasonable and
not a bit sarcastic. I was surprised by the final word and
I remarked that surely he would hardly be that at such
a time. But Jack said that you never knew when that sort
of man was going to be sarcastic and tell you to buy all
sorts of material which he knew perfectly well that you
couldn't afford, yet this fellow had been straightforward and
reasonable and had mentioned a truss of hay up the chimney,
which was fair enough because anyone could get a-hold
of that.

The dreadful insinuation contained in this argument made
me sit up and I went back across the road reflecting that
Jack was giving some of the people who come to address
us from time to time credit for far more brains, if much less
human decency, than I did, and I wondered then if the
fine old country gentry who are nearly all dead and gone
with their horses, their guinea tips, their grooms and their
leather hat-boxes, were not a deal more ingenious than I
had imagined if they bred a countryside always to expect
intelligence from them if nothing else whatever, for it sometimes seems that it is only a respect for superior brains and

the secret knowledge their possession entails which really makes men and masters. The Church, for instance, never showed any sign of losing her grip whatever abominable muddles she got herself into while the parsons were still the only people in the parishes who could read.

St. Nicholas Church.

Scraperboards by Youngman Carter

Norry Emeny at work in his forge.

5

DURING that first part of the winter the elaborate machinery of Civil Defence began to take some sort of shape in our district. To be honest, it was not a very definite shape then or at any other time during the first year or two of its life, and even now, when it is working like a cheerful kitchen clock, one could hardly describe it in detail without driving any reader to mild confusional insanity. The fact of the matter is that every authority, Rural, Urban and County, seems to have a separate and jealous finger in its administerial pie. These include the Police of each district, the Rural District Council, the Urban District Council, the County Council, and their various sub-committees, the Parish Councils, the Emergency Medical Services—incorporating in the case of Fishling and district at least three separate Medical Officers of Health—and so on until the mind reels. Moreover (and it is this which adds so much to the excitement), scarcely any one department of these various authorities would appear to know or have any desire to know anything whatever of the functions and responsibilities of any of the others. This sounds like the original recipe for chaos, but oddly enough in practice it does not work out like that at all. As far as the ordinary outside person can gather, the entire government of the country is conducted in much the same way.

I know it is a serious belief among some people that all this kind of government consists of a March Hare bureaucracy secretly controlled by large-stomached evil-eyed dishonest old gentlemen profiteering in the background, but one has only got to take a closer look at it to find that theory as wild as many other honestly held beliefs. The point that emerges is that this bulkheading, this watertight-compartmenting is natural to the species. It is not a fashion, not even a custom. Its spring is in the blood. It *always* happens. Make a man a village scavenger with a couple of mates under him and those three will instantly form a secret non-co-operative society even if they do not like each other personally. They obey their own immediate boss in the background somewhere and their own rules and they do their work, but they do not know or want to know anything about the arrangements of any other service in the place.

The great (if not instantly apparent) virtue of this extraordinary principle lies in the fact that the non-co-operation does not arise as a rule from any of the negative causes, laziness, nepotism or dishonesty, but instead from a very positive jealous pride of which a portion may very likely spring from a human desire to hold on to small powers but which is for the most part, I insist, a passionate determination to safeguard the minor freedoms of the office at all costs. There is nothing odd in it. A people who really will die for freedom, and have done so in vast numbers at intervals over a thousand years, must reasonably be supposed to struggle, quarrel, sulk and otherwise live for it also.

The advantage is, of course, that each authority is highly authoritative and never goes into a huddle with a colleague against the individual.

Time? Yes, it takes *time*, but, as Granny says her father kept saying so sententiously, "Time was made for slaves!" Considering the birth of local Civil Defence at a distance of two years or more, I think that what must have happened is best described by saying that everybody concerned, from the serious men at the Ministries in London down through the most astoundingly complicated channels to the if anything even more serious men gathered in council round our Auburn dining-room tables, envisaged the same dangers and privately decided irrevocably on slightly different ways of dealing with them. Sometimes the Ministry was right and sometimes, because it took no account of Auburn weather and Auburn temperament, it was abysmally wrong, but the result was the same. In time common-sense triumphed, or at least it came in sight of triumphing before the end of history.

The organisation has been achieved by the only perfectly safe method, which is trial and error. It has been handmade and cut to measure, and at tremendous speed too, for a couple of years is a very short time to create anything so big in such an incredibly thorough way. This insistence on the handmade, and each little corner being shaken to fit, infuriates our rational critics, who insist on seeing something sentimental and sweetly old-fashioned in it, but in Auburn we cannot follow that. In our opinion there's nothing sentimental in going to war in boots that fit.

However, to return to Air Raid Precautions, the amount of emotional upheaval, the *feeling*, which goes into the creation of an organisation like this is terrific and it is obviously this pain, this frustration and exasperation, this bitterness and angry endeavour, which gives it its life and which makes possible the remarkable fact that 90 per cent of the arduous and unpleasant work connected with it should be done entirely without reward, not even thanks, for until bombs began to fall these services were the source of much amusement, not all of it kind. However, a man will work himself like a slave without encouragement or reward out of cussedness quite as well as for any other reason, and if he has created a private scheme for saving his own and his unenthusiastic neighbours' families from death and disaster he will go to all kinds of extremes and limits of endurance to carry it out, sometimes even in the face of the said neighbours' active opposition.

The crisis has been a tremendous source of this kind of inspiration in Auburn and for the first time we all began to get a whiff of that heady air of active self-defence which became our natural atmosphere afterwards. It is no good pretending that it is not invigorating and rejuvenating, although it seemed very wrong to admit it then when we felt it most.

In Auburn that winter there were still many different schools of thought about what exactly we had coming to us. Something sensational was on its way, that was obvious, but our peculiar reluctance to envisage the full-scale Euro-

pean war which must have been evident to anyone in possession of the published facts was due not so much to wishful
thinking—the East Coast man is not by nature an optimist,
exactly—as to the remarkable behaviour of the Frenchies.

The vast majority of us were convinced that France could
not possibly have anything real to fear from Germany or
she would certainly be making more noise about it.

Our countryside knowledge of France at that time was
the knowledge of our ex-service men of the '14–'18 campaign, and that was of course bigoted, rural, intimate and
twenty years out of date, but naturally no one realised that
just then. Our convinced opinion of France was that she
was not only capable of looking after herself but of seeing
that we did our share to help her. Entirely wrongly, as it
now appears, we saw ourselves on land in Europe as France's
tough little brother. On land in Europe France was the
boss. French generals, any French generals, were the best
in the world, French soldiers the most heroic (not to say
foolhardy, if you were the P.B.I. supporting them), and
French men and women as incapable of parting with a
square yard of their "La-Belle-France" save over their dead
bodies as we were of relinquishing, say, Clacton beach on
any but the same terms.

At that date France's martial honour was above suspicion.
A lot of us think that is still true. In common with many
of our more informed countrymen we are convinced that
there was something "remarkably strange" going on at the
top in France and that therefore any sort of judgment is
impossible until "that all comes out." We also add (in-
furiatingly, to anyone who would argue with us) "likely
that 'on't be in my lifetime nor yours."

Meanwhile the one thing everybody did agree about was
that we could be certain of being attacked from the air and
so we concentrated on getting ready for that.

It is very difficult to recapture and bottle the exact mood
of those winter months. There were three main factors, all
contradictory, which made it a time of mental and emotional
confusion. In the first place nearly everyone in the village

was obviously stimulated. Ideas for self-protection, a lot of them insane in retrospect but some of them sounder than we knew, occurred to everybody. People thought things out in bed at night, or while they were working, and talked them over in the three pubs or round the fires in the evening with more force and energy than had been thrust into any other subject since the last war.

Secondly, there was a strong but secret sense of shame at this invigoration, for war was known to be wholly evil. No good dared be seen in it. Courage and "honour" in the Elizabethan sense were still right out of fashion and yet it was realised that if danger was coming we must somehow get into condition where we could look it squarely in the face and not see it too clearly.

Finally there was the sick crunch in the stomach of good old-fashioned physical fear whenever the utter enormity of the prospect occurred to one unexpectedly.

There were one or two unforgettable moments, nothing sensational as we now know sensationalism, but sharper probably than anything since because the protective mental blankets that one draws round oneself as the thing goes on were not then very thick. Many of us were still wearing the chiffons of a steam-heated civilisation when these winds began to blow.

The A.R.P. Officer followed up his personal appearance by sending us a lecturer in poison gas. This was no amateur but a grand Orkney Scottish ex-army instructor who conducted twelve two-hourly sessions at one-week intervals, and who took us very slowly and painstakingly through every conceivable aspect of the whole staggering business. He made no attempt to frighten the facts into us, but treated us as he must have treated generations of recruits, as if we were young boys, not too bright and if anything liable to be foolhardy. His complete genuineness and strong utilitarian note made the incredible things it was his job to teach us so ordinary that he slowly and kindly led us into the new world which was so rapidly closing down over our own like a second lithographic stone over a first printing. He taught us practically all that can be learned about air raids by mere listening.

One night he seemed to me to sum up the whole answer to the touchy question of personal risk in one immortal statement.

The entire scene was not without merit. The class, consisting of almost every responsible person in the place who could be expected to get about at night, had split itself into two tight clumps in the big schoolroom, one on either side of the blazing cinder fire with the high nursery guard round it. Mrs. Moore had borrowed a number of chairs from the hall next door, but the people at the back sat on the little desks which had held them as children. There we sat, as fine a mixed bunch as Illingworth ever picked to illustrate a country tale. We were not exactly the flower and crown of modern civilisation, perhaps, but we were all decent twentieth-century folk complete with wrist watches and false teeth and petrol lighters, bicycles, buses and motor-cars outside, and running water, main drains and telephones at home, while all about us, cradling us in a network of safety rails, was the magnificent medical and hospital service and as fair and sound a legal system as any in the history of the world.

The instructor stood smiling benignly at us from one end of the aisle. He had the blackboard beside him and there were still traces of the last lesson of the afternoon upon it, but over this he had hung a scarifying medical chart which showed a portion of a great pink arm with a stomach-turning blister upon it. Above his head, on the wall behind him, hung the school's own decorations, a collection of old German oleographs including *The Light of the World*, *The Infant Samuel*, and that one where the little child in a chemise is hugging a doggy-looking lion while a very clean vacant-faced lamb sits at their feet. The whole thing as a sight taken objectively was quite frightful. However, that was not the time for detachment and philosophic contemplation. The lecturer was giving us the soundest and most useful information it was possible for us to receive.

"Lewisite is a most perneecious gahs," he announced, his eyes twinkling kindly. "As well as its orrdinary prroperties it contains arrsenic, a substance highly inchurious to the human system. But if you get a high-explosive pomb on the top of your heid that's chust cholly bad luck. Aparrt from this, ye'll all be astonished tae discover whit a quantity of pombs can fall w'out doing any apprreciable damage to ye whitevrr."

He was quite right. I think we all have been astonished. It is evidently not quite so easy to kill everybody as we had at first supposed.

The process of hardening up is imperceptible. After the first effort the mental and spiritual muscles get going on their own. The unbelievable gradually becomes a common-place. The gas-mask loses its nightmare shape and becomes no more ugly than an umbrella. But there is a loss in all this as well as a gain. It seemed such a mercy and yet such a pity at the time, I remember.

Right: ARP: A Practical Guide for the Householder and Air-Raid Warden.
(www.blitzandpeaces.co.uk)

Below: Page 392 of the school log book.
(St. Nicholas Primary School)

> Many children have been absent this week with bad coughs & colds.
> Feb 13 Miss Colman visited school & stayed till 13 o'clock.
> 22 School used for A.R.P (mock air raids)
> 23 School used for Swearing-in of Special Constables.

6

I T would not be true to say that the gigantic war of
nerves which took up all the winter and spring, the
great Hitler–Mussolini cross-talk act, Mr. Chamberlain's disquieting speech comparing himself with the
younger Pitt, who, as everyone could see, had not been
very much like him, and the crisis which attended the reap
of the rest of Czechoslovakia, passed over Auburn's head.
They did not. But on the other hand they did not stop its
steady life any more than making tremendous noises round
a tree stops its leaves developing, coarsening, dropping off
and budding again. It may tremble occasionally but it goes
on doing what it has to do to keep living.

The invasion of the second half of Czechoslovakia, once
her defences had been seized by means of the oldest trick
in the world, presented the enemy to everybody "in one"
and immediately two things became obvious to every intelligence. One was that never in the future could honest
men accuse Britain of starting the new war, and the other
that she would have to start it verbally or go under; in
other words the Jerry had done it again. This made everybody very angry.

The individual point of view, which had begun with a
great many folk feeling and saying openly that they had
done their bit in the last war and hardly felt they should
be called upon to do much in this, gradually altered. The
hopeless old gentleman who boasted (in the Queen's I
think) that he "didn't care if the Germans did come, they
couldn't touch his pension," was sat upon and enlightened,
and one after another, privately and without discussion, we
each made the important and heartbreaking discovery that
our passionate resolution never to permit a European war
to happen again, a cry which had seemed so rational and
enlightened for twenty years, was only adolescent stuff,
naïve and silly and on a par with the resolution never to
develop pneumonia or grow a cancer. We discovered it was

no good just resolving and that Peace, like Freedom, is not
a thing you keep but a thing you have to go on making
all the time. It is a fruit, a perishable reward.

Preparations for Armageddon, or the one mighty catastrophe which some of us thought might take the place of
it (for people were still talking about Germany's fifty
thousand bombers due to arrive together instead of a
declaration of war) went on steadily. Auburn put "Gas" and
"First Aid" where it wanted them, tucked in between the
whist drives and the Women's Institute and other meetings.

P.Y.C. as Head Warden and Grog as his assistant dis-
tributed strange equipment to the ten villages between
Auburn and Fishling and, with the Deputy Heads, enrolled
Wardens and Messengers, filled in hundredweights of forms,
arranged lectures and exercises, attended stormy meetings,
and gave out among other things gaily coloured gas-masks
for youngsters between one and two and a half, and large
elaborate contraptions not unlike small oxygen tents for
young babies. At the same time all the other local services
were getting quietly into fighting form. The Observer Corps,
nearly all ex-service men, was mobilising under Mr. Eve
at The Hall. The Specials, still in existence from the last
war, appeared again, and First Aid Points were set up in
every village.

On the wireless and in the press all the drums rolled
sombrely except the little drum. That wicked, gay little
voice was not heard at all and its absence instilled a sneaking
doubt in the mind. Why didn't we need men? What sort
of a war was it going to be? How much of the whole thing
was bluff? There were stories everywhere of Hitler's difficulties. Every visitor from London, every commercial
traveller to Reg's store, every lorry-driver bringing steel to
the forge, had some tale to tell of splits in the Nazi Party
and a different date for the outbreak. March 20th was
given authoritatively, and then mid-May, but only the
Army was dead right so far as I heard. The Army always
did say September. The people who were utterly wrong
were the soothsayers, in fact popular soothsaying very nearly

died outright on the outbreak. *Old Moore's Almanac*, a respected and beloved handbook in Auburn and one Miss Susie swore by, and all the newspaper seers, who had been right about Munich, came a complete cropper the second time.

The winds blew hot and the winds blew cold. Sometimes the wireless was "dull" again, sometimes positively Ophelia-ish, uttering astounding statements between little snatches of wayward song, and sometimes it was itself again with the cricket scores coming in and the lawn tennis commentaries and Music Hall for morons and play acting for high-brows and nothing much for us in between. All the time there was no little drum, no call for men in thousands, no slogans, no mention of His Majesty needing anybody. The right type of man was invited to join the Army if he felt like it and the reserves were mobilised and demobilised until they felt giddy, but there was no pressure on the common chap. It was confusing until we heard in Auburn about the Maginot Line. Then one of the big picture magazines did a section on the great fortress, and I remember there was a theory at the time that the new Albert Canal constituted a line very nearly as impregnable right across Belgium.

Meanwhile Auburn went on living in the same way that it has gone on living through everything that has happened since. It is not so much that it is stolid and imperturbable as that it is up to its neck in work just living. For the first time that odd phenomenon which became so very apparent in 1940 began to show. Public life became melodramatic and private life formal and ordinary instead of the other way round, which is normal. Living in Auburn was like following a quiet domestic film which had been accidentally photographed on the negative of a sensational thriller.

However, a man may only be as angry, as hurt and as frightened as his heart will let him and, since all these things have their place in ordinary life in Auburn, it was difficult to conjure them up for outside things which had not touched us and which seemed just a little far-fetched, so the sober domestic tale at first remained much brighter and more convincing than the posturing of the shadowy giants behind it.

The change came slowly as the situation deteriorated, until in the June of the following year the two sequences overlaid each other in equally hard outline, presenting as terrifying a mental and emotional mess as ever confronted anyone. But in 1939 it was just that the mind had shadows which did not fit the current realities of life.

Homely anxieties were heightened and dramatised by the unnatural light of the world outside. Struan's confinement, I am certain, would never have shaken our immediate circle as much as it did had it not been for the pathetic sense of futility which hung about it.

Norry was as worried as a grandfather and old Mr. Saye, whose services he had secured as a horse-midwife and who spent whole nights in the lonely box over the meadow talking to the heavy-eyed mare in the deepest and most musical murmur I have ever heard, had to turn him out into the darkness which was every now and again disturbed by searchlights far more brilliant than any we remembered long ago. Norry scowled at them. He said they were enough to frighten the mare out of her wits.

Finally, when she disgraced everybody by choosing the one ten minutes when she was let out for a sedate constitutional to produce her firstborn in the middle of the field in full view of the scandalised village, and young Beau, born as flat as a closed deck-chair, was assisted to unpack himself and helped to stagger to his shaky feet, it suddenly seemed one of the smaller tragedies of the world to see his pencil-fine black head rise up so hopefully out of the yellow buttercups dancing in the cool sunshine of such a glittering Spring.

All the same I don't think any of us realised actually how far things had really gone until the August cricket party. A familiar landmark in the year like that is an inexorable gauge. You see yourself and everyone else by the light of other years at those times. On this occasion it was a shock,

I think, for most of us, like finding that a favourite old costume had mysteriously and unfairly become too young for one.

We had made the set-piece the Eve of Waterloo Ball, in that derisive spirit which is going to date our generation as surely as that dangerous adventuresome innocence which Ibsen crystallised and recorded has dated our mothers and fathers, and the sight of all the familiar folk in uniform, some of them borrowed and some of them faked, was suddenly not very funny any more. It was very easy to suspect oneself of hysteria and to be ashamed at wishing secretly that two Regular Army captains had not decided to come as the wounded cavalryman and his batman, and yet neither of them had returned from Dunkirk long before another August came.

The weather let us down for the first time in history. Albert and Charlotte and Alec gave up their lighting effects in despair. Even the great match was not up to standard with Pontisbright failing to score very heavily and Len knocking out Grog's front tooth in the middle of the first over of the fourth innings. It was still a great day, still an occasion, but the whole celebration was playing second fiddle for the first time in memory, and under the skin everybody felt another sort of party was due to come off at any moment and there was still rather a lot of preparation to be made for that.

Even so, there were still a number of us who did not, could not or would not see disaster coming, at any rate so soon, and I remember that there was a defiant mood in the air which made us insist over and over again on the permanence of this annual engagement. There were frequent references to "next year," suggestions that certain new impromptus should rank as full-blown customs along with the Frog Row and Jack Hargreaves' story of the Drag Hunt (a latter-day Grouse in the Gunroom); and an inscription appeared upon the new trophy containing the ashes of the Recorder's sun-hat from the year before declaring that the two villages of Auburn and Pontisbright should play on

August Monday in Auburn meadow "Every Year for Ever."
But it was no good: the peace had gone out of it all. It all
seemed a little childish and there was hurry and trouble
in the air. It was the same sort of sadness that one had on
growing up, an indefinable sense of losing something for
ever mixed with hoping to God it wasn't true. It was Cressie,
as far as I remember, who kept saying "when this is over
you'll all be old," like some dreadful lackadaisical Cassandra
about the place. It was an unpopular cry at the time.

Packing up after the party lost its ritual. More and more
A.R.P. equipment was coming out from Fishling and P.Y.C.
had made fast friends with his Wardens at Flinthammock.
This village turned out from his account to be not at all
the terrible Alsatia we had always supposed, but the home
of people only a little more unreasonable, only just a trifle
more independent, only just a shadow more cantankerous
than we ourselves. Indeed he seemed to find them even more
entertaining, which was thought pretty poor taste in him,
for, as everyone knew, Flinthammock and Auburn were oil
and water, and had been ever since the days in the middle
of the last century when there was a pitched battle with
sticks and fisticuffs between them in our cricket meadow
every Fair day as regular as clockwork.

Our local field was widening and at the same time the
neat little honeycomb compartments of life were being
broken up again. Makeshifts which we of our generation
had slowly learnt to abhor as we had painfully turned the
corner from demolition and had begun on construction
again were once more the vogue. We had to persuade
Christine to give up her new pantry in which Albert had
only just finished installing a sink and hot and cold, to be
turned into a First Aid Point, and there was the vital
question of whether to tape the living room windows against
blast or not.

This question of personal preparedness (setting aside all
the lecturing, newspaper conjecturing, threats and abuse
from the dictators and "dullness" on the wireless), the
question of how much exactly should we villagers really

do about saving ourselves, turned out to be a highly controversial matter.

Public opinion was very divided indeed. In retrospect it seems painfully clear that each held the views he did for obvious personal reasons; so-and-so because he had had experience of bombing, so-and-so because she was pathetically anxious not to believe that any twentieth-century human being could be so insanely violent as to want to kill *her*, of all unlikely people, so-and-so because he hoped to call attention to himself, and so-and-so because he had a horror of doing that very thing; but at the time it was simply all very confusing.

On the matter of black-out arrangements we were all more or less united because we really had learnt that lesson in the last war and most of us could remember the one really vital point about it, which is that there is only one way to counter the zeal of the voluntary official and that is to disguise the fact that one's house has any openings in it at all. Not only must the enemy airman several thousand feet up in a swiftly moving machine be unable to decide if you have gone to bed in the dark, but your neighbour, standing on his head in your flowerbed as he tries to get his eye on a dead level with your outside wall in an effort to peer upwards through a crack in the lintel, must be unable to decide the point also. For peace, safety and the ease of mind of one's friends the house must be inscrutable, as bland and as bald as an egg. This is not so easy to arrange, for light is as sly as water. There is simply no holding it in a makeshift.

Some Auburn people possess black-out arrangements left over from the last war and some from an even earlier day when brightly lit windows invited unwelcome guests. Those who had neither improvised hastily. Norry and Jack made thick sacking curtains and hung them outside the Thatchers, while Mr. Doe and some of the rest of us had big wooden shutters made and dumped them over the windows like a lid over a pan. All the Queen Anne houses, and there are quite a number in the village, have natural shutters hidden

away in the delicate panels and flutings round the windows.
Most of these had been unused for twenty years or more
and many layers of paint had sealed their joints and buried
their dainty hinges, but soon they came creaking out again,
slender iron bars girdling their narrow folds, fastening in
the light and out the flying glass.

However, if we were more or less agreed about the black-
out, after that point we began to differ considerably. Indeed
when Mr. Doe actually commissioned Albert and one or
two others to make him a real dug-out there was quite a
bit of talk. A stranger listening-in might have been misled
into thinking we all had personal grievances about it.

"Madness!" somebody said, and that word in the local
accent is slightly comic in its bleating gusto. "That's sheer
madness, so that is now." And there were others who
demanded in the clear forthright tones of the indignantly
logical "Will—you—sit—in—that—chair—and—tell—me—
honestly —what — wretched — German — is — going —to—
waste—a—bomb—on—Auburn?" The answer, of course,
was the dozens of lads who for some reason, private or
otherwise, never reach a better target, but no one thought
of that then.

Doey had the laugh on everyone too. I began to suspect
that he might when he showed me the neat concrete-lined
den in the patch of lawn behind the shop. It is a fine large
affair and will certainly do admirably, as he pointed out,
as a super-refrigerator after the war. I had not seen this
sort of fortification before and it reminded me irresistibly
of the inner chamber of a barrow. Such prehistoric tombs
are not uncommon in these ancient fields. Naturally I did
not mention it at the time and I hope he will forgive me
for saying it now, but it has got that same simple and determined aim towards permanence. He knew quite well what
he was doing. He had experienced bombing with the
Australians in the last war. Shells, he told me, were not
so bad because you could work out roughly where they
were going to fall, but bombing was all over the place.

All the same, very few people agreed with him a few

months before the war and in a way it was fortunate because
the making of underground shelters presents enormous difficulties in most places in Auburn, since water is liable to
appear as soon as you've dug two or three feet down and
that is the reason why so few houses here have cellars.

In the past, when the enemy was at least expected to
stick to the ground, our ancestors evidently utilised this, for
many of the farms are still moated.

Meanwhile things were quickening visibly. This was not
the familiar working up to a crisis, for that had become
rather tiresome in the past ten months. This time it was
much more like the final rush round before the embarkation.
Things were more or less ready. We knew or thought we
knew what was going to happen once we cast away.

'What wretched German is going to waste a bomb on Auburn?'

7

ONE thing Auburn had begun to notice was the change in the money situation. I do not want to suggest for a moment that there was any actual profiteering in our part of the world in the last war—that would be grossly untrue— but on the other hand, no one in his senses would deny that the entire agricultural population of Great Britain did good business in the years 1914–18. In the first year of that war money poured out over the countryside in a way it has certainly never done since. It was not only that all market prices rose beyond the dreams of the most ambitious, but everything else became so valuable. Scrap, for instance, fetched wild prices, while the Army of the day bought like maniacs. Nags, hay and straw brought in twenty times their normal value, and then the smart officer gentlemen were so excited that they made many mistakes and often the red tape was too difficult to disentangle, so that it did sometimes happen that a stack was sold twice over to the Army, it being no one's fault exactly and the money forced upon a man. These tales are hearsay, of course, and twenty-five years old at least, but I know that when I was eleven and at a prep. boarding school in Bastion my mother used to drive in once a month and take me out to tea in the town, and I remember very clearly the richness of those days of 1915. Everybody at all the farms round about us had grown very grand indeed and there was a great blossoming of furs and gaily coloured tweeds and motor-cars, which were thought of rather in the same breath as yachts in our part of the world at that time. The strain and anxiety was there under it all, of course, but on the top there was a veneer of tremendous gaiety and extravagance. The shops were full and very expensive and the restaurants were noisy and overcrowded all the time.

This was a disaster, as it happened, because it altered the value of each farm and put everything out of gear.

Round about our East Coast the farms are not the grand
kind. Save for a few exceptions, they are the sort of holding
which can provide a comfortable living for a man who will
work very hard himself and whose wife and children will
work also, sharing the labour of the farmhands, but in the
last war nearly every farmer suddenly, overnight almost,
became a big farmer; that is to say a gentleman-farmer
without the slur of amateur status. This change was so
universal that it altered the local view on farmers altogether.
The farmer himself gave up working like a horse, hired a
servant or two for his wife, took his children away from the
village elementary school and sent them to good secondary
establishments where they learnt much to put them off
working on a farm all their lives, and very few of those
private, nostalgic, indefinable things which keep people on
their own small native acres no matter what the rest of the
world has to offer.

   Some people insist that this was a pity in any case, even
if prices had kept up, and others that it was a good thing
to have happened, but however one looks at it there was
no earthly reason why the farmer should not have done
exactly what in nine cases out of ten he did do. He did not
lose his head, you see, nor become *nouveau-riche*, nor did he
do ridiculous things. (English farmers, from the great Dukes
downward, seem to be much the same sort of chaps at
heart; kindly, decent, pigheaded, over-pessimistic in speech,
over-optimistic in inaction, and much more independent
than anyone else on earth would ever dare to be in these
protected days.) He remained a farmer but behaved as he
would have done if his farm had spread to seven or eight
times its size under him. After the war came dumping and
the slump. This same farmer had to work like two horses
instead of one if he had no savings, but, what was almost
worse, if he had saved and could still live like a boss, he
seemed always to be trading at a tremendous loss. Work
which had seemed worth doing long ago when either he
himself or his children had done it began to look unecono-
mical if he had to pay high wages to get it done, and that

led to trouble all round for after all, it is the way in which
one speaks the phrase "there is ten shillings in it" which
really matters in this sort of trade. If the tone is contemptuous one is riding for a failure.

When the talk of war came up again no one was such a
fool as to want to see it come simply for the sake of a very
temporary spell of good business, but on the other hand
there was a very distinct recollection of the phenomenon.
Its reoccurrence was fully expected and was kept in the
back of the mind as some slight mitigation of the abominable
circumstances. However, early in 1939 it became apparent
that in this new war money was going to be very tight all
round this time and the economic frost was not just going
to pick off the middle and well-to-do. Norry, who had been
insisting not without a relish partly malignant and partly
anticipatory that it was going to be another farmers' war,
was very surprised when the Government stepped in and
controlled the price of scrap as early as June before the war.
Indeed, that was one of the pointers which made both of us
so certain the balloon was going up soon.

There was money enough for necessities, we were glad
to see. The babies' gas-masks, for instance, were elaborate
affairs costing twenty-five shillings each wholesale to the
Government and very carefully made, as you expect in that
kind of slightly medical appliance. One of these was lent
free to every baby in the Kingdom. The Army, what you
could see of it, seemed to be very well equipped too, but
there was none of that erratic generosity, that idiot prince-
liness of 1914–16. The War Office was the same wilful
unpredictable old party, but her family was not so rich.

As the final crisis came nearer and nearer, not with the
rushing winds and thundering hooves of movie symbolism
but rather with the slow tick of the dentist's waiting-room
clock, we began to make final preparations. They were still
reluctant. There was still a sneaking hope that Hitler might
really only be bluffing and might back down considerably
when he saw we would give way no longer, for there was
a very large school of thought among us ordinary people

which honestly believed that the man was *all* talk. It based its arguments most tragically on the simple theory that our Secret Service (so good at the end of the last war, which was the last time we thought of it) *must* have sent home the facts, and from the way our Government was behaving these evidently weren't as serious as some other people assumed.

So when war actually did come, it was one of that worst kind of surprises, the anti-climactic shock. It was as though the hero, in the very midst of the movie thriller, after swaying out over the rooftops again and again, had slowly bent forward as one had seen him so often before but had then quietly overbalanced and fallen to death in the crevice of the street below, while *Finis* scrawled across the screen. War came very slowly and smoothly and there was no shouting, no demonstrating, not even much talking, and no flags.

This was all on the Friday, the day the Germans marched on Poland.

Uncle Beastly (in those days the B.B.C. announcers were anonymous and had to have a convenient generic name in the family) made the statement in his "death's" voice and once again the button was pressed in Whitehall, and in Auburn I think most of us walked out in our gardens and saw them for the first time again in the blazing Lady of Shalott weather.

From that moment everything moved with a sort of slow, irrevocable violence. All disasters must come like that, I fancy, but in the normal way one is so excited that one does not notice it. This time everything had been thought over so much that there was not that muddle of ideas which is excitement's staple ingredient, and you could see your section of civilisation, the bit you had helped to build for better or for worse, cracking and splitting and crumbling as the shell hit it.

At that time, like the Guildhall fire a month or two ago, the damage looked as though it was going to be a good deal worse even than it turned out to be.

8

ON the Saturday morning, which was glorious, I dragged out about three hundredweight of depressing old books and made a wall of them half-way up across the breakfast room windows. Christine was furious with me.

"If you go on like that you'll *make* it happen," she said.

I was uncharacteristically incensed at this (half the difficulty of the ordinary person in this war has been to preserve a steady line of reasonable behaviour amid the shifting moods of a public opinion fluctuating daily between contempt for fearfulness and rage at foolhardiness). I said it *had* happened, and if she was anything but mentally defective she'd have known it when "they" marched on Poland. She flounced out on that but paused in the doorway to say her brother, the second eldest one, who was in the war last time, was very angry about the whole thing. He thought he'd seen to all that once, he said. A great many ex-servicemen shared his irritation at that time, certainly in Auburn and no doubt elsewhere.

As the day went on the tension was extraordinary inasmuch as it had this absence of excitement I keep mentioning. It was still a strain. All the breathlessness and the physical feeling of oppression was there but the novelty, and therefore the stimulus, was gone. The whole war has been like this. The actual thrust has come on an anti-climax every time. Doubtless it is intentional, one of those more complicated German weapons we start by ignoring, grow to admire, and end by thinking are rather silly and overdone.

Meanwhile the slow progress of the disruption of ordinary life was going on. The reserves were already called up and had gone to join their units. There was considerable activity round the searchlight camp on the hill. The Observer Corps was on duty, and P.Y.C. had got his Wardens' Post going; two men on duty at each Post night and day and the First Aid workers waiting to be called out on a Red warning.

He and Grog had commandeered the dining-room as their Post and they all, Herbert, Cliff, Sam, Reg, Driffy, Grog, P.Y.C., Johnny and two or three others took turn on the four-hour shifts.

P.Y.C. found a wall map of Europe which had belonged to the Old Doctor. It was enormous and we got it up with some difficulty. The date was 1804 and it is now almost correct again, but at that time most of the frontiers had to be re-drawn in pencil.

In the middle of the morning Norry and Jack arrived with the emergency lighting arrangements they were lending us. These were two old brass and black giglamps which they fixed up one each side of the map on great iron brackets Jack had hammered out in the forge. Norry had laid in a stock of the special thick candles some time before. The lamps looked very fine when they were up and had a rather fashionable outre air which added considerably to the cracking imbecility of the whole set-out, still astounding to me whenever I dared to consider it objectively.

What I have not cared to mention so far, but which ought to go in, was the emotional side of all this slow disintegration. There were a great many quiet tears, all ashamed naturally because there was nothing much yet to cry about, which proved that the weakness derived from emotional strain rather than from grief. Why it should be all right in Auburn to weep for grief but not for anything else I do not know, since so few of the genuinely grief-stricken ever do cry and tears appear to rise most naturally at something rather fine, which seems illogical. Still, there it was. There were a lot of private tears. It was all very difficult.

All through the day there was a tremendous amount of activity in the village although for the first time for weeks there were no planes in the sky. In our house, which tends to become a general headquarters whenever something is afoot because it is in the middle of the village, directly on the street, and used to belong to the old Doctor anyhow, there was a great deal going on. Cooee was off to help at a remount station and she and Norry had turned the animals out on to the Hall land where he could keep an eye on them. They were beset by a conviction that the Army would commandeer them (mares, foals, pensioners and all, in their more demented moments), and we had thought out all kinds of methods for saving the aged pets before we actually grasped the brutal fact that the cavalry really had turned over to petrol, and then, as far as I remember, we felt a trifle affronted.

Late in the afternoon my brother Phil turned up to make a brief call on his way down from the north. It must be ten years now since he went off and joined the fair people (as one member of our family always has done as far back as anyone can remember), and ever since then he has appeared unexpectedly every now and again, like a long-ago seafarer, full of fine stories about a strange and exciting world. His arrival is never heralded and is always an event. His car was laden like a caravan and he was in a tremendous hurry to get to London to pack up his affairs and join something. He is a terrific talker, as full of gesture as a Latin, and he presented a suddenly vivid picture of all the fair folk in England, all the gipsies, all those strange wandering folk who manage to live apart in a country not much bigger than a pocket-handkerchief, packing up the lights and the bunting and surging back to join the real world again to find out what was going to happen and what had to be done next.

He was very sick about everything, as we all were. His colourful affairs had been booming and he had been on the eve of one of his larger schemes. His age was irritating him. He was thirty-four and about as tough as they come, but at Munich time he had tried to join the Air Force and had been told he was too old. It had startled him, I fancy, and had set Grog and P.Y.C. back a bit too. Being far too young to take part in the last war had set a sort of seal of youth upon us. All our lives we had been a little young for anything we had tackled. This being "too old" was something new.

He rushed off again into the evening sun, the shiny

car glistening and glowing and all the brightly coloured things bundled in the back. He thought there would be a black-out that night and he wanted to make the city before it shut down on him.

Another overladen car arrived in the yard within fifteen minutes or so. It belonged to the Medical Officer of Health for the Rural District, who was saving time by distributing equipment himself. He was in fine smiling form, delightfully and comfortingly Scottish and unperturbed. P.Y.C. had been doing a little Pooh-Baahing and was Deputy First Aid Commandant as well as Head Warden, and we all helped him to pack the sealed dressings, bottles of Dettol and sal-volatile, bandages and packets of lint into little dumps, one for each village.

"It's not a great deal," said the M.O. apologetically in his gentle Highland voice, "but let's hope you won't need a great deal."

We were all very dubious if there would be enough, which seems madness now that we've seen modern high-explosives and we know not only what they can but what they don't do half the time. Then it was all a very unknown quantity and the spectacle of all this medical stuff presented to *us*, to the *ordinary public*, free by the local government, convinced us more than anything else could have done that the danger of death and injury was more than just likely. I remember looking at a new splint and wondering involuntarily which well-known arm that was for, then getting hot under the collar for being so theatrical, and then hoping suddenly that I *was* being theatrical.

While P.Y.C. went off in the car to re-distribute the stores I took a turn on duty by the telephone. It was still very warm and the gas-proof suits of oiled cloth which hung up just outside the door smelt of poultices. P.Y.C. had insisted on clearing the big sideboard cupboards for equipment and the one which held the seven pairs of new gumboots (of a very heavy quality and much approved by Auburn wardens, who are connoisseurs of the subject), cooked up an asphyxiating gas apparent whenever one opened the door.

Grog was fixing up a temporary wireless set and Johnny, who lives with his mother down past the church, was the other warden on duty. Johnny is a builder and has a one-man business. He and Cliff are great friends and they run an abusive cross-talk act which might almost deceive one into thinking they disliked each other for the first half-dozen times. They caused quite a sensation in the village a year or two ago by going to Le Touquet for a holiday, which is about as grand as you can get, but they were not proud or uppish about it when they returned. Cliff had grown used to the place when billeted there in the last war and always considered it then, he says, an "ideal little place for an outing."

That evening, when we were waiting for war to be declared (it took much longer than most of us expected) or for the one great annihilating raid which so many thought would forestall any formal opening of hostilities, we were, poor people, fairly confident. Our argument was, as usual, quite simple, for there is nothing complex about our mental processes in Auburn. Our Government had had with the French a full year to prepare for war. This was twelve months better than 1914, when, in spite of the most miserable unreadiness, we had not done so badly, so it was reasonable to suppose that we had a king-wonder or two in the bag for this Herr Hitler and his Nazis, who were not even the whole of the German people and were not to be confused with them so far as we could hear.

We were talking about some of these king-wonders that late afternoon. There were some head-tales floating about. (In Auburn "head" and "king" both mean "the tops.") The secret ray which affects the ignition of any engine at any distance was the favourite. Nearly all of us had met someone who knew someone else whose car had cut out mysteriously on the Southend Road or somewhere else equally unlikely, and who had not been able to start up again until released by an unseen military personage lurking in a tent or behind a wall somewhere near by. It is not certain where these wilder notions have their birth, but they

are very common with us and I think they are partially
suggested by the popular scientific writers, not direct but
through the "blood" writers of *The Wizard* and Sexton
Blake's weekly, who reduce difficult ideas to the near-magic
we find it most pleasant to read.

However, be this as it may, there were at that time many
mysterious contraptions about the countryside, as there always
are when troops get around, and these filled us all with the
most hopeful anticipation. We expected we had something
sensational in the way of defence since such horrors in the
way of offence were promised us. By all present accounts
we appear to have been greatly mistaken. If this is so, it
was all part of our original mistake in believing Mr. Chamberlain trusted us as implicitly as we trusted him.

On that evening, when we waited for war to be declared
or for the great air attack to develop, we assumed that as
a large army had not been called up we did not need a
large army. This argued that the German war machine was
not at all what it used to be in the days when France had
fought to her last man, America had had to come in to win,
and we ourselves had lost a generation dead in our own
footling long-abused little way. It may seem paradoxical
to say that this very circumstance made the situation even
more depressing that Saturday night, but the fact remains
that there is a great difference between going into an all-in
fight for your life and the right to go to heaven in your
own private pigheaded way, and in going into a fight which
will make a mess of you, teach someone else a lesson, rob
you of the best years of your life—which are always the
next five if you're healthy—and which you ought to win
with one hand tied behind your back.

To everyone's relief Mr. Chamberlain, whose stock was
still very high indeed, had definitely decided on a firm stand
and was clearly determined that we should teach this Herr
Hitler (an incomprehensible "bloody awful little man") the
lesson of his life if he did not withdraw from Poland, which
seemed unlikely, to say the least of it. Mr. Chamberlain was
angry all right, but his anger was not the kind of anger

that the common people of Auburn experience just before they begin to hit out. He seemed "sort of schoolmasterish angry" as Sam said, "not fighting riled."

It was very close in the dining-room that night with the shutters up. I had embarked on an ambitious list in a copy-book of every household in the village, showing water facilities, ladders, able-bodied men present and so on (the scheme which Grog was to do much better in a cross between a map and a chart some weeks later) and Johnny was supplying valuable information about wells and mains, while Grog was still fidgeting with the wireless, a disembowelled affair which spread like a vine and which had begun to show signs of strain as the crisis progressed. The same Uncle Beastly appeared to have been on duty for days on end and his death-voice had grown hoarse with exhaustion, while the records he played of the old war songs struck a false, unpleasant, weary note. There was no bravura, no sudden quickening of the blood, no secret feeling of exultation and anticipation of the conflict. *Land of Hope and Glory* sung with feeling simply made one feel slightly sick. We seemed to me to be going to war as a duty, a people elderly in soul going in stolidly to kill or be killed because we felt it was the only wise course to take. It was insufferably depressing. I began to hope (feeling very glad nobody knew) that the air raid would begin at once and the worst happen quickly.

Alvar Liddell ('Uncle Beastly').
www.radioacademy.org

9

P.Y.C. came in, and Driffy, who has a fruit farm, took Johnny's place as the hours dragged on. About nine at night, when we had put up the black-out very carefully, Doey arrived unexpectedly with a case full of books and forms. A man had just come out from Fishling with the news, he said. They were coming, ninety evacuee kids, eleven o'clock down at the school the next morning.

I was frankly delighted to have something to do. I had taken a look at my own work and decided it was beyond me, probably for ever. We had a moment of exasperation soon after we settled down at the breakfast-room table. We discovered that the local authorities had decided to ignore all the careful work done in the village during the year under the new "visiting and investigating" scheme, and, over-riding our scrupulously honest recommendations, had returned to the *five-rooms-three-in-family-two-billetees* formula. In fury I wrote "rubbish" in blue pencil over one form, and we had to spend nearly ten minutes trying to get it out. At the time, I remember, we felt I might get into frightful trouble for doing it, which shows, now I come to think of it, that we must have been getting rather nervy without realising it. I know Doey moved all the papers away from me, and I resented that secretly.

We got our ninety children fixed up very easily on paper, and Sam, who was still about in spite of the time, went round on a bicycle and informed the chosen householders that their promises of earlier in the year were going to be taken up. It was after midnight when we finished, and when we called in at the Wardens' Post (as P.Y.C. and Grog were then calling the dining-room) we all had the faint beginnings of that curious look that a day or so later everyone in the world seemed to have developed. It was that same look that actors have behind the scenes on a first night. We were unreasonably tired, not at all sleepy, and slightly hot round the eyes.

At eleven o'clock the next morning Mr. Chamberlain made his famous speech and, still like the family solicitor, so kindly and so very upset, told us it had come. We were at war.

Still there was no band, no cheering, no noise; only this breathless feeling of mingled relief and intolerable grief. Poor Mother Peace was dead at last after all her sufferings.

Grog and P.Y.C. were in the Post alone. They would not leave the phone. They were convinced that the great raids, with gas and everything else, would start on London and Paris the instant the German Government received the declaration, and that our raid on Berlin would begin the moment a Nazi plane crossed our coastline.

So I went down the garden alone, mainly because I felt emotionally unreliable, and also because I could see from the paddock across the cricket meadow to the school gates and I wanted to be present when the evacuees' bus arrived. There was no sign of it, and I went on round down the lime walk to the yard gate and stood for a minute looking out at the Square. It was a real Sunday morning, not a soul about and sunny. The forge was closed, and I could see from across the street the worn grey paint blistering round the mobilisation notices on the doors and the sale poster for the Gate Farm. Reg's shop door-blinds were down.

I went back into the garden, which is and always will be just a garden and could never conceivably be called "the grounds." No landscape artist designed it. The Old Doctor and Herbert Bullard's grandfather merely decided on it, and they were principally gardeners; which is why you find a fine row of delphiniums and a neat row of onions running parallel with a smart row of yellow lilies, a threadbare grass path lined with fan-shaped apple-trees, and a nice sound trench of celery—all equally beautiful to their way of thinking, and also, I admit, to mine.

I went down to the end and sat under the laburnum and the fancy red oaks. I could smell the sea, and I watched the sky over the rookery in the Vicarage elms, more than half expecting that I should suddenly see the warplanes coming like starlings in the spring, making the sky black. If the boys were right, they were just about due.

I thought: "Well, it's come; this is the terminus. This is the explanation of the extraordinary sense of apprehension, of the unaccountable nostalgic sadness of the last few years. This is where our philosophy led. This is what was in the bag for us after all. This is what has come of curbing our natural bossiness out of deference to the criticisms of the sophisticated cleversides of three continents. This is what comes of putting up with wrong 'uns. This is what comes of not interfering when you see something horrible happening, even if it isn't your business. This is where we've been going. This was our portion after all."

I spent much of my childhood alone in a garden, and I have never lost the habit of hanging about in one in times of stress, waiting for a comforting thought. I do not mean anything fancified, of course; no visions or voices, naturally; but I do expect to get in that sanctuary a momentary clarity of mind which will give me a definite lead at least as to the next step in whatever I may be about.

On this occasion the thought which came into my mind arrived with the vehemence of a command. "Whatever happens, *whatever* happens, never go pretending that things were going well before the war. Never deceive yourself that you could not foresee a dead end." I knew what I meant, although I had not been able to nail it down before. There *had* been a growing sense of dissatisfaction (none of it acute) in most of our generation for some time. Following the logical conclusions of our early disillusions, most of us were arriving at full maturity without a faith and without a hobby—two rather serious deficiencies in the adult. Some revolutionary change of popular interest had been indicated for some time. Now we certainly seemed to be going to get it, although it seemed criminally silly that we should have to find it in another war.

I took another look at the sky over the estuary. It was as empty as the future.

After a while I gave up idling and wandered over to the

comfortable shabby little school, where I found Mrs. Moore
and Mrs. Gager, the assistant mistress, with Miss Christie
waiting with the teacups and boiling water. They had turned
off the wireless, but the Prime Minister's voice still seemed
to hang about the room. Obviously they too had been
emotionally shaken up as I had, but since it was both
genuine and general none of us mentioned it except to say
that he had been "very good."

Doey was already installed in a little reception office in
the middle room, the one Mrs. Moore has blacked out and
where the children get down under the desks in a raid. He
had all the billeting vouchers and the great loose-leafed
book of accommodation, the one I had mutilated, one page
for every house in the village. Mr. Moore was with him,
and we went over our prepared list of addresses again. The
visitors were very late, and we began to get mildly impatient.

I don't know what sort of invasion we all had in mind
apart from the initial nice little girls and tough little old
boys, but we were not unduly optimistic. We had certainly
been warned. From the beginning the evacuation scheme
had come in for criticism. To read the country letters in the
newspapers just after the Munich crisis you would have
thought that everybody in the country thought that everybody in the towns was a vermin-infested T.B. carrier; and
naturally in the face of such a howl of fury the newspapers
did what they always do when confronted by the really
unpopular and shut down on the whole story like a clam.
This was particularly unfortunate, because the scheme could
have done with an airing, especially that part of it which
affected adults.

As we sat there in the cool shadow of the room, looking
out through the back window under the elms, across the
Vicarage meadow to the church tower dancing in the heat
haze, we were talking about it as we kept one ear open for
the buses, and of course, in a sly half-disbelieving way, for
possible enemy aircraft.

We agreed, I remember, that the bulk of the countryfolk
were by no means dead set against the idea of taking in

children, and that the money—ten-and-six for one child
and eight-and-six each if you took several—was pretty good,
or at least it was fair; but unhappily the people who did
object so strongly were just the sort who could and would
be able to write to a newspaper. Such an accomplishment
is fairly rare in and around Auburn. I do not mean that we
are illiterate, but it is no good pretending that ninety-five
per cent of the population writes with pleasure. The kind
of people who wrote and advanced good cases, although a
very important minority in the country which they adorn,
educate and improve in the main, were not *really* of any
importance in the matter; that is to say, as far as bed space
was concerned. There were not enough of them.

We all agreed there was no need to worry anyone who
didn't want evacuees. I was particularly vehement about
this, I remember, because I felt with a passion left over
from my own childhood that the important thing was to
put the youngster where someone wanted him first and
worry about his living space afterwards. "Better a dinner of
herbs . . ." in fact, every time. And there were in Auburn
literally dozens of people who said yes yes, they thought
they had room for another little old boy or a nice little girl.

Meanwhile the time went on and on. One by one we
slipped home for lunch and raced back again, but still no
one came. I was frankly fascinated by the evacuation
scheme, and had been from the beginning because it seemed
to me to be the most revolutionary of all the Government
measures, not excluding conscription. After all, one's own
fireside is the citadel of freedom, and it did seem extraordinarily dangerous if any local authority could legally
invade it. However, since the art of being governed is to do
the necessary voluntarily and in one's own way before
anyone starts shoving, and since Britain has that art at her
finger-tips, I did not anticipate any real trouble; but I did
feel the whole scheme might have been better had it been
given the usual thorough shaking out in the high winds of
Parliament and Press before it became law.

At that time no one knew much about it, for it had never

been published out of Hansard as far as I could find out.
All we knew then, and that mainly from hearsay, was that
when an adult was billeted on you you got five shillings a
week from the Post Office, and she was expected to buy her
own food and cook it on your stove if you let her. It was
made pretty clear that you were expected to let her do that,
but no other details appeared to have been considered at
all. Nothing about washing up, nothing about bedding,
nothing about fuel, nothing about cooking utensils. It
sounded like a fine source of trouble and quarrels all round
to us, "worse than the war," and we congratulated ourselves
on the ninety children. Whatever a child does you can't
very well quarrel with it, and in our experience in Auburn
half the trouble in a lifetime comes from quarrels.

Meanwhile it was nearly three o'clock in the afternoon,
very hot and very dusty. We began to worry they would
not get down in time for them to have their tea and get
safely installed before the black-out. Mrs. Moore hoped they
hadn't been travelling all day and wondered if they wouldn't
be starving, and Doey said he'd been informed that they
would all have rations.

Presently Mr. Moore shouted from the playground, and
we all popped out; but it was only a big coloured van
arriving. It swung down through the elm avenue and pulled
up outside the school. The driver and his mate turned out
of their seats like automatons, opened the doors, and began
to drag out wooden food cases. They did not smile or speak
or look at us. They brought the stuff straight in, dumped it
in a corner and went back for more, moving quickly and
as if they were working in their sleep. It was the first time
war strain had come to Auburn, and it was odd and
impressive, like the first puff of ack-ack fire in a blue sky.
They looked as though they had been at work for seventy-two
hours, as they probably had. There were red rims round
their eyes, and their faces were grey and dirty. When someone asked them about the evacuees they snapped at us, and
one man took off his coat, rolled it in a ball and threw it
in a corner. Then he put his head on it and went to sleep.

Thinking it over, we were curiously unexcited by all this when one considers how interested we usually are when anything a little bit different arrives. We expected excitement, I suppose, and were saving it for the children. At any rate we took no notice of the sleeping man or his lorry, as far as I remember, apart from regarding them both stolidly. We examined the stores. There were quantities of it; bully beef, two sorts of tinned milk, and a considerable number of tins of biscuits as well as several quires of brown paper shopping bags.

Doey said suspiciously, "There's a lot there, isn't there?" But at that moment a message came over from the Lion to say that eight buses were on their way. This delighted us all, and Mrs. Moore got the kettles boiling. We were fidgeting about making last-minute preparations, when Doey, who had been thinking over the message, suddenly said, "*Eight* buses?"

I said, "Oh, they'll be those little old-fashioned charabanc things." And he said, "Very likely."

I was wrong. Mrs. Moore, who was by the big window which looks on to the road, saw them first. There they were, as foreign-looking as elephants. There were eight of them, big red double-decker London buses, the kind that carries thirty-two passengers on each floor, and as far as we could see they were crowded. They pulled up, a long line all down the road, with a London taxicab behind them. A small army of drivers and officials sprang out, shouting instructions to their passengers.

It was a difficult moment. We locals were all doing arithmetic. Twice thirty-two is sixty-four; eight times sixty-four is five hundred and twelve; and the entire population of Auburn is under six hundred and fifty. We hoped, we trusted, there had been some mistake.

It was at this point that Doey made the second discovery. *They weren't children.* They were strange London-dressed ladies, all very tired and irritable, with babies in their arms.

We attempted to explain to the drivers, but all the time we were doing it it was slowly dawning upon us that we should never succeed. The drivers and the officials expected us to be hostile. They had read the newspapers. They were very tired, and moreover they were so nervy and exhausted, more with the emotional effort than anything else, that they were raw and spoiling for trouble. Doey and I, on the other hand, were just plain terrified. Finally we persuaded them to wait for just ten minutes while we found out if there had been a mistake, and we all went into the Lion to telephone authority at Fishling.

Authority at Fishling sounded a bit rattled also, and we gathered that our difficulties were as nothing beside the troubles of others, and that we'd kindly get on with what God and the German Chancellor had seen fit to send us. So we said "All right," and went back. It was the beginning of the war for us in Auburn, the first real start of genuine trouble.

Fortunately there was plenty to do. As a reception committee we had hardly shone, and the immediate need seemed to be to remove any unfortunate first impressions.

To our intense relief the buses proved to be not quite full. There were just over three hundred souls altogether, many of them infants, but they looked like an army. They trooped into the school, spread over the rooms and the playground and sat down, all looking at us with tired, expectant eyes.

There appeared to be no one actually in charge of them now they had arrived. The bus drivers went away with the buses, and the two schoolmasters and one young schoolmistress who had come down with them were due to rush back as soon as possible to rejoin their own schools evacuated somewhere else in the east country.

The utter forlornness of the newcomers was quite theatrical. To our startled country eyes their inexpensive but very fashionable city clothes were grand if unsuitable, and with the myriads of babies in arms and the weeping toddlers hanging to their skirts they looked like everybody's long-lost erring daughter turned up to the old homes together in one vast paralysing emotional surprise.

They did not talk much, except to catch one's arm and say, "Get me off soon, please. I'm very done up," which was piteous in the circumstances. They had no luggage except brown paper carriers containing the babies' immediate necessities, which was fortunate, for they had had an air-raid warning or two on the way down and had been bundled into shelters and out again. Moreover, they were not the ordinary East End cockneys, with whom we have some kinship and whom we had expected. These girls came from the suburbs well our side of the city, and most of them were obviously better off in actual spending money than the majority of Auburn families. Somehow this made it more difficult.

What we did not understand at all at the time, and which would never have occurred to us if some of them hadn't told us about it afterwards, was that they were nearly all great cinema-goers and had been seeing newsreel pictures of refugees for months, so that when their turn came they dropped into the part more or less automatically. To us who did not know this, of course, their silent hopeless gloom, indicative of utter exhaustion, was terrifying and incomprehensible. After all, they had only come thirty-five miles, and that in a bus. In normal times they might easily have done the trip for pleasure. We wondered what in God's name was happening up there in London.

Meanwhile, of course, our position (Doey's and mine) was rather delicate. It's one thing to arrange with a valued neighbour and client to receive two small girls, and another to send her instead two weeping young women and eight children under seven between them.

Also another problem had arisen. It was Anne who produced it. This was the first time I ever saw Anne. She came up, forcing her way through the crush and roaring with laughter. Her gaily painted face was quite different in its happiness from almost everyone else's, and she was hatless. She touched my arm, and I saw that she was wearing a wildly patterned green and purple silk dress, which, like the lady's in the ballad, was "narrow . . . that

used to be sae wide." Tony, nearly two, clung to her neck
and screamed with delight.

She said, "Here, I say, where's the clinic?"

The word rang a faint bell. As far as I could remember
there was a welfare clinic at Flinthammock which was held
every Thursday afternoon, or something like that. This did
not sound as if it was going to be much use to Anne, however, for she said she was "due" in ten days or so, and that
there were about twenty others like her. They 'had ought'
to have had pink tickets, she said, but what with the rush
and one thing and another they'd come along without.

Since it seemed to be our business, I assured her it would
be quite all right. I had come to the conclusion that this
was probably the end of the world, and that Dante was
evidently going to have a hand in it, as I had always feared
he might. I also felt wildly indignant that it should be
Englishwomen who were being herded about in this abominable way. I do not defend this insular and prideful reaction,
which shocked me out of the corner of my eye, so to speak,
at the time; but I feel bound to mention it because it was
so strong.

Meanwhile we were getting a move on as best we could.
I sent as many people as I dared over to Margaret and
Christine, and Doey sent some home to Mrs. Doe. Mrs.
Moore and Mrs. Gager somehow got tea for everybody, and
at the same time we sent out a general SOS. There was
nothing formal or resounding about it, as far as I remember,
but rather an agonised shout of "Somebody come!"

Miraculously Auburn responded. It turned up like the
Navy or the Fire Brigade or one's parents, and, having
taken one horrified, outraged look at the scarifying sight in
the big schoolroom, it took the situation in hand.

It was extraordinary. People who had no room, who
loathed the idea of strangers, and who had declared in all
honesty that while they were prepared if necessary to die
for their country, they could not and would not stomach
a child in their house for ten minutes, came up to the sunny
playground with unwilling, conscience-driven steps, paused

at the doorway of the big school aghast, and then went in and collected some weeping young mother and her infants and carried them home with tight lips and grim eyes.

The entire business became more and more unreal as it went on. We went back into a Bret Harte or Dickensian world in which stony hearts dissolved in acid tears and piteous rosy-faced babies smiled their way into private fortresses. It was a frightening experience, a sort of return to simplicity by way of an avalanche; or as though God, tiring at last of our blasted superiority, had taken us and banged our heads together.

The most elementary emotions, without any modern fancy-work about them by way of complexes or inhibitions, seized everybody and churned up the concrete like butter. I fancy everyone wept, except perhaps Anne and Tony, who sat and laughed on the gravel in the sun.

Even so, however, even with the entire village doing a little more than its utmost, a quart will not go into a pint pot. The time raced on towards black-out. The babies cried, and there still seemed to be dozens of strangers left un-accommodated in the schoolroom, which was gradually growing dark under the trees.

It was somewhere about this time that Jane and Mark arrived on the scene. They were newcomers themselves to Auburn and had been in Captain Brice's old house for about a week, and so were still mysterious. Mark turned out to be a well-known author and Jane an economist after-wards, but at that time they were just thorough Londoners who, according to Albert, had a lot of books, and who seemed to be heaven-sent liaison officers between us and the new arrivals. Gradually certain facts began to emerge about our newest visitors. One of these concerned the size of the families. The amount of very young mothers with quite remarkable broods, say three babies under two, or an expectant mother with three children under four, seemed quite out of all proportion until we realised that of course the kind of family which would be forced to leave the city would be just those who like these would find it impossible to keep getting up and down into shelters.

Then there were the Steins. There were about eight of them, and they settled in a corner of the schoolroom in their good shiny black clothes and their hats with quills and ornaments, bright-eyed, self-possessed, tolerant, and as completely Oriental and foreign to our northern green as so many exotic black parrots. They appeared to be the only people on the horizon who knew absolutely and exactly what they wanted. They were wonderfully polite and patient, and they wanted to know what was the best there was going. Jane and I explained, and they seemed doubtful for the first time. It transpired that they did not want to be parted and, while not actively averse to taking lodgings, would prefer a house to themselves. This seemed to be the only possible solution, since there were so many of them. Authority at Fishling had said that we might commandeer empty houses, but not those with furniture left in them. Auburn is not the sort of place where you find empty houses unless there is something a little bit wrong with them, say condemnation order; but Doey, who has an encyclopaedic knowledge of the district, knew of an empty three-roomed cottage in the Heron Hall row which was perfectly sound, and I promised glibly to find some furniture.

Mark offered to take the Steins down there and was apologising for the half-mile walk when, to everybody's astonishment, the taxi turned out to belong to them. It was owned and driven by a relative, who had followed the buses down. They set off, but unfortunately the trip was a failure. The cottage was not at all what they wanted. There was no running water, no electric light, and no gas. Mark said they poured out of the house and sat in the hedge, and wailed at him, "No gas! No gas!" as if he were personally to blame. In the end he persuaded two families on the Fishling road to take them in; but they left early next morning and went off in their taxicab, very disgruntled by all accounts. Whether they went back to London or dropped in on some other evacuation scheme in a village where the amenities were better we never knew.

While all this was going on, and the numbers in the school seemed even more now they were spread out a bit, I looked out of the window and saw another bus. It took me some seconds of panic-stricken gaping before I discovered that it was empty. Authority at Fishling had softened its heart and sent us a relief.

With the departure of a whole busload of the more impatient souls, who had begun to complain of arrangements which no one on earth could reasonably have called good, things began to look almost manageable. There were still groups of homeless strangers waiting about, but not so many nor so big. It occurred to me at this point that we were only one village out of hundreds, probably thousands, all suddenly confronted by this remarkable invasion, and that all over the country startled people must be opening their doors like this to tired and sometimes angry strange girls and their heavy-eyed children. Somehow that reflection did not make our immediate problem seem any more simple.

Meanwhile Jane had discovered the Ring Farmers. They were not called that yet, of course; that came later. At this time they were just one vast loving family who did not want to be separated even for a night. There were nineteen of them: a matriarch who had been married twice and her younger children, two families of her married daughters, a daughter-in-law and at least one baby apiece. Most of the girls were remarkably pretty, Jessie Matthews types, and they were very smart if in a rather dressed-up way for Auburn. They all had soft voices and that delightful impudent direct intelligence which belongs to the city. Mama outshone them all, however. She was well over fifty, and looked like some fine Shakespearean actress playing the Queen of Denmark before the trouble started. Her expression was imperious and her carriage regal. She was wearing a black halo hat which suited her, and she drew me away from the others and said, "How about letting us stay here till the morning? You know what the girls are. We ought to get the kids to sleep. We'll be all right by ourselves. We don't *want* billets, my dear, not to-night. Just find us a few necessities, and we'll manage."

Well, of course they couldn't stay there because there was no black-out in the big room for one thing; but we did fit them up for the night in the schoolroom behind the chapel, and the big old-fashioned pew forms fitted together made cribs for the babies. Mr. Spooner, who looks after the chapel, worked like a slave to make them comfortable. Bill got out his lorry, and Albert and Charlotte, and Alan their eldest, loaded it with camp beds dug out from the junk cupboard and mended at speed. Everybody lent something, blankets or crocks or food, for the night.

Mama received everything with the gracious ease of a Duchess at a bazaar. She was never hurried, never hesitant, and always charmingly smooth and polite. If she needed anything we had forgotten, she indicated it rather than mentioned it. Someone said she couldn't have taken in things better if she'd been a sausage machine.

When the flow ceased she dismissed us gently with thanks and a Mona Lisa smile. There was no need for us to think of them for quite a time, she said. They'd manage.

As I came back I saw Albert and Charlotte in the Queen's yard, and we eyed each other very thoughtfully for a minute before we all burst out laughing at the same thing. The old woman thought she was pretty smart. The joke was, of course, that we weren't being done; we were just being generous. I wondered if the old lady, with all her town intelligence, would ever get the exquisite subtlety of that one.

This slightly peculiar humour of ours, which is scarcely ever understood or even suspected by the townsfolk, may be a little hard to follow, because of course on the surface the townee always appears to come off best. On this occasion Mama had our crocks, our beds, our blankets and our food, and we had no means of knowing if we should ever see any of them again. However, the whole thing goes far deeper than that and is the outcome of a thousand years' experience

of living next door to the same families. We had certainly
risked a few odds-and-ends, but think of the position in
which she had put herself. If she and her family were pro-
posing to live amongst us for any length of time the definite
information we should have in a few days' time about her
innate honesty, her reliability as a borrower, her generosity
and her cleanliness was practically beyond price.

They were putting up the black-out when I got into our
yard, and when I opened the door I saw to my astonishment
a replica of the schoolroom of earlier in the day, with
Margaret grinning and Christine looking doubtful in the
middle of it. The home situation appeared to be delicate
too. All through the evening I had been sending round to
Margaret anyone whose difficulties had appeared insoluble
at the immediate moment. For instance, there beaming at
me was Elsie with the four children, whom I had first met
when she called to me in the schoolyard, "Hold the baby.
I'm going to faint," and had put her youngest in my arms.
There were five others besides these, and also there were
those school teachers who couldn't leave before the morning
and one or two neighbours who had come in to help.

However, all this influx was not the trouble. The thing
that was occupying the house's attention was the formal
inspection of the A.R.P. arrangements by the Chief Warden
and his deputy, and a decree had gone out that no evacuees
were to be billeted on an official Post, which sounded
awkward. I sought out P.Y.C. to get his co-operation.

I found him with Grog and Driffy waiting for the inspection. The bomb map of the district, virgin and sinister, had
just been hung up. I had forgotten the raids. In the excitement and upheaval at the school my mind had shied away
with relief from the exhausting waiting which had gone on
so long, and which the others had experienced in its most
acute form all day. They were much more weary than I was.
I had forgotten the war. I wanted to talk about the crowd
at the school, but they were concentrating on the news and
the arrangements for fire-fighting, whether Bill's lorry would
do as an auxiliary ambulance, the Flinthammock Stretcher

Party, rotas, lights, methods of getting the news of incidents
from outlying parts when there was no telephone, gas-proof
clothing, discussion with P.C. Me on the registration of
aliens, and so on in vast detail, for they had a wide and
scattered area to serve.

Practically for the first time in our lives we three all had
important and different interests at the same time. We were
by no means the only centre of activities, either, even in
the one village. The Observer Corps was going through the
same sort of experience, the Specials were out on patrol and
the tradesfolk had the Food Committees to think about,
and all this in Auburn which itself is no bigger than a small
Canadian field, no richer in population than a short London
street, no more important or peculiar than any other pin-
point on the map of Europe and a good deal less than some.

All this was doubtless very good for one's sense of proportion, but it was alarming too when one considered the
variety and strength of the emotional strain packed into
those few hours in the school, a strain now diffused into
every home in Auburn, and realised how little or how much
it mattered.

It was about then that I began to realise one of the first
elementary lessons of the war, which is that the whole world
is bounded in your understanding, and that however large
it may be, or however varied, it cannot exceed your conception of it or hurt or please you beyond your capacity.
There is nothing new in this naturally, and I do not advance
it as any sort of discovery; I merely mention it because it is
one thing to know it and another and very comforting one
to realise it. Coming out of the Post and going into the
kitchen just then, you would have thought the entire
universe hinged on Elsie's baby.

After a hasty consultation Christine and Margaret and I
decided that concealment was out of the question, Chief
Warden or no Chief Warden. It is not feasible to hide fifteen
strangers in any ordinary-sized house, even in the heap of
upended egg-boxes which ours is inclined to resemble at the
back. I said very likely we'd have to alter things a bit in

the morning. Margaret, who had taken to the children, pointed out that we couldn't be without evacuees. "Not when you've been putting them in other people's houses," said Christine, with that devastating directness which is all Pontisbright. I agreed with her fervently, and we decided to get the fifteen in somehow that night and to think again in the daylight.

"There'll be a lot of thinking twice to-morrow, I bet," she said darkly.

I thought she was probably right. I wasn't at all sure that the forms we had been giving out at such speed were all in order, for one thing. They certainly had nothing about adults on them anywhere, and mentioned ten-and-sixpence and eight-and-sixpence specifically. They were all we had of course, and if there was a mistake it was hardly ours; but still, long experience of the playfulness of fate did not let me be deceived into thinking that there might be any comfort in that.

There were other circumstances too which made me hope everything was better than it looked. The school teachers, who were charming and very kind, could not be altogether helpful, although they tried their best. Their job was school-children. These mothers and babies had not appeared until the very last moment, they said. Some were properly registered, but some might not be. As for the mothers-to-be, no one liked to mention them very much. Two, whose adventure was fairly imminent, I knew were next door with Jessie, who used to be the Old Doctor's housekeeper, and who knows as much about medicine as makes no difference; but I had no idea where Anne's twenty-odd could possibly be, for it was not a matter anyone could have gone into at the time of the rush, and no one had shown me or Doey any pink card. Thinking it over, I fancied there might be quite a lot to do the next day.

When at last everyone had been fed and all the visitors had gone to bed, I went into the Wardens' Post to hear the midnight news, which told the same tale—no action on the Western Front. Driffy went home at midnight, and Cliff came on duty. He and Grog were going to share the small-hour watch. P.Y.C. was astounded at the absence of raids. He still clung to his theory of the one smashing attack on London or Paris.

"But they *must* do it," he said irritably. "It's their one chance before we're ready."

"Good God!" I said. "Aren't we ready?"

"Well——" P.Y.C. was getting embarrassed, as though it was his fault as political expert and head of the family, "we never are quite ready, are we? They say that if they come over now we'll bring down twenty per cent of them; but if they've got thirty thousand planes, you see . . ."

I inquired how many bombs they carried, and he said, as far as he knew, the Junkers carried five high-explosive bombs and five hundred incendiaries.

"They won't bomb *us*," he said. "Our danger here is only from planes coming down on us, or chaps unloading before they get to the sea. We're practically safe. London will be in a mess, though."

"What, to-night?" I demanded, for it was getting on for one.

He stuck to his opinion. He said he couldn't see why they were waiting. France and ourselves were the big enemies. Once Hitler had put us out he could do what he liked.

I said I wasn't frightened, and felt what a liar I was, and suspected too that he was also, and that three-quarters of the families in England were saying and thinking the same sort of thing at the same moment. As a rule it is rather irritating to become very conscious of oneself as just one of millions of others, all roughly similar, but on this occasion the notion had a comforting side. We were all in it together, anyway.

About an hour later, just after I fell asleep, Cliff came up and tapped on the door, and murmured much as he must announce his people's morning tea:

"Air-Raid Warning Red, madam."

All through this war there have been scattered moments of real drama, little half-hours when the thing for which one has been waiting too long suddenly does happen. Nearly always they have turned out to be anti-climaxes, but that has not prevented the first fifteen minutes or so from having certain merits. It never seems to come a second time. We must have had thousands of Red warnings since, but we never recaptured the frightened excitement and the ashamed but undeniable stimulus of that first alarm.

The Wardens did their stuff. P.Y.C. put the rest of the warnings through on the telephone, trying not to quaggle and even to sound reassuring to the equally excited hiccups on the other end of the line, and Cliff and Grog went out with whistles. You could hear the thin eerie noise echoing through the blackness and going further and further away.

Meanwhile I wondered what on earth I was going to do about the household. Like everybody else, we had a fairly clear idea of the general plan of family campaign when the raids should begin. Those of us who happened to be on duty at the time would be up and about anyway, and the rest of us were to stay in bed or get under the stairs as our fancy dictated (at that time, by the way, getting under the stairs and falling on one's face were still considered a little childish and over-enthusiastic). However, that night we were suddenly twenty-one in family. The stairs might have sheltered three people, but not more. The house is not really very big, we had no dug-out, and in view of the congestion when all the Wardens turned up and all the First Aid ladies arrived at their point it really seemed doubtful if the ground floor was any safer than anywhere else in the building. I went out to try if I could hear any planes, making up my mind that I'd get all the evacuees down as soon as I heard one. It was misty and only fairly dark on the lawn, and you could hear for miles. There were no searchlights and no engines. I heard the tramp and swish of rubber boots on the tarmac right over on the other side of the cricket field. It was deathly still.

Suddenly the White message came through; not even *Raiders Passed*, but *All Clear*. It was over. Done. The raiders had gone. We were astounded and almost annoyed.

It was absurd not to be profoundly grateful, of course. We realised that. But it did seem rather amazing that we'd not heard anything at all. The night was so still and the air so carrying.

We all discussed it in the Post, and most of us thought that something extraordinary must have happened. Had the fifty thousand planes been met in mid-Channel and defeated? That sounded doubtful, but the whole perishing business from start to finish could hardly be called likely. Had the ridiculous mystery ray by chance been a fact after all? Had the Luftwaffe funked it or gone humanitarian and refused to bomb? These Nazis were not like the old German Army. They were all war-babies, all rickety, nervy, hysterical types most of them. It was a proper mystery, so that was. Very strange and sinister. The threat must be real—it *was*, obviously—terrible and immediate, or we should hardly have had to house half our own population again at half an hour's notice. And yet what kind of an air raid was this?

As I went back to bed I heard Elsie's baby howling wrathfully. I wondered how many more of the new babies in Auburn had been wakened by the whistles. Poor Nurse, I recollected guiltily, had three brothers all under two, including twins of nine months and their mother, who was soon to have another child, in her house.

P.Y.C. and I stood on the landing, which had that chilly surprised look which well-known day places do have in the middle of the night. There we were, two among the millions, I thought suddenly, all getting cold, our familiar houses packed to the rafters with complete strangers, neighbours sitting up all night in the dining-rooms, careful preparations for the most scarifying casualties in the pantries, gas-proof suits and steel hats hanging up in the back halls, sideboard cupboards bursting with gumboots and Civilian Defence Respirators, windows shrouded and sealed like jampots, and sudden death liable to drop on our heads at any moment; but otherwise everything remarkably and pleasantly as usual. No guns, no cheers, no flags, no glory, no anaesthetising panoply of battle.

I said to P.Y.C. that it wasn't much like a war at all.

"No," he said, with his perpetual interestedness. "No. More like an earthquake, or something *completely* new like the Day of Judgment. *I* thought that. Better get some sleep. More to-morrow."

"I wouldn't be surprised," I said.

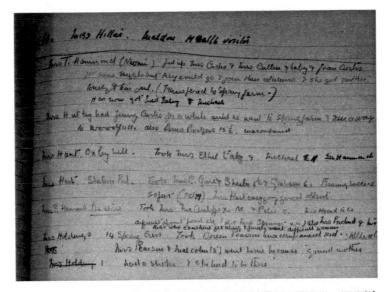

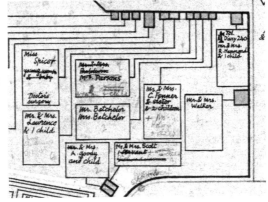

A page of Margery's billeting book and detail from Grog's map.

10

THERE was another Red warning just after six the next morning and we remembered the great daylight attacks on Barcelona and especially on Guernica. Looking at the place, it seemed pretty impossible that any such thing should happen to Auburn, but then the terrific bustle and movement inside the house as the evacuees began to stir did not seem quite credible either. The Wardens appeared out in the square at once, looking a little self-conscious in their new tin hats as they stood about in the sharp mother-o'-pearl morning. Norry came trotting along ostensibly to let a horse out, but he too remained standing with everyone else at the meadow gate, waiting. Small companies of farm hands cycling down to the fields, each with his little cardboard gas-mask box (still ridiculous and shocking) on his hip, came by. They did not dismount but looked up every now and again as they rode. Still there was no sound of engines and the weather-cock on the maypole was the only strange bird in the sky. No one talked much. And then suddenly, far out in the distance beyond the three elms, came the first ack-ack fire we had seen, little puffs of white smoke against a clear sky. We could hear the firing too, not quite synchronising with it. It was a tremendous moment. Grog went upstairs to collect the evacuees and I trotted in to prepare the others in the kitchen, who, in spite of my admonition, promptly came out to watch.

And then suddenly and almost disappointingly it was over. First the Green message came and then the White, and once more there was the now familiar sense of anti-climax.

As the Wardens came in it was noticeable that the sense of being mucked about was growing in Auburn. We had experienced it in the collective political sense far too long already, but now it was getting personal and intimate. The far more than half-forgotten dislike of the Jerry as a boor and a highhanded vulgarian of a type we sometimes breed ourselves, and therefore loathe with the hatred of experience, began to return. It was like seeing again the characteristics which one has resented before in a family which one has decided to like and live with at all costs in the interests of peace and quiet after the most frightful row of all time. It may sound illogical that some of us should have felt this then when a raid had *not* happened, but this leaping out of bed with one's heart racing, only to be left flat, differed from real attack, which at any rate has dignity, inasmuch as there was insult in this.

As the sun rose higher the back doors of Auburn began to open (we very seldom use the front) and out came all the visitors, dozens and dozens of them, young women, toddlers and infants in arms. They were in every conceivable emotional condition from reckless gaiety to hopeless tears. They swarmed over the village, filling the Square and the narrow main street with the four houses on one side and the eight on the other, and wandered in and out of Reg's shop and Albert's old shop (which was and is now kept by little Jose's father and mother, Albert's father having gone to live at Goldenhind, the next village along the Fishling road), and asked where the other stores were. Most of them were hatless, bare-legged and remarkably unself-conscious, utterly different from us and tremendously interesting.

Our familiar views of the village, the ivied wall of the Post Office, the big walnut tree behind the baker's, even the narrow roads themselves looked different and warmer as this new life poured and surged round them. It reminded those of us who were old enough of the village we had known as children, when the regular size of a labourer's family was "twelve with father and mother," and there were two or three hundred youngsters at every village school.

Mind you, the effect of this sudden burgeoning, this great unforeseen burst of fecundity and flower, was quite as overwhelming as it had been in the school on the day before, but it was by no means so piteous. Mrs. Bouttell, who lives in the Street, chuckled whenever she saw them and so

did most of the older women. It was such an almighty
set-out.

That morning the newcomers ceased to be a crowd and
became individuals, living women, potential friends or
enemies perhaps for a lifetime, for it is a peculiarity of ours
in Auburn to expect things to last for ever. Naïve we may
be, but it was a tremendous shock to most of us to find that
on the whole these strange girls were not happy in our
glorious village. The very superior ones, who looked like
summer visitors, were the least satisfied and this was disconcerting to the native because Auburn was at its most
expansive best. It was a dizzily sunny day. The sun shone,
the wind danced, the fruit hung ripe and heavy in the trees,
flowers blazed in everybody's garden, and the richness and
prodigality of autumn was in full display. We had no
illusions. If a person did not like Auburn on that day the
chances were that he would loathe it on most of the others,
for even the hedges round Auburn all bend one way as they
crouch before the villainous wind which blows half the year
from the estuary.

It may as well be admitted at once that Auburn came
as near panic on that Monday morning as it has yet ventured.
The fall of France and the first bombs by the church both
shook it up considerably, but by the time those things
happened it was becoming innured. On this occasion it was
still sensitive to shock.

Besides, the variety, the universality of the trouble those
girls got into! Not one single one of them or us had a quiet
time. Everything that one could possibly imagine happening,
except death, did, and it happened at speed and with
emotion, lifting us off our flat country feet, shaking our
hearts up, kicking us in the wind and tweaking us by the
nose until we had no idea if we were going or coming.

Much of this was due to the disproportionate numbers
of the visitors, no doubt, but the rest, I fancy, came of the
initial shock on the Sunday. That shock made each householder's experience a private and slightly emotional
adventure.

There had been no billeting at all. Each host had been moved by sudden pity to take in a young mother and her babies and the subsequent disillusion was therefore a personal business.

There were some good moments. Mr. Eaton, the farmer who drives his milk cart round Auburn like a Roman emperor in a tweed pork-pie hat (singing sometimes when he feels like it), took Elsie and the children down to Mrs. Eaton on the farm. Their departure was fine. He stopped at the *Queen's* and bought Elsie some stout and the kids some sweets, and then, when she was grinning and the children were roaring with delight, he flourished his whip and away they went like an illustration to Dickens, a great floatful of noise and enthusiasm, the cans and bottles rattling, the pony snorting, the children bellowing with joy and the war as far away as Poland.

Elsie was one of the lucky ones. She was down at the farm for months. Phoebe was not so fortunate. Phoebe had been unlucky from birth, I am afraid, and her children looked as though they were going to inherit the trait.

It was Phoebe who started one particular ball rolling. She brought up the homely subject of "things in the head." It sounds hardly credible now, but in those days we had to seek out people in Auburn who knew what the creatures looked like and what their abominable habits were, and when at last we did discover an informant the chances were she asked us in and shut the door and whispered.

Since the evacuation a great deal of scorn has been poured on country people as a whole because of their attitude towards this subject, and it is quite true that in Auburn at any rate we did have a complex in the matter. However, in Auburn there is always some very good and obvious reason for any complex, and the origin of this one can be traced directly to our first-class county medical authority (schools department), and doubtless the same sort of explanation applies to other places. In the last twenty years the country school medical authorities have made head lice a social error of real magnitude. While most of the genuine sins on the calendar have suffered a grand letting-up all round, and in years when the social code has permitted more and more laxity in almost every direction, hygiene alone has stood its ground as a disciplinarian. Hygiene, in the person of school doctors all over the country, has said definitely that things in the head are social death. We in the puritanical east country, home of Spurgeon, nursery of non-conformity, have never taken kindly to the relaxing of discipline of any kind. Each innovation has been forced on us most reluctantly and it almost looks as if we welcomed hygiene as some sort of substitute, if only a poor one, for our departed doctrinarians who once kept us living a life as rigid in code as many in Tibet.

Phoebe, on the other hand, had missed most disciplinarians, hygiene amongst them. When I first met her she had left the cottage where she had spent the night, had returned to the school, and was being interviewed by the Relieving Officer from Heath. He had appeared by magic and turned out to be a nice polite young man, but with a line in adroit professional questions which would have brought dawning respect into the eyes of a detective inspector.

Phoebe reduced him to tears.

I had missed her in the crush on the previous day and now she appeared as something quite new in Auburn's experience. Practically all the other evacuees were on the smart side but Phoebe and "her three" had never been in that category. As a group they had as obviously been designed by George Price of the *New Yorker* as if he had signed them. There was the same slightly leery gaiety and general waggliness of outline. Daisy, the eldest, a brilliant thirteen, was the one real brain in the outfit and she swung on her mother, prompting her occasionally with a sort of malicious caprice, as if she were the living materialisation of an evil impulse. Denis hung on the other side, snuffling and dripping, as did also Eveline, who was in arms. Phoebe smiled affably from toothless gums and gave herself and her family to us apparently for keeps.

No, she said, she hadn't registered in London for the

scheme; didn't know you had to. Yes, she'd left her husband at home. He was out of work and a baker. How did she get here? Well, there was an air-raid siren (an all-clear) and she'd seen a lot of people getting in a bus to get away from the bombs, and so she'd got on too. No, they had no luggage. Any money? Yes—proudly—eightpence. (This eightpence kept reappearing throughout the whole evacuation and I could never understand why it should be that exact sum until someone, I think it was P.C. Me, explained that fourpence constituted "means" and prevented you from getting taken up as a vagrant, and so by a rather charming mental convolution, two fourpences constituted if not affluence at least comfortable respectability.)

The delicate subject of vermin was touched on insouciantly, but Phoebe had no inhibitions there. She was devastatingly honest and confiding. She also mentioned she was going to have a baby.

The problem had enormous difficulties. Mrs. Moore and I, who were inexperienced social workers to put it mildly, could see that. The newspapers said that no householder could be forced to take in verminous folk (which seemed reasonable), and at that date, so far as we knew, no free money for food was available, since an adult evacuee was required to buy her own and her children's victuals. To date Phoebe and her three had been fed by the householder, whose entire home they had promptly reduced to bad stable conditions, so they still had their iron rations, but these would scarcely last for any length of time.

Public Institutions (looked upon with horror in Auburn) were reported to be cleared for casualties, and anyway Phoebe had come on our buses and the problem appeared to be the village's own.

She remained placid and smiling, as though she sympathised with us but only as an outsider, and Daisy, wildly expectant and dancing with avid delight, chattered something about what we were "forced to do" for them in triumphant glee. The R.O. said helplessly that by rights they ought to go back.

Phoebe looked at us all blankly and said in astonishment, "To the bombs?"

That was the end of the red tape, naturally. Phoebe's was not a very extraordinary case, but it made a tremendous impression on anyone who had anything to do with it. It marked a new step in the upheaval, although even at the time we saw that there was nothing unique about it.

(It was odd how one kept realising the universality of the breaking up and knew as if by sympathetic telepathy that at that moment startled countryfolk all over Britain were getting shot out of their normal social machinery just as we were. It was like a very rapid visible retrogression into a less ordered past. Old ideas, old ways and means, presented themselves promptly like long-disused furniture in a junk shed coming in handy again after a fire at the house. It was a great relief to find it all there. It made one feel solid and still secure.)

Phoebe was fixed up without much difficulty. For a time she was accommodated in the kitchen wing of the Vicarage, which had a bathroom and happened to be empty since Auburn was "between Vicars." Since she had no host on the premises she was billeted on the owner of the living and he handed over the cash thus obtained (five shillings for Phoebe and three shillings for each child: fourteen shillings in all) to Mrs. Fenner, who lives opposite the Vicarage back gate. She bought and cooked enormous meals for the whole family with it until after a general clean up and a return to health Phoebe was able, with money from the Assistance Board, to take over, and afterwards I am afraid, with Daisy's sinister help, to get into the same sort of catastrophic muddle again. However, that process took months and in the initial stages, when the family was eating like horses and Mrs. Moore was assisting in the cleansing, everything was lovely and Phoebe's life problem appeared to be solved for the time. The fourteen shillings would never have fed them all later in the year when the bounty of harvest had vanished, but by that time the man with the bags of money from the

Unemployment Assistance Board had made his somewhat sensational appearance.

No one knew about him at this early stage and his materialisation was one of the jollier surprises in store for everybody.

It was this element of perpetual surprise which made nearly all the real strain in the evacuation, at least so far as Auburn was concerned, and the blame for that, I honestly believe, must belong almost solely to those literate but unimaginative few in the country who raised such a howl in the beginning. To my mind these folk were at fault. They violated the one great principle of the immortal art of being governed. They did not find out if a thing was a vital necessity in the opinion of the rest of the nation (in other words if it was coming) before they objected to it, and also they did not take the trouble to find out that, astounding though it must have seemed to them, they were in a remarkably small minority. If they had only held their fire we might have found out something about what was going to happen to us and have been prepared for all the mitigating circumstances as well as the depressing ones. If the newspapers and the wireless had discussed the scheme in its entirety, as they certainly would have done, since it was news, without provoking a bellow of fury, the ordinary village Billeting Officer would have known just how much had been thought out and prepared against. He might also have acquired some idea of his job, which was complex.

Many things had been worked out astonishingly well and one of these was the money. However, it is no good being all right for cash if you don't know it, and there was an anxious day or so all round when it became generally realised, both by the village and by its guests, that the Government grant would not cover food, and that most of the large and healthily hungry families had arrived with a couple of shillings only until their menfolk should send part of the next week's wages. As some of these fathers had been called up and had no addresses at the time the position was disturbing. As it was, into this situation the man with the bags of money arrived like Santa Claus at the orphan asylum, a lovely surprise from uncle at Westminster. But surprise is a heady wine and you can have much too much of it in a week.

There were other things too, services we should have known about, schemes we ought to have understood. There was no book of the words, no guide for the use of those about to be a Reception Area. In Auburn's startled view there seemed at first to have been a conspiracy to keep the country, even Authority at Fishling, in the dark. We knew it was not a real conspiracy, naturally, because as a nation we are not given to playing the goat in times of emergency, but it did seem to be one of those natural reticences hidden in the private mind of everyone concerned. The towns—and really who could blame them?—appeared to have it firmly fixed in their heads that the countryside was madly antagonistic to the scheme and must therefore be given the dose as one gives the dog's medicine, swiftly, unhesitatingly, and before he realises quite what he is getting.

It was a great pity because it made for a lot of emotional upset, a lot of muddle and no end of overlapping. Emergency schemes were improvised everywhere and then the real ones appeared, and all the time there was every now and again an irritating assumption that one was doing one's best to get out of doing one's duty and it was astonishing if one did do it, and that was ruffling and insulting to that countryman who, because he was prepared to take whatever came as a matter of course, had not troubled to write to anyone to say so.

Another very wretched aspect of the affair was the tendency of the Indignant Hearted to accredit the letters to one class only, which is of course absurd. In a country village there is very little "class"; only "sort." People go by nature, not by blood or possessions. A man will share his fire or he won't. It really makes very little difference what sort of hearth he has.

11

URING the morning we borrowed the old farm
paying-out office in the Street opposite the
Thatchers and conveniently near Doey's shop.
In the days when farming was a thriving trade,
and not the emergency food supply service it
seems to have become in this century, the farm hands used
to line up here on a Saturday to get their money, but now
it is never used.

Jane and Mark and Betty, a friend of theirs who was
staying with them, installed typewriters and afterwards the
first and last card index system ever to be seen in Auburn.
There was no affectation about this; it was a necessity, we
discovered. People swapped homes so fast there was no
keeping track of them without it.

The office is a little house about as big as a toolshed and
it stands sideways to the Street with a small creeper-hung
yard, which is open to the road, running alongside it. Miss
Gene (Norry's sister and named for the Empress) lent us
some garden seats from the Cyclists' Rest, which she and
her sister, Miss Beattie, kept opposite. (Miss Beattie, by the
way, was once in service as a cook to a Duke in Scotland,
and in his castle, as she loved to relate, she once sneaked up
the back stairs to put on Queen Victoria's royal Inverness
cape, which was lying in the hall, just to say she had done
it. Whether it was due to this incident or not I don't know,
but she certainly resembled the great Queen to a scarifying
degree and would give you quite a turn if you looked in
absently and saw her sitting there in black satin with a
white tucker, white hair parted in the centre, and an air of
indefatigability which would have stopped a tank.)

We put the garden seats in the yard and a notice which
said briefly "*Enquire Here*" (it was assumed, naturally, that
no one would want to enquire about anything but the
evacuation) on the side of the house, and within ten minutes

it began to look as if we were conducting a three-cornered election with highly controversial programmes on every side. This atmosphere lasted for about three weeks and gave those of us most nearly concerned a temporarily detached outlook on the rest of the war.

The main problem, far transcending the things in the head, the letters to the Army Paymasters, the quarrels, the babies who cried all night and kept labourers awake, the money, the children who had never been house-trained by mothers who could see no prospect of success even if they should bring themselves to attempt an experimental elementary course, worse than all there was the dreadful business of persuading people to stay and not to scuttle back to their own homes, as yet perfectly safe and only thirty miles away.

The very nature of the scheme, which was compulsory for the villagers and voluntary for the evacuees, made this trouble inevitable, because in their passionate anxiety to prove that they too were acting voluntarily (compulsion has an intolerably bad taste in Auburn) many of the householders developed a positive horror of losing their visitors without having good sound discussable reasons for the change. Private discomfort is often much more bearable than public suspicion and Auburn on the whole is only deeply charitable in deed. In speech it is inclined to be a slightly malicious old party with a genius for attributing the lowest and most human of reasons to any action of anybody's (thereby often scoring a staggeringly acute bullseye), and this put the householder almost entirely at the mercy of the evacuee.

Fortunately by far the larger number of the guests had no idea of this. All they saw was that their billetor was desperately anxious not to lose them unless the fault was clearly and obviously and publicly their own, and that led to their depressing habit of slipping away without any explanation whatever, a proceeding made easy by the fact that they had no luggage. Several of the girls departed on the Monday but the same sort of thing went on all the time. Sometimes they would drop in at the shed to report that they were going without telling because they "did not want to hurt *her* feelings," meaning, of course, that they did not feel like being present when *her* feelings were hurt. It was this sort of misstatement which depressed Auburn, who, with its vast and ancient knowledge of every shade of human frailty, is very clear thinking in that sort of matter. Sometimes they just vanished after accepting a deal of kindness and left the whole household angry, wounded, and wretchedly suspicious that its best had not been thought good enough.

This propensity of theirs to fade quietly away worried us all so much, particularly since we had this awful libel of antagonism to live down, that we hunted out the explanation assiduously in nearly every case. Most of the excuses given were frankly unconvincing, but there was one stranger who, although less skilled on paper than most of the new arrivals, went out of her way to explain in writing. Mrs. Doe, in whose house she had stayed a couple of nights, had been very kind indeed to her and had touched her so deeply that the conflicting emotions moved her to write a letter which to my mind practically achieves the expression of that which cannot be told. I have copied it down exactly, spelling and all.

> *Dear Madam,*
>   *I wish to say From the Bottom of my Hart how I long to stop at This Place. But my hart is so sad as to wont to go Back to My Own People. I have been most Happy and* (the) *Lady I have been staying with has treated me kindly. She has done her Utmost to make me Happy. I connot say otherwise. I was made Happy. Sorry too, my Hart is in the Rong Place to stop here. So at my wish they Let me Go. Behind it all I shall be sorry for it will be all my own fault. Thanks one and all for Kindness to me. I remain closing with a sad Hart,*
>   *from Mrs. B.*

I heard lots of tales breathed confidentially in my ear on

Miss Gene's garden seat, awful tales about "she," and sad
tales about "him mad for me to come home," wicked tales
about mothers-in-law left behind "putting him against
me" or women at "the house where he's lodged going after
him," and depressing but dimly comprehensible tales about
sweet, fascinating Auburn being dead and alive; but, packing
them all together, I fancy Mrs. B. came as near the bottom
of the holy well with "my Hart is in the Rong Place to stop
here" as it is possible to penetrate.

Now that the bombs really have come most of the adult
Londoners still stay in London. A small minority goes to a
shelter at night. The great majority stays where its heart
is, albeit in the basement. Logically this is madness, but
the heart has never been a logical organ, and if your heart
happens to rule your head, as the Didikye say, there is
nothing very logical you can do with yourself. It has taken
the war to teach some of the smartest of us that. Perhaps
it is only to be expected that once you start realizing that
there are things you really do love better than your life,
your courage and/or foolhardiness must appear astonishing
to anyone who does not share your passion and may very
well startle you a bit too. Moreover, behind it all, as Mrs. B.
pointed out, you "will be sorry, for it (all the idiot might
of the Luftwaffe) will be your own fault." I am not at all
sure that attitude is not half the secret of the British ability
to put up with the Luftwaffe. Nothing is intolerable if you
are honestly under the impression that you are bearing it
voluntarily. It is this question of freedom again. In Britain
it always seems to come back to that.

It is not easy to describe honestly those first few days of
the war in Auburn without sounding slightly cranky. However, I suppose most of the soberest people have experienced
at one time in their life the phenomena of what I can only
call "things turning out all right." The thing that made
the Auburn occurrence so startling was the size and duration of the performance. It began to remind me of one of
those glorious stories of my youth in which every mortal
thing happened miraculously for the best. The Swiss Family

Robinson were the playthings of a cruel fate compared with
us those first few weeks. To need a thing was to find it. To
discover a problem was to receive the answer. The reason,
of course, now I come to consider it in cold blood, must
have been that the original shock and the spontaneous
emotion of genuine disinterested pity engendered by it set
up a village-wide effort of co-operation. Public opinion was
in a generous and exalted mood. It gave way to pressure
in the end, of course, and died down, but while it lasted
there was a fine old lying down of the lions with the lambs,
miraculous emotional changes of heart in people one had
known, and never known apparently, for years, and as each
breaker of an impossible problem rolled up on top of the
last it faded and dropped and melted into a wavelet as
though before some fierce natural magic, which is just about
what it was probably.

One of the most unexpected harmonies, to be honest, was
Jane and myself. I venture to mention this because I am
writing this book in the only spirit in which such a book
dare be written, as though each word may possibly be my
last. Jane and I met at the crisis, worked together about
twenty hours a day for weeks, and grew first to respect and
then to like each other enormously, but it is still astonishing to me, and I fancy to her too, that we did not kill each
other in the first few days.

Jane was something quite new on my horizon. She turned
out to be very Left Wing, brilliant, a little more informed
about facts than about people, Indignant Hearted, and full
of what to my mind was complete misinformation about
the country upper classes. As soon as I persuaded her I
was honest I began to suspect that I had lowered my social
status. Meanwhile, to my astonishment (in Auburn, where
we are all true blues first and independents afterwards, I
seemed to have no politics at all), I turned out clearly to
be a sort of female Blimp.

Jane and I had no political arguments. Life was too full,
and the barnstormers' melodrama was happening too quickly
all round us for much talk to be possible, but as soon as

we began to work together the two different governing principles which controlled each of us became apparent at once.

Jane was obviously an idealist and was certainly one sort of realist as well. She seemed to be determined, right being right and all men being equal in value, that everyone should be kind, generous and honest towards each other, if necessary at the point of the gun. The inhumanity of man to man scandalised Jane. Not only that; it infuriated her, and she was quite right, of course. Even I could see that. It will probably startle her to say so, for she is Jewish and of Russian extraction, but she appeared to me to be bent on enforcing old-fashioned British Christianity with a mallet, while I, who am East Anglian and middle Church of England, was equally vehement that nobody must ever be forced into doing good and must only be forcibly restrained from doing evil if he is actively harming somebody else.

In our brief period of power I was frankly all for compromise (now I come to think of it "appeasement" is nearer the term), for bargaining, for coaxing, for bribing; for anything, in fact, so that the individual liberty of evacuee and billetor was never even questioned; while Jane was for frank honesty of purpose and, if necessary, the bang on the head. Her policy mattered to her enormously because she believed in it as she believed in right or wrong, but then my policy mattered desperately to me too because my world was infinitely smaller than hers and within its green hedges lived friends and neighbours with whom I trusted to spend the rest of my life. On paper there is no question whose was the nobler motive, but in self-defence I must say at once that I had no objection to living in a nobler Auburn. I was only against enforcing Christian principles by legislation in Auburn, or anywhere else, because I thought that if there had been the faintest hope of the plan not putting people off Christian principles in the long run someone would have done it already. Moreover, all fancy speculation apart, I knew for a fact without any thinking that one touch of the whip and my thoroughbred Auburn would drop on its haunches, pull back its ears, stick in its toes, and then God alone knew where we'd be. Sitting up thinking things over in Flinthammock, probably. Gone, anyway, would be all this growing constructive co-operation and we should beat in vain against a will which machine-guns alone might conquer.

Jane did not spare me. She pointed out my earthy motives and suspected me openly of much worse. To be honest, I was rather astonished to find my motives were so low, but since my very home life was at stake I stuck to my ground with the obstinacy of pure terror. Jane put the fear of God into me and I almost begin to sympathise with, if not to forgive, Mr. Chamberlain's terror of what must have been much the same thing in a much larger way when I remember it.

However, curiously enough, this complete difference of outlook, this battlegrip in which we worked, seemed to improve our joint legislation enormously. It imposed such rigorous discipline on us both.

Although we became friends, and the odd thing is that we did, we never let up the fight and it went on all the time in a positively parliamentary style, she watching me like a lynx for favouritism and me watching her lest she should try to cure some case of scant generosity by wishing an unfortunate girl and her baby on it.

Where I found Jane miraculous was in her knowledge of the vast and complicated social welfare system of our blessed and astonishing country. Most of these schemes and grants and aids and reliefs had been fought for by people like Jane in the teeth of people like me, or so she said, and I would not be at all surprised, for people like me need people like Jane to prevent us from seeing some things so much more clearly than others. At any rate these improvements were certainly useful, not to say providential, at the time and I was more than relieved to take advantage of them.

At this distance, and thinking it all over, Doey and I would have made a muddle of the evacuation without Jane and Mark, but I still maintain, and I know that she will forgive me and not agree with me, that they would have had a bloody revolution without us. As it was, there were, amazingly, hardly any complaints and we became genuine friends.

Where the aids, grants, schemes and improvements were particularly useful was in the matter of Anne and her sisters.

Until this first full day of the war Auburn was perhaps a little old-fashioned about the expectant mother. The Victorian theory that any lady in such a condition is an indecent spectacle and must be hidden at all costs was dying down a little in most quarters, but we had by no means reached the Roman matron's proud display stage. However, the sudden arrival of seventeen or so unembarrassed young women floating round the village like galleons in full sail, or as Mr. Spitty said rather better to P.Y.C., "like little old molehills," delivered a blow to old-fashioned prejudices which was swift and annihilating. Auburn gasped, grinned and succumbed.

All the same, there were still reticences. We came up against a serious one in the beginning. The dreadful fact had to be faced that no one knew where all these girls were, exactly. Somewhere over the five-mile length and three-mile breadth of Auburn they were sitting in someone's parlour, waiting to be notified about the clinic, or at least about the arrangements made for them, but where it was impossible to determine. There was no way of telling from the counterfoils in the (wrong) form-book if Mrs. So-and-so, mother of Lucy and Peter, was also expecting a Jim or a Mary in the near future. A house-to-house enquiry (Have you a lady here who is going to have a baby?) was thought to present certain difficulties and we fell back upon notices to be put up at strategic places throughout the village. The exact wording was another difficulty. War or no war, Auburn was quite capable of being disgusted and offended by any official bluntness.

In the end a somewhat remarkable sheet, which said, "Will any lady *specially interested in maternity* call on Mrs. Carter in the Street?" was stuck up on the school notice-board, on a telegraph post in the Flinthammock road, and at sundry other scattered points throughout the length of Auburn. In the meantime we had to find out what arrangements had been made for them and these were disturbing. Something like eight thousand expectant mothers had arrived in the county when round about two thousand had been expected we heard, and therefore it had been decided that the girls should remain in their country billets until the last moment and then be rushed into hospital in the county town twenty miles away by voluntary transport or A.R.P. ambulance. Auburn was against this from the start. Shy of the subject it might be, but it did know a little about it and about local transport. "That on't be good for a dog, that on't," was the general verdict. "No no, that's asking for trouble, so that is now."

The solution was one of those small miracles which was part and parcel of a miraculous and renascent period in Auburn's history. The Mama's House appeared. It was down at the end of Chapel Road, the local lovers' lane, and belonged to Cynthia's mother who lent it to us free. It happened to be getting empty and was the old coastguard house, a well-built little brick box with four rooms upstairs and three down, and from the windows you could see far over the ploughland to the silver estuary and hear the gulls scream as they flew inland. When Norry's father, the redoubtable Abraham (who must have looked, from his photograph, like Clark Gable in a pioneer film), was a boy, there were some terrific times round that house as the smugglers bundled the old coastguard out of the way on important nights, but this was a new chapter in its experience. From the moment the idea was born there was a ridiculous but classic race to beat the stork. The notion was simplicity itself. In Auburn's opinion the best place for a girl to have a baby is in her own home, if it's suitable, and it seemed to follow that if a suitable home was provided the problem would be solved. Oddly enough it was so. The entire equipment of the Mama's House was lent. The

Women's Institute had a meeting, subscribed eleven pounds
on the spot for linen and medical supplies, and promised
loans of furniture and bedding. Bill got out his lorry and
went round collecting a chair here, a table there and a
washstand somewhere else. The departing tenant even lent
the bath. Albert colour-washed the entire place out and
lent the lead pipes we had to instal for a new sort of bath-
drainage system he and I thought out, and which was called
by its inventors on several official forms "the Buried Soak-
away." There was also a remarkable hot-water system
whereby a rotary pump we found in the shed was fixed
up over the bath upstairs to suck up the water from the
copper in the kitchen below.

As a rule something sad happens when this sort of slightly
fantastic local enterprise runs up against officialdom, but
the Mama's House was conceived on a lucky night under
a fortunate star. The County Medical Officer (whose personal appearance in the matter at all was one of those
remarkable strokes of fortune which seemed to be the fashion
at the time) turned out to be a man of imagination and
enthusiasm, and with a genius and speed quite out of keeping
with any municipal government ever heard of in England,
entered gallantly into the great race against the stork, who
was hovering dangerously over Anne. Even so, the entire
project might have crashed had it not been for Bea and for
Mrs. Foster. The one rule the medical authorities will not
waive, if the skies fall, and for excellent reasons, is the one
about a resident midwife always being on duty in any
authorised nursing home. This looked as though it was
going to be the end, for Nurse, although she lives in
Auburn, is shared by two other villages and could not
forsake her ordinary work, which is arduous enough
in all conscience, to move down to the end of lovers'
lane. However, at the crucial moment Bea, Driff's sister,
a C.M.B., an ex-matron of a hospital in Africa, appeared
to the rescue. She took the responsibility without a murmur
and Anne, who had been waiting in our house, moved in.

In the course of the next five months five fine babies

appeared at Mama's House, each one heralded by Auburn
as a triumph and a remarkable thing, as indeed it was. In
that time the continued safety of London and the gradual
enlargement of the grander nursing homes nearer the town,
depleted the numbers of our expectant mother evacuees
until none were left, but the Mama's House served its purpose and was never regretted. None of the many dangers
which beset the young at such a time ever even threatened
the girls who stayed there, and the babies might have
had Oberon's own blessing on them:

> "Never mole, hairlip nor scar
> Nor mark prodigious such as are
> Despised in nativity
> Shall upon their children be."

One of the oddest things about the concern was its finance.
It cost the County thirty shillings a week; the Government
its billeting money (five shillings per adult, three shillings
per child), and five shillings per week special lying-in grant
paid to householders for the fortnight period of their confinement. The girls paid sixteen shillings a week for their
food and joined the local Nursing Association, which cost
them six shillings but entitled them to have the benefit of
Nurse's skilled attention at the baby's birth and for a week
after for one guinea. And that was all. Bea did the house-
keeping and everybody who stayed there grew fat. I do not
attempt to explain this, but no other money went into it.
It was Bea's miracle. She and Nurse did it between them.

I do not wish to suggest that Auburn went soft on this
project. On the contrary, the criticism was quite as bitter
as usual and there were many misgivings. The rosy view
was not taken by everybody by any means, but the idea
happened to be a right thing at the moment and it took
root and flourished like a vine. There was no stopping it
any more than one could have stopped the arrival of the
younger Anne.

It was an extraordinary interlude altogether in the beginning of a great war and I for one found it remarkably satis-

factory and hopeful and in some inexplicable way a sort of sign. This estuaryside country may be a trifle empty, grass-widowed by men who have left her for the cities, but there is nothing barren about her. There could, and please God will, be at some time a flowering here as luxuriant and prodigal as any ever seen anywhere in any age.

Above: The school log for September 1939.
(St Nicholas Primary School)

Below: Jane Degras (left) with George Bolsover, Vernon Aspaturian, Jacques Freymond, Isiah Berlin and Leopold Labedz.
(Stephanie Kleine-Ahlbrandt)

12

AMID all this good excitement there was a great deal of bad excitement too.

In Auburn and district there is always this penetrating distinction. Joey, who came to put our house in order once, observed that the Old Doctor, our predecessor, had made more "bad improvements in one house" than ever he'd laid eyes on in the whole of his plumbing career. For a start in those first few weeks of the war everybody began to drive their cars as if they were taking secret dispatches through no-man's-land. Auburn, with its five blind corners, two bottle-necks and one S-bend, became more of a deathtrap than ever—and that when, for the first time for twenty years, the place was swarming with toddlers. The evacuees too were not the only unhappy people. The average Auburn householder developed a way of bearing everything in stoical silence until a final straw brought a light of panic in his eyes and relief from his intolerable burden (a rather helpless girl and four recklessly insanitary children can be a burden in a small cottage) became a matter of pressing urgency. This peculiar way of going on is very irritating to some people, especially officials, to whom it seems very unreasonable, but as one who possesses the weakness personally I can guarantee that it is natural and unconscious and you can't cure yourself except by years of experience. What happens is, I think, that you almost enjoy the discomfort for a bit and you watch it piling up on you with a sort of detached interest to see how outrageous it can possibly get; and then one morning some trivial extra, *unforeseen* (that's the touch powder) incident brings the whole thing home to you, and you realise that it is you, you mug, who is putting up with it all, and quite probably you get blindly and unreasonably angry. This happened quite a bit in Auburn, and we were always being dragged out before breakfast or during a meal to see to some balloon which had suddenly gone up.

However, not everyone was of this difficult persuasion. Some people started off right from the beginning without any misleading and silly detachment. George's mother, up at the Council Houses, was one of these. Her evacuee was one of the lah-di-perishing-dah variety. "That's quite a nice sideboard," said she, with condescension. "I wonder you don't keep your silver on it. I always keep my silver on my sideboard." "Do ye?" said George's mother. "That's a wunnerful strange thing, my girl, but I don't. I'll tell you where I keep my silver. In my purse, and that's where I'm goin' to keep it. Time you made your bed, ain't it?"

The food money was a problem, although it presented nothing like the difficulty I had thought it might, for to begin with nobody took any notice whatever of the instructions concerning the loan of cooking facilities. In only one instance out of all those which I had anything to do with did I hear of an evacuee buying her own food and proceeding to cook it. In every other case she joined in the household as a lodger and a reasonable being, for the houses were all small. The householder did the cooking, as she always had done. That was arranged independently and without any appeal to official opinion.

Money was more difficult. As far as I could gather the question of paying did not even come up for a day or two. Then there was an extraordinary amount of shyness, refusing to say, whispering and detective work generally about what "she" wanted on one side and what "she" *had* on the other. The girls used to crook their fingers at Mark and Jane and me on the street and take us into corners and whisper about it, and then confess that they were broke until "he" wrote. If there had not been so many of them it might not have been quite so alarming, but in any case by that time we had begun to hear rumours of the man from the U.A.B, He had been heard of in Flinthammock and seen in Bastion and Goldenhind was awaiting him too.

(The notion of all this wrestling, urgent excitement and upheaval going on all over the country was still comforting and consoling. It also made Auburn cautious. We did not want to show up worse than anywhere else—Flinthammock, for instance.)

In the meantime it seemed important to get at a reasonable general figure somehow, something as a basis of argument, anyway. Norry's brother Jack, as landlord of the Thatchers, Alf Goody and his wife (Alf worked on the roads and had taken in a family), Margaret as a housekeeper and Reg as storekeeper were consulted, and after a good deal of figuring out and adding up, and deducting ha'pence for the season and the numbers, it was generally decided that ten shillings for an adult, five shillings for a child over five, or two shillings for one under that age, when added to the billeting money, constituted an absolute minimum for board and lodging.

There was obviously no profiteering about this, and it only really applied to the majority of householders, who live very carefully. As soon as the farms came under review, where living was "high" as we say, the figure shot up; but there was plenty going there and room for an extra one or two. The minimum only applied to Auburn. In Flinthammock, which is more of a town, fifteen shillings for the adult and five shillings for a child of any age proved nearer the figure, so we heard.

Having got a rough idea of the cost, the next thing was to get the cash, and one day the happy announcement "*Money gone into to-day*" went up on the side of the shed in the street. There was a very large crowd at once and a great air of expectancy. The man from the Government was due, and after a breathless wait he turned up with a secretary, two great bags of money and a couple of ex-prizefighters, or so they appeared.

I cannot hope to explain how remarkably foreign and astonishing this entourage appeared in Auburn. In Auburn no man is ever just an official. The stranger arrives complete with a temperament, bad and good habits, background, possible relatives, politics, laundry and taste in food. All these important attributes hover round him in spirit like so many interesting, unopened parcels. These four people on

their unusual expedition were no exceptions, and they
responded to Auburn's inquisitiveness charmingly.

As the weeks went by the bodyguard disappeared, and
the official once brought his wife with him on his weekly
visit and made it a proper friendly outing. However, that
was later. Their first visit was an experience. They had had
some rather disturbing adventures in some of the larger
places and were all suffering, I fancy, from the same sense
of shock which I had experienced in the school—a feeling
of outrage that English folk should experience such an
indignity.

Once again I apologise for this, which looks so revealing
and shocking when written down.

Anyway, the pug-uglies were very shaken and upset.
Terrible work it was, they said.

The head man was an ex-sailor, we found out, and a
senior official. He was one of those pink-skinned, very
blue-eyed people who convey confidence, and he certainly
had the cash, quantities of it in silver.

I have had the U.A.B. emergency system explained to me
and I have seen it in action, but I may as well make a clean
breast of it at once and say that I never understood exactly
how it worked, and I swear that none of the evacuees did
either. What happened was this. Those girls who needed
money waited outside on the garden seats and came in one
at a time. They told the tale, gave their husband's name
and address, and related the state of their present finances
and the number of their children, and they received a
mysterious sum—seven-and-six, ten, twelve, fifteen, eighteen
or more shillings—according to the problem worked out by
the official on the back of an envelope. The really remarkable thing was that, although no mention of the current
rules of board-lodgings was ever made, each woman always
had just about enough to meet her requirements and scarcely
any margin at all. I am aware that the whole story sounds
miraculous, but I can only say that it looked like a miracle
to me. In Auburn, where most women have to work very
hard for a week for eighteen shillings, there was a certain

amount of tacit interest to know whether this bounty by any chance came out of the rates; but, that point being satisfactorily cleared up, there was no more questioning and it was accepted as one of the Government's doings. One of *our* doings, in fact, and probably—no, obviously—a good thing. Certainly no one starved, and there was no real hardship.

To see Mama (now removed with her brood from the Chapel schoolroom to Ring Farm, a house which had been untenanted for some years) telling the tale was an experience. Jane, Mark and I, who were acting as referees (from opposing teams), used to stand by in respectful admiration. She was superb. Sweet reason lay in every word she used, and on her noble face beneath her Statue of Liberty hat there was always a patient, reserved and never com-plaining smile. She never lied, but she used to squeeze my hand before she went in to the interview as if she was going to sing an aria at Covent Garden. The ex-sailor understood her. He used to look at her under his light eyelashes and grin a little. She always got her fair share, but nothing extra as far as I could see.

While all this was going on outside in the village it was like going into another and grimmer world to step home and find the war and the wireless and *The Times* and the maps and the vigilant wardens sitting doggedly by their tele-phone. News from old friends scattered about the country brought fresh aspects of the situation. As far as we could hear, there was an inexplicable rush to change jobs. There had been a great deal of talk ever since the last war about conserving brains and how wrong it had been that intelli-gence should have been thrust into the front line, while inferior minds conducted things inefficiently behind. The determination not to let this happen again—laudable, God knows—seemed, however, to be producing even more of an upset than ever before. Businesses closed as their staffs rushed off either to get into some more useful business, into a Ministry, or into uniform. There was a wild milling scramble, as far as you could gather, not so much to get a good job as to get a different one. People were still not pretending that they wanted to dash out and die for their country, which as late as that seemed a useless thing to do, God forgive us; but there was a great deal of altruism left, notwithstanding the sneers of the perpetual critics to whom mankind is such a poor thing you wonder they can bear themselves. People were throwing up their careers all over the place, at any rate, and in view of what has happened since one can afford to forget those who insisted that this was merely done in an ignoble effort to save their own skins.

War had come, and the whole country was leaping up to begin. But there was no fighting, no start. The two great machines were not pitting their real weight against one another. It almost looked as if we were waiting for the enemy to tidy up his second front. It was very mystifying, very cold and depressing.

Looking back, it is baldly and cruelly clear that the men in charge at that time and in the few years before had no conception whatever of the calibre of the cattle they were required to ride nor of the dangerous standard of the race about to be run. That was not their fault. No man on earth can help his size. It is no good grumbling at him. The root of that disaster must have lain where Auburn in its simplicity always dreaded it might—on the Somme, at Passchaendale and among the sedges of the Marne. It may well be that this is an observation which would come better from a man of forty-six or so, solid, established, experienced and in the height of his mental and moral powers, instead of from a youngish countrywoman; but such men are terrifyingly scarce, and so I venture to make it for some chap ten years older than I who died with thousands like him in France when I was eleven. It seems to me that we have mourned these men too long poetically as ever-glorious youths. It is the *use* of them which is our bitter practical loss; now their maturity, long after this their experienced age.

Probably the most alarming aspect from our point of view of these early days of this new half of the old war was the complete absence of any but medicated news. The censorship shut down like a lid on a box. In normal times, and even now when the country is well under way again and the new values are settling, there is all the while a continuous undercurrent of what I can only call public and private notions about affairs. I do not mean rumour. Rather it is almost a wordless communication, carried by looks and frames of mind, atmospheres, personal deductions from scattered clues. At the beginning of the war all this vanished. It shut off like a light. The Press boys were bewildered, without a single secret to keep quiet about between them, and there was not even any "I could an' if I would"-ing going around. Like most country people, we had certain contacts in town from whom we were in the habit of getting a general view of current affairs. It is extraordinary how informed one can keep in peace-time by visiting the city once a week and having a circle of widely different acquaintances. In these days P.Y.C.'s weekly gossip hunts produced nothing. The city knew less than Auburn. Normally well-informed circles were startled by their own ignorance.

This silence was so complete, the harping on the necessity for secrecy so continuous, that most of us assumed that something considerable was being done very quietly indeed. At the same time it looked odd that the call-up was so slow and there was no great talk about munitions. Some of us were silly enough to think we must have got some put by.

Norry and Jack said "that seemed strange," but apart from a general worried frown Auburn showed no great sign of anxiety. Experience, and the instinct which derives from it, has taught the countryside in times of doubt to sit powerful tight.

Pip Youngman Carter ('P.Y.C.').

13

THE one evidence of bustle which did reach us in Auburn was frankly dispiriting. One of our small nearby factories where two or three of the local boys worked was said to be making corpse-racks. The possible use of these was discussed with a certain amount of not unnatural interest, but no satisfactory explanation was forthcoming until Jane's evacuee's husband came down to see his wife. He was a builder working in London on what, as far as we could gather, was a chain of super-mortuaries, as you might have a chain of cinemas. Naturally we discredited three parts of what he said and believed the rest. We had had an idea that London expected casualties. Fifty thousand a week, some people said (without mentioning the number of weeks they thought it was going to continue). However, this looked like confirmation of some of it.

There was so much secrecy about all this, such complete quiet in the Press, that I fancy we were not the only folk to assume that, since such thorough arrangements were being made for the dead, equally sound arrangements had already been made for the living, and that all over London there must be hidden deep shelters. In this, as it turned out over a year later, we were mistaken. Such an astounding anomaly seems almost beyond belief, until one realises that under the peculiar and complex system of local government which manages these things a corpse and a casualty are both concrete public nuisances, directly the concern of the appropriate municipal body, but the living citizen is largely his own responsibility. In normal times this arrangement works out excellently. The public is informed of every possible angle of its probable needs in the near future through the Press and the wireless. Gradually it makes up its mind exactly what it wants to do about them, and then it grumbles until it gets what it wants. Unfortunately this silence, this censorship, this sudden cutting off of air and light, destroyed

134

all that in an afternoon without anybody realising it. The pity was that not half of it seems to have been particularly necessary.

From the beginning there was an extraordinary anxiety in official circles not to alarm the public. Even now in 1941, when the same public has viewed with stoic calm time bombs in its front gardens and the whole centre of the city blazing like a page from the *Inferno*, one still sometimes hears the phrase.

Altogether it was a sad thing to see, for in the past this nation has been trained by giants and can take a giant's hand.

It was at that time that the tremendous importance of the wireless to us ordinary country people first became so very obvious. The news on the wireless, although not very full, is at least not muddled. It sounds like gospel, and the announcers do their best to be as impersonal as print. This has had one most interesting effect on us in Auburn. It has isolated news in our minds. To the ordinary Auburn man news now means one thing, and opinion means another. This is fresh. It has put the newspapers into the category of entertainments. Let me say at once that I do not believe myself that the B.B.C. is always entirely unbiased or that it never, never makes mistakes; but it sounds as though it is as near the limpid truth as maybe, and by its extreme caution and conservatism it does preserve this impression.

The newspapers, then, have developed a new status, for even though opinion is valued and very carefully considered in Auburn it is recognised for what it is, just opinion and not necessarily better than yours or mine. Everybody takes in a paper and most people read one, but not, I think, for the news. P.Y.C., who used always to take in two papers, used to read the *Express*, so he said, for Coop's cat, William Hickey and Beachcomber, and to see what was going to happen. He then read *The Times* to see if it ought to have happened, and he listened to the wireless to see if it really had happened. And there are others like him.

The rest of us—excluding a few who, like Norry, buy only

the local papers in which there are a couple of columns
headed "The War," and all the rest is about local sales and
deaths and prosecutions and small paragraphs of gossip from
each village—take in one of the popular dailies, but not
necessarily for their letterpress. This is largely their own
fault. According to Sam, they all copy each other, and are
consequently all six of one and half a dozen of the other.
He and his friends have taken in each of them in their time
because of the presents. Before the war door-to-door travellers
used to come round and try to persuade you to change your
paper for the one which employed them. As a reward you
could save up coupons and get a present. The idea was that
by the time you had got a present or two, and had been
taking the paper for three months or so, you would be so
fond of it you wouldn't want to leave it. In effect, of course,
when you'd got all you could from one paper you changed
to its rival, which was very like it, and got a lot more
presents. Sam has quite a library of cook books, gardening
books, home doctors and children's painting books all
obtained in this economical fashion. He also got some toys
for Roy and Barry and a fountain-pen. It is true that when
war started and the whole circus came to an end for a time
he was left with the *News Chronicle*, which does not suit his
politics at all and frequently scandalises him, but he won't
change until the "present" system returns and so may be
a constant reader for the rest of his life. All the same he
won't agree with it if he doesn't feel like it. In the matter
of politics Sam would get on much better with *The Times*
(he once reduced a socialist up at the factory to purple-faced
impotence by insisting that "this fascism will goo right out
of fashion. It'll die after it's failed, same as your Labour did
when it come into power.") However, *The Times*' literary
style defeats him, and it is a great pity from his point of
view that that austere organ does not run a junior edition
for its less erudite Blimps. Sam is quite as Tory and quite
as austere politically as P.Y.C. or any other *Times* reader,
but the paper's magazine content does not appeal to him.
The Greek pun leaves him cold.

To return to the war and the wireless. If we did not get action in those early days, we did get talk. Addressing the nation became a mania like diabolo, or so it seemed to us who were addressed. We were addressed like billy-o and, knowing just how important we were and how unnecessary it was to convince us that we had anything to do but fight, we were often dismayed.

Once or twice the talk was impressive. The King's speech brought everyone to a sudden halt, because for the first time his voice was so uncannily like his father's. We were rather in need of the "old squire" at that time, and the same voice which had said so tremendously at the Christmas broadcast, "This is to the children. This is the *King* speaking" sent a shot of the old pride, the pride we most of us deride and hide and abuse and treasure privately, through everyone.

Unfortunately that was almost all of warmth. After that came the steady rain. There was Sir Samuel Hoare's speech, which had to be heard to be believed, and all the other depressed ministers, and the Archbishop of York, who spoke like a statesman rather than a churchman and who made the one good political speech of the first period.

In the midst of all this uninspired oratory—for, apart from the King, who alone touched the hungry spot in the waking countryside, the tendency was all to dwell on the disaster rather than on the heights to be scaled—there suddenly came the speeches from the Dominions representatives, and they were a revelation and an experience.

One of the wardens—I cannot remember who it was— summed up the surprise by saying, "Sounds like *us*, don't he?" This is not an easy thing to explain, because to country ears very few people indeed talk like us. Most of the world, London included, is a bit on the foreign side. These Colonial accents, however, are country accents, and when the Australian came out with no measured commiseration, no yarn about us all being in trouble—which was after all a fact none of us was likely to forget—but made instead a fine vigorous offer to come in with us and take the enemy's hide off him and enjoy it (as they have), it was the first word of the kind we had heard. It was indescribable. It was terrific. Here was the great draught of new blood we needed, not foreign blood either, not even Frenchy stuff which is a bit hot and sometimes a bit thin, but our own blood, good comprehensible stuff suitable for fighting. This, everybody knew instinctively, was the only thing we were a mite short of—the real old solid stuff, the stuff the Old Doctor was made of long ago, and George Playle and Long 'un and Bill's brother who was "the best of the lot," and all the other dozens of country chaps who had no time to get sons before they died. There was an old man in Suffolk once who told me about the last war when I was a girl.

"Ah, they cut down the seed, you see," he said. "They cut down the seed."

The South African chap too went down very well with us. His "we're on your side because it suits us" line was recognisable as a home product all right. "Sounds honest anyhoo, don't 'e?" said Auburn, with a dirty chuckle. While the Canadian, with his more urban but still virile talk, confirmed our conviction that once we only got started things would not be so bad. We beat 'em once, and we'd beat 'em again.

Alongside these voices from all over the world came the metallic affectations of Lord Haw-Haw, the German pro-pagandist. Auburn listened to Haw-Haw with a deep and particular satisfaction extraordinary to anyone who did not know us very well. The explanation lies in a racial, or at least a tribal, foible of the district. In describing Auburn it may be that I have been so anxious to give our point of view that I have ignored those considerable eccentricities which do sometimes make us awkward people for the stranger to like and understand. The fact is—it has to be faced—that we have in some respects a cruel and perverted sense of humour, and few things strike us as being more funny than the liar who is unconscious that he is entirely disbelieved. I cannot hope to explain why this is so. I can only record that such a spectacle to most of us does rank with "man treading on rake" or "fat person sitting on absent chair." I do not defend it, but I may as well admit that it makes me laugh too, although not for so long as some of us. Some of us can laugh at this joke for months continuously, or even years. There used to be a summer visitor who fancied himself as a connoisseur of these parts, and one of the local sports, ranking almost with cricket or making wine, used to be to get hold of him and coax him into telling tall stories of his own and others' prowess on the water or with a shotgun. He would be kept talking for evenings on end, fed assiduously with hints and led on with vacant and bemazed expressions of wonderment; and all the time the whole tap-room would be in secret convulsions. He was never told. No one ever let on. They just enjoyed him. The wilder he grew the better he went down, because he was lying and they knew, and he didn't know that they knew. We'd laugh about him afterwards until we cried. This is a dreadful confession. On paper it looks like a betrayal. But there you are: that is the main reason for Lord Haw-Haw's success in Auburn. The night he said that Bastion was in ruins, and the bus had just come in and reported that not a plane had been seen there all day, was one of his greatest triumphs. If he told the truth, I don't think anyone would listen to him.

In the house we never heard him much, because P.Y.C. wouldn't have his voice in the place—mainly, I believe, because he thought him a trespassing Hun, whatever his parentage—but the rest of us once had a good evening listening to the sins of an English Secret Service which was entirely supported by voluntary contributions and door-to-door collections like a hospital, and which made a bit on the side in the white slave traffic.

It may be that German propaganda is so good and so subtle that the mere fact that Auburn listened at all poisoned its ears. Many people believe this. But I do not think Auburn has had its ears poisoned. It has never altered its opinion of the enemy from the day it discovered it was an enemy again, except to decide that it was stronger than it had been led to believe. The real propaganda against Germany and the

Germans was put out by them twenty-five years ago. Since
then they have merely brought it up to date. Bill, who was
put in charge of three hundred of them in the great retreat
of 1918 (and given an interpreter who he began to suspect
was on their side), says they were extraordinary people
when fighting. "They'd *gre-owl* at ye," he says.

Apart from the speeches there was little news on the
wireless until the Russian descent on Poland, which startled
everybody. It filled P.Y.C. with the darkest Tory foreboding
and shook other people to their Left Wing hearts. Low's
caricature "Idealism: the First Casualty" had a great vogue.
Auburn noted the move, realised "we couldn't do nothing
yit," and went on grappling with the evacuees.

When Warsaw and her heroic Mayor went down together
in as fine a tale as any in the classics, our turn, it seemed,
must come soon. The Wardens clung to their telephone with
renewed expectancy. The First Aiders sat up again, and one
listened slyly for the scream of wings.

I went out in the garden for the first time for what seemed
a year or two one morning about then with the idea of
having a bit of a pause.

I avoided the top garden, because it was usually full of
the visitors and we had made it the quarrelling place. The
girls' husbands used to come down over the week-ends, and
there had been a growing tendency for the marital fights
which invariably ensued over going back or not going back
to take place in the yard outside our official shed bang in
the middle of the street. They had the sense not to fight in
the billets, but they used to come up to us to do it, expecting
us to be mugs enough to take sides. I had protested at this
custom because I could see we were all getting a bad enough
name already, what with the things in the head (which had
been caught in the bus in some cases, given to the householders' families, and discovered simultaneously by both
parties, each blaming the other), to say nothing of the
insanitary children; and I did not know how long Auburn's
saintly patience, none the less a virtue because it was a bit
conscious, was going to hold out. Still, as everyone knows,

if you want to quarrel with your husband it is your unquestionable right to do so, so the cricket-watching cartshed was put at their disposal. This was in the top garden and three hundred yards from a house. They used to go up there and say what they liked to each other as loudly as they liked, and no harm was done and nothing repeated afterwards.

Since I felt like being quiet that morning, I went round to the Lady Garden, wondering how long before the heavens would really fall. As I turned the corner I came on Albert and Alec. They were re-roofing the conservatory. It was a job we'd been considering for years. Every time P.Y.C. and I took Albert round to look at it Albert stuck his penknife into the woodwork, and great chunks of it came away like stale bread. All the same I was a bit startled to see the neat heaps of new timber and crates of fresh glass set out ready for the repairs. Albert regarded my expression with astonishment. He said it was then or never. The war might go on ten years. Alec was going to get into the Air Force, and God alone knew what price glass and timber would go up to. "You don't want the whole thing coming down, do you?" he said.

I said what about the air raids? We were taping up the windows round the other side of the house to prevent splintering.

He said that would be all right, for it would never get hit until the last nail was in, and he wouldn't quite finish it for that reason.

I said acidly that I betted he wouldn't for the usual reason, for there never was such a man for leaving one job to start another, and I'd known him conduct seven simultaneously in our house alone. All the same I said I didn't see much sense in mending anything, the way this man Hitler was going on.

Albert sat up on the spidery roof and pointed a trowel at me.

"You don't want to *give way to him*," he said. "He can't upset you if you don't let him."

After that I went back to the evacuees. The conservatory

is still up and still intact. The eucalyptus and the passion flowers are in perfect health, and when even the nearest bombs fell later they did no more than shake a pane out and break the heavy flowers from our twenty-year-old begonia. The roof is still waiting for the bit of timber at the top over the fanlight, which Albert has not seen fit to finish, and it may be that it will still be standing to-morrow, or next year, or in fifty years' time.

Right: 'Idealism: theFirst Casualty' by David Low. (*Associated Newspapers*)

FINLAND.— FIRST CASUALTY

Below: Margery in front of her conservatory in the 1950s.

14

THE first part of the war, the part which we called "funny," and which in America they called "phoney" (both countries meaning very much the same thing, probably only America as usual saying it less ambiguously), was in Auburn dominated almost entirely by the evacuees. This was not really very odd, for, as everyone knows, people to stay—even relations—can revolutionise one's outlook on life more thoroughly than anything else on earth save physical pain. All the same there were people who kept their sense of proportion. One of these was Martha Cracknell. She was very old, could neither read nor write, and was dying. She used to lie close to the open window in her cottage in the baker's square, not to be confused with the real or Queen's Head square, and nearly opposite our billeting shed, and she would often call out to her acquaintances as they passed along the Street.

"They're a'coming on," she shouted one morning, as I came by.

Since the whole place was swarming with little children, very pretty in the sun, I said Yes, and wasn't it nice to see them?

She eyed me with cold amazement. "Oh, I don't mean *they*," she said, with terrific contempt. "I mean the French."

There were many other activities too in the village at this time. Cynthia and Joan were running a working party at The Court, making Red Cross supplies. Pauline had another, knitting comforts for the men at the searchlights, and later for the Observers and the Wardens, and later still for the Home Guards, not forgetting the real sailors and soldiers from the village. However, even with the invasion of Finland and our impotence because we were not able to get there to help, and the wrangling in Parliament and the general impression that some terrific effort must be going on like fun under the blanket of secrecy, the actual urgent anxiety of each day usually turned out to be something to do with the visitors.

The trouble was they remained visitors. Nothing we householders could do would make them other than guests, if they stayed in billets. By giving some of them empty houses and lending them furniture and diverting the rest of the billeting money after the few shillings rent was paid as an allowance for heat and cooking facilities, we did get a few to make an effort to live here rather than to make a call; but their "Harts were in the wrong place to Stop Here," and gradually as the days grew colder and colder and London seemed safer and safer, more and more of them went away.

Not all of these departures were entirely willing. Sometimes it was a husband who insisted. I remember Jenny particularly. She had been a Barnardo's girl, and was the gentlest and smallest person I ever met. She had a splendid baby half as big as she was, and there was a most pathetic scene in our kitchen one Sunday afternoon when her husband made her go home. They had come up to see me and Margaret because Jenny had been staying with Margaret's two old aunties in Pansy Cottage by the pond. (This picturesqueness is Auburn's, not mine. It is a most absent-mindedly picturesque place.) And they had advised him not to take her back. She did not want to go. She was still frightened of the bombs for the baby.

I was in a most difficult position, because I did not want her to go either, and we were under definite instructions to keep people here if we could; but I could not tell her husband, as she wanted me to, that he was not to take her away. I could not go forbidding a man to take his own wife and child home whatever the danger. It would have been different if the thing had been put to the country, and it had been decided by general consent that in view of the circumstances women and children would keep out of the city. In that case this husband would have been in on the decision. As it was, as I tried to tell Jenny, I couldn't and wouldn't interfere, and that no responsible person in Auburn

would either, because to do so would have been against our
principles, which by the enormous efforts of our ancestors
constitute the law of the land.

In the past generations we've had enough fuss about that.

So I gave it the man as my honest opinion that I thought
it was criminally silly as well as a wicked waste of money to
take them back. I also said that if he got them home and
something happened to them and not to him, he'd never
forgive himself.

He was a little tiny young chap, no bigger than Jenny,
not at all bright in mind but desperately sensitive to feeling.
He got himself between me and her (she was crying and
holding on to my apron as if I were Barnardo's itself), and
he did a most disturbing thing. He spread his arms out so
that he almost hid her.

"I'll save 'em," he said in his little sparrowy voice. "I'll
save 'em from the bombs."

He meant it too, poor chap.

We all had some tea after that to get the tears out of the
atmosphere (people who are contemptuous of tea cannot
understand it. It is a very remarkable herb), and off they
went on the bus.

When the bombs did come it was very difficult to forget
those three.

The same sort of thing happened to Tiff and his missus.
They took in a very nice young woman and her little girl,
and Mrs. Tiff became devoted to the child, who was particularly charming. One Sunday afternoon the father of the
baby came down, and the child clung to her hosts. There
was a most unfortunate set-out, and home they went immediately, instantly, without pause, leaving Tiff and his wife,
who is a darling, naturally very hurt and unenthusiastic
about evacuees.

Sometimes it was the other way round. Joan and her
husband had the most impressive quarrel I was ever
privileged to witness, lasting for twenty-four hours without
pause, because she wanted to take the children home, and
he didn't think it a good idea. They brought the problem

round to the billeting hut, where I was keeping shop alone, just when everybody was going to evening service. We are still reasonably sedate about the Sabbath in Auburn, and I persuaded them at least to go down the garden for the shouting. But they came back in what we call the evening time, which is the few minutes from sunset to sundown, and were still completely at war.

Finally Joan, who was beautiful in that tortured way which makes one think of snakes for hair, strode off down the road to London (on which the last bus had long gone), wheeling the pram with the baby in it and the other children snivelling at her side, while her young husband walked two or three yards behind her repeating his arguments. I thought very likely it would work itself out, as such quarrels have to in Auburn, where, bitter as the fight may be, there is no chance of going away without a tremendous upheaval of relations and luggage, in which the original cause of the trouble may well be lost. However, very early the next morning one of the Ring Farm sisters—Joan was a sister-in-law—came round with a tale of what sounded like serious trouble, and Mark and I went down there to find a Hogarthian scene. That term is often used too lightly. Real Hogarth has turned over plates on brick floors and dogs and bare-seated babies and children stealing food from the bowl of the woman who is feeding the infant at the breast. There was all this there that morning, and drama too. The room is one of those real farm kitchens with a nook by the fire, a low ceiling and not quite enough light. Joan sat in the ingle with a stony expression and a silent baby in her arms. She was stiff-backed and imperious, and she had remained like that, as far as we could gather, for about twelve hours. The rest of the family moved about dramatically in various conditions of undress. They looked very pretty, most of them, for they were natural beauties, part Italian and all so very young. Mama was the exception. She stood like Hecuba, elf-locks streaming. In fact, Mama was more like Hecuba than Gertrude of Denmark now I consider the matter. There was the underlying and magnificent

guile of the Greek in her. The husband, though Mama's
son, was not the same stuff as his sisters. He sat and nattered.

Mark, who is probably the most sensitively polite person
in the world, inquired if we could be of any use to them,
and Joan burst into tears. This brought a dreadful cry of
triumph from the rest of the family, who saw it as capitulation. I mumbled something about a nice new billet for Joan
and leaving the family for a bit; but you might as well
have tempted the Sphinx with an orange. Joan was going
home. If she stayed she would stay with the family, but as
it happened she was going home.

Home in the end she went.

This last experience was rare naturally, because there
were not enough largish houses to take in very big families
who wanted to stick together even to the breaking-point.
The Ring Farmers were remarkable people anyway, more
like the Didikye than anything else in our experience, but
they had their place in the composite picture.

There were two things only that the majority of our
evacuees had in absolute common, sex and age, for they
were nearly all young; but, although I am almost incapable
of seeing people as groups and not as individuals, even I
began to notice other things about them as a whole.

One of the oddest of these was this lack of house-training
among their children. All young things need house-training.
It is one of the jolly reminders that civilisation, like peace,
is a reward for effort and not a free gift for a lucky nation.
The training of some youngsters takes more effort than
others, especially if their general standard of physique is not
so good, but these suburban children were uniformly first-
class. The whole of Auburn remarked upon it. With very
few exceptions the children were fine, fit, rosy and beaming
with health, yet the habits of nearly all of them would have
disgraced any two-months-old pup.

After a lot of listening to the main difference between
Auburn's inconveniences and the luxuries of town life a
dreadful suspicion came into my mind that it might be that
to a certain temperament these new labour-saving devices

with which urban homes are crowded might create a situation in which it would be much easier to clean a floor, do unlimited laundry and wipe down the furniture than to train a baby; for it needs more than physical work to teach a child, or indeed any other little animal.

There were other evidences of the same sort of thing too. Herbert and his wife took in a gentle young mother who expected a child and had a toddler with her, and she was quite willing to help if she could. Mrs. Herbert gave her some beans to string, but she had no idea how to do them and could hardly believe that such a fatigue was necessary. Herbert thought it odd but not, I think, wrong. After all, there is no great virtue in stringing beans, and if one can afford a tin and town beans are unpalatable (as we firmly believe, although we send our best produce to London) to an ordinary country mind there does not seem any sin in opening one. What did bother some of us, though, was the paralysing discontent of a number of the young women. Being intensely inquisitive people (Auburn will deny this indignantly, but any Arctic explorer would recognise the fascinated penguin in our elaborately expressionless stares), we located, after a good deal of diffident detective work, some of the main reasons for this.

The fact had to be faced that for a certain section of the newcomers the bottom had been knocked clean out of life by their transplantation. These were those girls who, though of varying incomes, had been used to buying everything at Woolworth's, wearing it or using it until it got dirty or torn and then throwing it away and buying fresh. Without Woolworth's, not only their milliner, hosier, grocer, ironmonger and furnisher were gone, but their laundry and seamstress also, and, even more important still, half their occupation in life as well. Unfortunately, too, they relied on the cinema and their husband and friends for the rest of their reason for existence, and there again they were without.

Their children's remarkable health depending on the free milk, free baby food and free advice given by their local clinics was only partly a flower of their growing too, and so they were terrified when they found that, although we were able to get them a clinic in Auburn, it would not be open all day and every day.

Besides, in Auburn, where floors are very seldom covered with thick linoleum, where constant hot water is a great luxury, where laundry facilities are only on hand two or three days in the week and incomes do not always run to tins, the girls were as helpless as French aristocrats during the revolution. (This, of course, only referred to those girls who had modern homes often costing them as much as twenty-seven shillings a week against our seven shillings for a cottage. Some of our evacuees had houses as hard to manage and as deficient in modern improvements as any on the coast. They found things easier, of course.)

There were Auburn people who were inclined to dis-approve strongly of this new-fangled way of life which seemed to depend so vitally on things instead of on human character, but there were others who at least saw the idea and saw one aspect in which it could be considered advan-tageous. Albert was one of these last, and Christine, for one, did not agree with him. He said buy a thing not made to wear, buy it cheap, use it new, then chuck it away. Thus you made trade, you made work and you did away with drudgery, since there was not a lot of sense in mending or washing for their own sakes. Also you encouraged change and new ideas.

It was up to Christine to produce the snag we all had to recognise. It was the one point which could not be ignored. She said, in effect, that this lack of training in the children, the absence of constructive effort in the girls which made that lack of training possible, and the helplessness of the whole family if anything went wrong with the plumbing or the shops was plain wrong. It was, of course. It was also dangerous if upheavals like this were going to blow up; no one could deny that. You could see what had happened, how the lack of the little disciplines and drudgeries had made the young women soft; but what exactly to do about it seemed more difficult to suggest. Obviously they needed a discipline if they were going to be happy, and if you did not want them to have the physical discipline of well water and no Woolworth's you would have to provide something moral, the discipline of some snobbery, some code or some religion.

It is one of those things which will have to be gone into in the great exciting days of reconstruction to come. Meanwhile the whole question remains as one of the reasons why people on the wireless and in the newspapers—who talk grandiloquently of war aims and new social orders, but who are discovered, when we work out what they really *are* saying, to be thinking rather vaguely of bigger and better municipal housing schemes and co-operative, all-embracing Woolworth's—don't cut a lot of ice in Auburn.

If it did nothing else, the evacuation convinced a good many of us that man and woman don't live satisfactorily by bread alone, even for a week, and that those folk who say "Get the body right first, and we'll see to the rest later" are laying up a mighty lot of work for the time when they can get round to "the rest," as they call it, if they get on too far with the physical side before considering the other two.

Apart from this large general difficulty, there were plenty of others more simple and individual. There was the fire, for instance, that little four-year-old Derek must have lit, staggering out with a box of matches into the yard of the farm-house where he was billeted. He found a stack of loose straw and made a little hole under it on the windward side. There was a good stiff sea breeze blowing, and the surrounding countryside had been baked in a strong sun all the summer. Derek's simple idea was to see if he could make a fire. He could. They just got the animals out of the barn before the tar caught, and eventually, by hacking down the furthest of the buildings, saved the rest of the stacks. The wind by the grace of God was not blowing towards the house. Fortunately the farmer had insured, and also the soldiers up at the lights happened to see the first crackling sheet of flame and cut over the fields to the rescue.

The bright spot in the incident—for no wind is entirely

ill in Auburn—was the practice it gave the new emergency fire brigades, who were several days on the job. The Flint-hammock outfit excelled itself and gained much experience towards that far greater fire-fight on the banks of the Thames much later on, when it worked for forty-eight hours without rest and only paused when the engine broke down.

The delightful thing about the Flinthammock emergency fire brigade is that it is really the Flinthammock and district funeral parlour in a newer and gayer guise. The personnel is the same, and this chameleon changing from black to red, from snail's pace to glorious speed, has a most satisfying quality of poetic justice about it. We have seen them so often advancing sadly down the narrow Street; Dick Houlding in front, large and impressive in top hat, black gloves and long frock-coat, the little bier behind him covered with posies, the bearers walking on either side, and Mr. Maskell himself, plump, fatherly and firmly kind, in charge of all. And so to see them now, alternately so to speak, speeding round the Thatchers corner in a crimson box, their red steel helmets glowing in the sun, their leather belts and shining equipment glistening, their faces alive and confident and usually extremely jovial, is an odd but strangely inspiring experience. They won the shield for the district and were heroes in the blitz.

Derek's experiment gave everyone concerned a lot of anxiety, however, and did not do much to add to the popularity of evacuees generally. This popularity, which had never been exactly high after the first twelve hours, began to wane fast as the months dragged on, largely because they would not or could not settle, and gradually their ranks grew thinner and thinner as even the very few unaccompanied children began to be taken off home.

Meanwhile there were other things to think of. Gradually, as the position in France solidified, or seemed to, young folk from Auburn, which was already a thought over-old, began to go away.

15

APART from the Major up at The Court, Albert Clover was the only man in the Regular Army from Auburn when the war broke out; but his brother Sam was in the Reserve and he went off at once at the beginning of the war, and so did George Bouttell. The others went one by one, and the cricket team began to disappear fast. There was Joe, who after his medical was promptly put into the Guards and had some fine tales when he came back looking no longer a big but an enormous chap, although he showed Grog a photograph of himself with some of his mates in which he looked almost small. He had been on guard at Buckingham Palace and was fed and housed, so he said, like a lord. Fred Cockle went into the Air Force and injured his bowling hand almost at once; but when P.Y.C. and I met him in the bus some time later he said he reckoned it wouldn't put him right out in the future. The others went as their time came. Alec got into the R.A.F., and so did Stan Goody and Geoffrey Townsend; while Mr. Ford, the newcomer to old Mrs. Seabrook's house, had had two sons, one in the Fighter and one in the Bomber Command, since the very beginning. Later on more and more went; Fred Braddy from the cobbler's shop, Smiler from the store and his brother Tiddles, Alf Goody who was a Warden, and Frank Hart from the station, and the Spooner who used to be the baker, and Harold Curtis and Mrs. Chaplin's daughter's husband.

George went, but had to come out again because he was wanted on the land, which was shorthanded enough before the big agricultural drive. There were the sailors too; Johnny Burmby, and Mr. Todd on a submarine, and Tony, the brother of Francis and Brian. He came home on leave when we were having first-aid lectures, and he came up to one or two of them. His ship was unknown to most of us then, and it would have sounded a strange outlandish name

without the blaze of glory which now surrounds it. The
Rawalpindi; an odd name for a ship.

Flinthammock, of course, is a nursery of the Merchant
Navy, and the finest yacht crews in the world are born
down there. Every day you heard of another boy gone off
to help keep the North Sea clear.

The girls went too. They seemed to go first. Cis from the
Lion went into Air Force blue and Betty James, and so did
Miss Smith from the Wick; while Cooee joined the A.T.S.
as a transport driver.

P.Y.C.'s sudden decision to get into the Army was
naturally the most important departure to me personally.
The inactivity of the Wardens' Service exasperated him.
Our A.R.P.O. had gone back to his old job in the R.A.S.C.,
and P.Y.C. made up his mind to join him if he could. It
was not a fighting service, but it didn't seem to be out of
the fighting, and was the only thing he could get into.
Getting in wasn't so easy at that time, because rising
thirty-seven was considered pretty old; and anyhow, there
was a good deal of waiting about and interviewing and
forms to be understood and signed, and it was not until
much later that the whole thing went through.

Many very well-meaning people, when talking to me
afterwards on P.Y.C.'s adventure, said, "Ah, they like to be
in it," and I began to wonder if that really was true in his
case, because ever since we were all in our 'teens together
we have never worried much about being in anything but
our own private world; and in that respect I think we are
very much like a great many other British families, especially
those in the country. It may seem an odd unfashionable
thing to say, but I fancy P.Y.C. joined up because he
honestly disliked the Germans to the point of wanting to do
what he could to help in their destruction, and I think the
reason he disliked them so was primarily because he saw
them as the arch-trespassers of all time.

P.Y.C. has a bee in his bonnet about trespassers, and
always did have. One of the most hospitable people on earth,
a man with a horror of being alone and a good habit of

bringing every stranger he meets home with him, he yet has a spot of blind loathing for the person who wanders into his own or anyone else's house, garden or meadow unannounced or uninvited. It used to happen quite a lot at one time that people who had heard of the Old Doctor's garden would come walking in through the side gate in that gentle, interested way which garden lovers have, and you would come across them, pink, sly-eyed and a thought defiant sniffing at a border or hesitating on the edge of the lawn. My reaction to them was, as usual, partly shy and partly unbearably inquisitive. Grog and Cooee were both blithely indifferent and would have suffered them to wander about for weeks or even years so long as they did not actively interfere. But P.Y.C. would always bound out upon them in icy fury, only too clearly controlling murderous instincts with the greatest difficulty. My impression was that the private personal quarrel which he and the hundreds of Englishmen like him (for the trait is by no means uncommon) have with the invading Hun lies largely there.

My father hated the Germans. Long after the last war it used to astound me that such an extraordinarily tolerant and logical man should grow so coldly savage whenever he spoke of them. "They have the gift of offence," he used to say, and I think it may be there is more in that than I realised. My father believed in Tolerance. It was his particular version of that Christian liking of mankind which is the simplest key to the comprehension of the universe, and in his case I think it was probably this which the 1914 Germans had attacked and all but destroyed, and he hated them for that.

Other men had other reasons obviously, but I mention these two, for they were the ones I knew about.

It was later on in the next year that we ordinary people really saw the new German experiment for what it manifestly is: the plainest and most elementary attempt to gain the world by laboriously and meticulously backing the downward drive in the universal equilibrium—at one time the most gigantic and most naïvely mistaken project since

Lucifer got himself kicked out of heaven; an undertaking comparable in execution with the highest achievements in organisation civilisation has ever known, but in aim, inspiration and ultimate result simple blood brother to Derek's idea in the stackyard.

Before a menace like this hatred wanes. Private idiosyncrasies and dear ideals become personal foibles and the fight becomes clear, unhampered by doubt or intellectual argument, a simple battle for the continued existence of man as a civilised animal in the generation after next.

However, at that time—Christmas, 1939—the problem still appeared comparatively small and complicated, and there was room for private reasons for going off to war.

Christmas was the last of the feasts. There was talk about sacrifice and economy, but no real signs of it. The Wardens had given up waiting round for an attack that never came, and the Post had been transferred to the studio, although the sideboard was still full of boots. With the restoration of the dining-room much of normal home life returned, and in that, I think, our house was fairly typical of Auburn.

In the beginning a great many people had been in the habit of getting out their gas-masks and going downstairs on a raid warning; but now, as night after night went by with no interruptions, gradually things settled again and we were "lulled into a false security," as the papers said afterwards so angrily, as if we had lulled them and not they us. Most of the evacuees had gone from the village, but there were still a few for whom we had been able to find houses of their own, although even these were beginning to wilt before the weather. Christine had nearly given up grieving after Tony, who with one or two others had spent a long time with us while his sister was being born. She had also given up pouncing on me with a toothcomb every morning, and she and Margaret had ceased the nightly precautionary hunt in the kitchen.

The time was almost normal save for the ever-present underlying sensation of waiting, and, to be honest, a new sociability and life which had not been so apparent in the

village before the great upheaval. We had all come out from
behind our lattices a little, and I for one had found the
experience rejuvenating.

The war still absorbed practically all our spare attention,
but because of the great lid of secrecy and silence, which still
almost alone among all the emergency measures appeared
to be absolutely efficacious from the outset, it was not at all
easy to get any vivid picture of the position anywhere. To
most of us blindfold in Auburn, going about in much our
usual way now that the first shock appeared to have been
a false alarm, the situation in France, with the two armies
facing one another in consolidated positions and a no-man's
patrol ground in between, suggested a sort of new-fangled
Somme with a certain amount of modern comfort for the
troops. Poland was a horrible tragedy, a murder and a rape
which could only be avenged and repaid when we could
get at her; and meanwhile the magnificent Finns were setting
our imaginations on fire and carving an example for Greece
and us to follow, and we were eagerly expecting a Scandina-
vian entry into the war and a French and British Norseland
expedition.

At that time, and again now I should say, real secrecy in
war-time on the part of the Government usually suggests
one thing to the ordinary person who has helped to put the
reigning party in power and who believes in the Prime
Minister, and that is that some important move to frustrate
the enemy is being planned and put into execution. All
these generalisations of mine refer only to the rank and file
of Auburn, and not to the students of the times or the folk
who make a serious hobby of politics. Some of these people's
ideas are even wilder and sometimes they are nearer the
mark, but I can only hope to explain what it has all looked
like from an ordinary point of view, like my own or, say,
Sam's, or any other busy person's who has had his own
urgent affairs to look after as well.

I thought the Government was working like a fiend to
get ready for a smashing Spring offensive, probably in the
north, and I thought we were incomparably better equipped,

especially in the air, than we turned out to be. I thought that the reason I did not see any factories going up was because they were being built in safer places, and I thought workmen were not being called up faster because they were not needed. It never occurred to me that we were in such extraordinary danger.

Remembering what other people said at the time, I don't think I was alone.

At Christmas, therefore, we were sanguine enough. We were being given time, we imagined, to build up a colossal war machine, the Jerry seemed to be in no mind to attack us from the air, and it felt as though it was going to be all right to have a few mild celebrations after all.

For us at home it turned out to be a curious, Jane Austenish Christmas, involving two separate but exactly similar midday parties in the same week for the two halves of a Searchlight unit with whom P.Y.C. had made friends in Mr. Spitty's pub, and who had been moved on to a bleak ploughed hillock close to our old house down the road to Bastion.

Cooee in khaki and Joyce, my young sister, on leave from the Wrens, were anachronisms, but the spirit and atmosphere were ridiculously alike. The Terriers were mainly young and decorous in mixed company, as the young are in England to-day in direct contrast to ourselves ten or fifteen years ago, and even more different from our immediate elders, the war survivors, who as a class have even now in full middle age a gift for playing the goat on festive occasions. They were both good parties, and there was a great deal of genuine jollity, a lot of eating and much martial thumping on the wood floors. The soldiers were living in uncomfortable and intolerably dull conditions, and yet with all the freedom and fun of being a gang of lads together. Their need was for formal civilisation instead of the reverse, as had hitherto been more common.

The weather, too, all that winter was old-fashioned and together with the petrol control, produced conditions which I had forgotten since I was a child. Probably it was this, the sudden return of distance, which was the first physical change after the brief return of the children which the war produced in Auburn. It gave me, at any rate, a most extraordinary sense of the untrustworthiness of time as anything but a convenient short-term gauge. When I was a child Bastion was a morning's journey away by buggy if the weather was good. Just before the war it was scarcely round the corner by car. Now it is a long slow bus journey, sometimes entailing a call in at Mudlarking out in the marsh. Time and distance have lost that constancy with which I used to credit them, and their falseness is found out. They depend on other things.

It was an unusual winter, though, for any age. Norry was roughing horses all day. The school bus had to turn back on the Fishling road several times. Birds froze on the trees, and the gulls, so lovely on the wing and so clumsy and out-of-drawing on their feet, came clamouring round the house for food.

In spite of the inconvenience, the frozen pumps and the burst pipes, the absence of papers and mail, there is a peculiar sense of safety and cosiness in this kind of crisis in a village like Auburn. I used to feel the same thing very acutely when I was small in the hard, paraffin-lit winters of my youth. We could be comfortably marooned for days, safe from the terrors of boarding school, the horrors of the dentist, and from the fear of Granny being called away or a governess coming down. If Mr. Whybrow, the carrier, could not get into Bastion on his weekly visits, we were cut off indeed and the situation approached the calamity stage which I always secretly enjoyed, being at that age and in private rather a one for calamities. However, I learnt then that to sit by a fire after battening down the house before a tearing blizzard off the sea and to listen to the frustrated howling of the elements is one of the great pleasures in life, one of the most precious fruits of a triumphant civilisation. In the past our Auburn ancestors must have listened to such fury much as we now listen to the Luftwaffe without this sense of safety and security. The time will come, no doubt, when that insensate growling will be heard with grim satisfaction. But that hour is not yet.

However, it certainly was a sensational winter which all but took Auburn's mind off its sorrows and anxieties.

The *Rawalpindi* had been our first real tragedy and our first great pride. To come from the same village as a man on the *Rawalpindi* is a fine thing, as good as having had a great-great-uncle on the *Victory*. Yet now there was silence for a little, and on land only the magnificent Finns still gave us that daily inspiration which had to come from somewhere.

Up at the Mama's House the last evacuee baby was born, and when her mother, bundling her in blankets, hustled her back over the icy roads to the city in spite of our protests the house was dismantled, the furniture returned to its various owners and the remainder of the equipment packed in an attic to await the next emergency. Albert took his lead pipes back, and new tenants moved into the house. Bea and Nurse had performed their miracle and seemed to think there was nothing very odd about it.

As the ice melted the pains returned. There was some very funny talk in the papers about supply, and the Government began to get restive. Nor was any help for the Finns forthcoming, although everybody you met seemed to know for a fact that an expeditionary force was fitted out and waiting, and all the time there was this dampening secrecy, only lightened by the impression that a great move must be being made somewhere, although there was no actual sign of it.

Phil had been out in France entertaining the troops, and came back wildly enthusiastic about those members of the R.A.F. whom he had seen. He had met Cobber Kain and the group of youngsters round him, and was unexpectedly excited about them. I say "unexpectedly," for of a disillusioned generation he is perhaps of all of us the least impressed by most new things, having seen much in his time of human nature, most of it extraordinary. If Phil said a gang was exceptional, you knew that he had found something breath-taking. He was not so enthusiastic about

anything else, but innocently we put that down to the fact
that the Army would hardly appeal to him. He was very
restless and exasperated by the cracking insanity of the
whole thing. There was no fighting save in Finland, and
we did not seem to be going there. Joining up was difficult,
recruiting still being so controlled that there was a real
doubt in most of our minds whether large numbers of men
were actually needed unless they were of a certain type and
age. Any special appeal was answered so promptly that the
demand was over practically before the B.B.C. had finished
making the announcement.

Meanwhile Auburn was getting on with the spring sowing.
The unexpected winter had caught almost everybody nap-
ping. Very little autumn stuff had been planted, and there
was therefore a great belated bustle going on everywhere.
Feeding stuffs were going to be short too, as far as one
could hear, and the meadowland was to be ploughed.
Rationing, which had been very slight to begin with, had
begun to tighten up, and at last it was more like war-time.

Fordie, as yet a stranger, was devoting his considerable
energy to salvage, and there was an ecstatic moment when
he unearthed Norry's private store of mild steel, the foundations of which had been laid down no doubt before the
Boer War, and which he keeps under the grass behind the
forge. Sam and I defended our pig-pen railings too, struggling
with a natural desire not to appear unpatriotic before a
newcomer but appalled at the prospect of losing an essential
asset. To be sure the pig-pen storeroom had been used as
a cricket pavilion for some time, but that had been only
a concession to times of plenty. As far as we could hear,
pig-pens might be coming in again.

In Auburn all sorts of curious iron contraptions are
heirlooms of immense private value, but they are left
standing around deceptively, and it is only when someone
attempts to move one of them that the outraged owner
appears, wild-eyed and indignant, to defend his property.
There was a good deal of stray scrap about too, however,
apart from the ploughshares lying temptingly along the

verges which are reputed to have been too much for our
enthusiast, who was not then a countryman, and a fine
dump was soon collected, while the Women's Institute
organised paper and tin hunts with the splendid folk from
Poynter's as organisers-in-chief.

From Ring Farm, Mama went home quietly and with
dignity. She said good-bye sadly and with great courage.
On the staggering table amid the wreckage of smashed
window glass, broken crockery and unspeakable bedding
which she left behind there was a touching note of tribute
to the people of Auburn, expressing gentle gratitude for all
their inestimable kindness. It tickled Auburn and took some
of the edge off its tongue.

Meanwhile Norry and Jack were busy in the forge. Norry
did a brief but satisfactory trade in wheels. With the revival
of agriculture, old farm carts had become scarce, and
whereas everything else on a cart may be patched, a wheel
is a wheel, ancient among the assistants of man and still
almost impossible to manufacture in a hurry. So Norry, after
waiting a decent interval, went round to the long grass
behind his chicken-houses and out of a cache there produced
a fine horde of the precious necessities, laid aside carefully
in the prudent past long before the pre-war craze for using
up and throwing away had taken hold. He and Jack shoed
them as Tiff repaired them, and presently they trundled
down the road again.

Shoeing wheels is one of the forge's specialities, and is a
sight to contemplate. I was round there one sunny morning
and, together with P.C. Me and a corporal from the Lights
who was hanging over the cobbler's fence, watched the
whole process.

It is a tiny yard out at the back there, and in the centre
Norry has constructed a low circular wall of loosely arranged
bricks. Within this circle is another wall of chunks of old
iron, and in the gap between a trough of fire is built of
green ash and sere oak, a combination which will give more
heat for a short space than any of your special coals. In this
fire are laid the iron tires, and the whole stove is then

covered with old bits of corrugated iron. The heat in the
cold windy sunshine is considerable, and the two smiths in
their goatskins preside over the stove like priests, each armed
with the kind of pincers the Devil carried in the Mystery
plays. At the psychological moment, decided upon by Jack
and assented to by Norry, off comes the corrugated iron.
A darkling tire is then pounced upon by the brothers and
carried at enormous speed to the shed, where the wheel is
already mounted on a flat platform of steel. The tire is
clapped on to the wheel, the pincers are discarded for the
long-handled hammers, and the iron knocked on into
position amid a great smell of scorching wood. Cans of water
stand ready and are then poured over the whole, while a
steam like an inferno rises. Clang goes Jack's hammer, clang
goes Norry's, alternately round the rim, and the long nails
previously made are brought in for the final fixing, the
whole performance being conducted in an atmosphere of
tremendous excitement.

P.C. Me and I were properly impressed, and Norry said
that in the *Daily Mail* a year or so ago there were some
pictures of some lads doing the very same thing. The pictures
were headed *In the Ancient Manner*, he told us, and he was
mildly contemptuous.

"They don't know what they're a-talking about," he said.
"Ignorant persons. That's not ancient. That's modern. *I* do
it every week of my life."

Meanwhile at home the sense of waiting was becoming
electric. The fall of Finland shocked us out of any com-
placency, although I think it wrong to call Auburn's almost
vegetable determination to go on growing naturally in the
intervals of being threatened, shaken, blasted, smothered
and subjected to extremes of hot and cold, by that oppro-
brious name.

The sinking of the submarine *Thistle* and the tragic loss
of Mr. Todd in her was another shock to the village,
and in the next two or three weeks there was a renewed
restlessness, a new anxiety to get down to the worst, whatever
it was.

"Let that come," said Jack. "Let that come and be done with."

P.Y.C., who had almost given up hope, suddenly received a bundle of documents as big as a barrister's brief and went off to get a uniform. The A.R.P. season began, and there was a great spate of exercises with stormy inquests after them. Bill came along and harrowed the meadow, since a good hay crop seemed imperative, and Sam decided to go all out on potatoes.

Some of the strappings had warped off the windows, and Christine had to be persuaded not to scrape them all off. Sometimes you could see little feathers of practice ack-ack fire over the estuary and there was the booming of mines exploding at sea, but there was no real war on land in England yet and very little in France, and none in Norway, Denmark, Holland or the Flemish lowlands. In Auburn, in spite of the forebodings, in spite of the continuous threats, the bad omens and the warnings, it was almost incredible that it should ever come.

That was early April. In late May the Scots Major took me down to look at the cricket meadow and the tents there and said shyly that it was the first time his troops had been in the front line. In the interval and immediately afterwards a very odd thing happened in Auburn, and obviously in the rest of England too.

Very lately Mr. Churchill, talking of Yugoslavia, said that nation had found its soul. That sounds a very flowery, high-falutin way of talking and not the thing he would have said of anyone who had not the decent covering of foreignness to protect him; but, like all nakedness, there is nothing embarrassing about it when it is completely stark and in one's own home. In those weeks in May and June I think ninety-nine per cent of English folk, country and town, found their souls, and whatever else it may have been it was a glorious and triumphant experience. If you have lived half your life's span without a passionate belief in anything, the bald discovery that you would honestly and in cold blood rather die when it came to it than be bossed about by a Nazi, and that freedom to follow your heart or not is literally, like air or water, an actual necessity in your life, and that you are not alone in it but that everyone around you, from the most obvious to the most unlikely person, is of the same mind— then that is something to have lived for.

I myself am a physical funk. I wince at violence, and the sight of blood makes me feel sick. But even I, most morally inferior and over-complicated beside most Auburn folk, who are not wavering and never have wavered, am profoundly glad I was born in these days when all the tragic grandeurs of the past fade into perspective and become small battles and local encounters, rehearsals, trial runs before this simple gigantic fight to the death between the up-pull and the down-pull, freedom and slavery, right and wrong.

It has just occurred to me why this is so. Until that experience I would have been afraid to admit such a thought had I had it. The chances of being misrepresented or mis-understood or of offending, which are so great, would have appalled me. Now the timidity is gone. With the rest of Auburn and the thousands of villages like us I have found something out, and there is a rock under my feet. Physical fear, recantations under torture, are weapons of the enemy. *They are not truths.* If we are not free to-morrow, we shall not be happy to-morrow. There will be no living in false content. That in all the world is certain. We have touched something solid and eternal after floundering for a genera-tion in a sea of muddles and unsatisfying things. Whatever comes after, we have got back something vital which had been lost. With it you live always; without it you die.

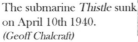
The submarine *Thistle* sunk
on April 10th 1940.
(Geoff Chalcraft)

16

THE actual day-to-day history of those two months, April and May 1940, is now known to everybody who can read, and, completed from all the various sources, it makes a savage but coherent tale, one thing following ruthlessly and logically upon the next, but at the time in Auburn (who was like the child in the crowd at the barrier, not seeing any the better for being in the front row) nothing seemed at all logical.

We got to hear of things in a slightly different order from the true one. Some of them, the evacuation from Dunkirk for instance, we got wind of before many other people, but others, like the shakiness of France, we realised long after most, so our picture was not only over-vivid because of its nearness but often monstrous in its apparent irrelevancies.

Out of the chaotic muddle, when people "didn't know *what* to think, didn't really *like* to think," and instinctively kept their eyes in the boat and rowed on, a more or less coherent procession of events emerges.

Someone, I think it must have been Albert, said the German advance was like dry rot, as not only one board in the familiar structure of Europe gave way before a penknife thrust as brutal and enquiring as his own, but the shutters and wainscots too crunched and crumbled and came apart in one's hand in the short afternoons between one news bulletin and the next. Uncle Beastly's death-voice became his natural tone and the newspapers looked like theatrical props for a spy drama.

The first great shock was the most dangerous although it was less obvious than the others. This, in Auburn phrasing, boiled down to nothing more or less than the sudden and paralysing revelation by Mr. Chamberlain personally that he was "a wonderful vain old man who had nothing particular up his sleeve." As P.C. Me put it afterwards, "we thought he was getting on with it. Instead of that the old blighter was mucking about."

The effect of this discovery at that particular time was almost indescribable. It was like suddenly noticing that the man driving the charabanc in which you were careering down an S-bend mountain road, with a wall on one side and a chasm on the other, was slightly tight and not a brilliant driver at the best. This was a particular sort of horrible experience, far worse, to my mind, than anything physical that has come after. The ordinary country chap is peculiarly loyal, however, and instinctively just. Even in that hour it was seen that the Prime Minister was well meant, honest, very astute in a business way, and that his greatest fault lay in his lack of size and consequently in his vision. However, most people saw that none of these virtues was of much use in the new situation.

The actual revelation came, I honestly believe, by one of those providential series of accidents which do seem to protect the simple faithful people of the earth, argue against it as you like.

It began with the wink. When Mr. Chamberlain said that Hitler had missed the bus ("Yes, but he caught the workman's," said P.C. Me), the Germans had not actually invaded Norway, and Denmark was still free, but everybody knew that vast concentrations of troops and transports were waiting on the Baltic coast. That fact was one of those half-mentioned, half-rumoured but entirely understood things, and it was the point uppermost in the mind of a public which has a gift for grasping essentials. The next factor was the theory (which generations of experience in being governed well has implanted in the ordinary country chap) that anything we know has been known very much longer by our Government who has already done something about it. We are only now just beginning to grasp that the change in the speed at which news travels has annihilated distance and that therefore this cannot be so true as it used to be. Another chance fortunate for the country in the long run was that the phrase caught the fancy of the Press and the wireless and was publicised freely everywhere for two or three days after it was first used, the B.B.C. announcers putting the colloquialism into inverted commas and often being a little arch about it. The result was inevitable. It was taken as a wink. The ordinary chap trusted Mr. Chamberlain to be a statesman, to know and love his country, and to recognise its intelligence, talking to it as to a less well-informed equal as adult as he was. The difference between the statesman and the politician, after all, is largely the difference between the man who goes to the pub and sees a lot of his fellow national intelligences and the man who does the same thing and sees a lot of common persons easily to be converted into a crowd. Britain has had a vast experience of the two in her time and has learnt to recognise the great by their ability to assess their superiority over the rest of us accurately and not to get some fantastic idea that they are a different species altogether. A giant is only half as tall again as his fellow men, past that he becomes a monster.

Therefore, at a time when the Government was being criticised, when alarming little scandals about Supply were still in the mind, and when all eyes were fixed on the enemy concentrations, and Mr. Chamberlain winked at the country, when he gave it the little encouraging personal dig in the ribs for which it had been waiting so long and murmured the untranslatable "he's missed the bus," it was assumed by many simple people and with immense relief that there was a bag waiting for the tiger.

Some news is forgotten in a day but not a personal whisper from the Chief. Within the next few hours, or so it seemed —in fact there was a day or so between the utterance and the enemy's leap—Norway was captured and, with the fleet steaming away to Narvik, virtually the whole of the price-lessly valuably coastline from Denmark to the north was in the hands of the Nazi and an unprepared Norway was struggling like a sheep with a rogue dog.

In more sophisticated circles Norway's earlier mistaken efforts towards neutrality were bitterly criticised, but in Auburn not at all that I heard. Auburn is chary of criticising foreigners. It does not understand them, never has and knows

it, and "judge not in a hurry" is graven on its seamy old
heart. Besides, Auburn had something far more serious to
worry about than even the loss of the Norseland coast.
Auburn was worrying about the Prime Minister.

In this respect Auburn is perhaps typical of a people so
old that self-preservative policies are instinctive, for at any
rate it saw at once where the real danger lay, and the whole
of the country seems to have done exactly the same thing
at the same time.

"Naught shall make us rue, if England to itself do rest but true."

That is the basic rock, the ultimate secret belief of the
instinctive Briton, the touchstone, the magic ring, the root
of his pride, the cornerstone of his remembered history.

"Resting true" means what it says, too. It is not only
resting honest, according to one's own or anyone else's lights.
True means true. True as a line or a weight or a wheel is
true, true like a ship's compass or a horseshoe or a gunsight
or a heart. Steady and true, honest and true, true love, true
sovereignty, true as all the things that have made the
country great.

In the days that followed Auburn waited for news of even
greater importance than military success or failure in Norway, of greater importance even than the safety of the B.E.F.
What Auburn wanted to know was what had gone wrong
with the tiger bag? Failure it could and had faced. If you
have a sense of history like Auburn military failures mean
very little unless they are consistent and prove inherent
weakness in an army or a fleet. Auburn wanted to hear the
rights of a failure, what had gone wrong with the timing,
who had muffed it, where the enemy had outwitted us.

The debate in the House was followed by everyone. The
P.M.'s defence was scrutinised like a casualty list and slowly
the dreadful truth emerged. There had been no tiger trap.
The wink meant nothing. It was capricious, a handkerchief-
rabbit to amuse a child.

That was a very terrifying moment. It was not as if Auburn

had really been a child. It recognised the type of man at once. God knows the Government has been full of such men up and down the years.

For myself I have never been more abjectly frightened in all my life, but even the stout hearts, Albert and Charlotte, Sam and his missus, Norry and Jack, P.Y.C., Grog, Christine, Reg and Dorothy, Bill and Basil, the farmers, the ladies and all the other folk who pass up and down the square round the maypole, began to look drawn and anxious and pale round the eyes and to keep very non-committal.

Mr. Churchill saved the Government and saved the country and saved Auburn too. In a week it was over and all was safe and true again, whatever the outward danger.

Mr. Churchill's appointment as the new Prime Minister was never questioned in Auburn for an instant. It was unanimous. But neither was the importance of the choice underestimated.

It is believed by some less simple people that Mr. Churchill, after having been neglected for years, was suddenly remembered in the hour of stress. Auburn does not see it in that way at all, as far as I can gather. From Auburn's point of view, and the place is obviously not alone, Mr. Churchill has been perfectly recognised and liked and trusted to be true to himself and faithful to his country ever since he first appeared in Parliament. However, never until now has the country come into line, come into the true that is, with Mr. Churchill. He is not a man to rise to an hour. The hour has had to rise to him. His is a fixed compass. The Auburn kind has always enjoyed him and known him as they knew his father and mother before him, and his tremendous qualities and tremendous peculiarities are not only known but understood by the people whose hearts rule their heads as well as those who think first, and that is for a very good reason indeed.

Mr. Churchill is the unchanging bulldog, the epitome of British aggressiveness and the living incarnation of the true Briton in fighting, not standing any damned nonsense, stoking the boilers with the grand piano and enjoying it mood. Also he never lets go. He is so designed that he cannot breathe if he does. At the end of the fight he will come crawling in, unrecognisable, covered with blood and delighted, with the enemy's heart between his teeth. Moreover, he always has been like this as far as anybody remembers, and his family before him. After half a century the country has got into the true with him, but it is its fighting not its normal angle.

In handing over his own precious bit and bridle to Mr. Churchill the British horse gave himself the master whom he knew to be far more ruthless in a British way than anything possible to be produced elsewhere in Europe. Mr. Churchill would ride his horse to the death and die with it as a matter of course, and be sublimely confident of its thanks as they trudged off to join the shades together, and, which is tremendously important, when Auburn and all Auburn kind were quietly depending on his appointment, they knew that as well as, and perhaps a good deal better than, anybody else in the world.

For the rest, of course, as a general, as a tactician, and above all as a technical rider, Mr. Churchill is superb. His hands are light and strong and his instructions intelligent, unhesitant and inspiring. There is no jagging, no uncertainty, no tricking, no coaxing. He demands a schooled warhorse without vice and with a great heart and he has one, obviously, between his knees.

Also, and this is still dangerous ground, with Mr. Churchill returned some of the sublime exhilaration hidden in the heart of good fighting. It seems that a race is either martial or it is not. There is no peculiar moral virtue in being a fighter, a badger rather than a rabbit, but no badger can pretend to himself to be a rabbit satisfactorily or vice versa. That results in a pansy badger and a ridiculous rabbit. The natural fighter has an extra gadget, that is all. The very existence of this gadget or asset in the British has been denied and explained away for twenty years and those who are rediscovering it in themselves are still feeling startled and a thought guilty about it, but it is a very real and ancient attribute and it contains its own compensation and generating power.

In the actual fighting there is a secret joy. It may not be "quite the article," as the Cockneys say, but it is there all right. Look at the faces of the people in the rescue gangs and on the troopships and on the fire lorries.

It has not been possible to put down all the little scraps of evidence which have made it so clear that the ordinary people knew all this about Mr. Churchill, because country people in England so seldom speak unambiguously but rely on the most subtle combination of nods, winks and parables to convey their mind even if they want to, which is not often. I doubt if the ordinary chap cares two penn'orth of gin, as he says, if you know what he thinks or not. He is thinking it. He has got it right and you can work it out for yourself. However, the fact that from the beginning everybody chuckled when Mr. Churchill's name was mentioned, and does still, is one piece of evidence, and the conversation that Nerney heard in London between two charladies who had turned up to clean an office which had disappeared overnight was another. One of them was completely taken aback and temporarily demoralised. The whole mooring post of her existence had come out of the rock in her hand. The other one was telling her off.

"My dear ole gel," she was saying, "blubber away. But *you can take it from me*, while one bloody brick stands on another ole Churchill will never let us give in."

Mr. Churchill has made a lot of fine speeches but it takes more than words to convince the ordinary man and woman personally. For personal conviction one has to know the man, to recognise the mood he epitomises in oneself. When Mr. Churchill came into power Auburn said yes, well, now we're for it, and it said it with complete satisfaction.

Detail from the first edition cover of *The Oaken Heart*.
Drawn by A. J. Gregory ('Grog')

17

HOWEVER, while all this was taking place in the big theatre outside and in the deep heart inside, Auburn and district was still conducting its own comedy-drama at home. For example, on the Wednesday of the invasion of Norway, the blessed day when she decided to fight for it, there was an inquest in Fishling on an Air Raid Precautions exercise which had taken place in Flinthammock some time previously. You would think that in a country which really did realise its tremendous danger no sensible person could get wildly upset about the safety arrangements for a place the size of Flinthammock, which has a reputation for looking after itself anyway. Compared with the big issues at stake the whole thing was puerile, but then none of the men concerned could do anything at all about the big issues and they could do a great deal about Flinthammock.

P.Y.C., who had been stationed at Bastion by one of those freaks of luck which do seem to keep cropping up to help one along, had been lent by his Colonel to umpire that exercise and I went along with him to the inquest because I had inherited his Deputy First Aid Commandant job and my ambulance, stretcher party and First Aid Point had been involved in the performance. I have never attended any meeting at which feelings ran so high or at which more active brains or so many personally disinterested men were so deeply concerned. It was an extraordinary gathering because it was only the relative importance of the matters discussed which made it so trivial. It was like the battle for the school, just as difficult, just as hard and bitter a fight as if the safety of a continent and not a village on a mud flat was involved. The same sincerity and drive and complete recklessness of effort was there. No one was being paid for anything and no one was toadying and everyone was stirred to the utmost limit of his capabilities.

I could not help thinking that if only there had been half

as much of the same all-essential life in the parliamentary committee meetings before and even after the war we might possibly have been a bit better equipped.

As we drove back over the narrow lanes, which were lit up like day by the searchlights, the enormity of the whole thing returned to us. You could almost feel the whole vast structure of the old world cracking and splitting and struggling in a mighty but very slow explosion, each fractional part a replica of the whole bust-up, until you got down at last to the essential basic atoms which were the private and personal integrity and steadfastness of each ordinary chap.

The next period of Auburn's experience is very difficult to record because it was the time when the outside shadow-show of world events, against whose screen we had been living for so long, began to get so vivid and three-dimensional that it ceased to be part of our scenery and became part of our play. As our ordinary life is usually quite enough for us to manage, this intrusion made values very hard to assess (in my own case it was further complicated by the fact that I was trying desperately to fulfil my engagements by finishing a thriller, and so I was living in a third world as well for the best part of each day, and many people who are as absorbed in their work as I am had the same experience). It meant one had to take a very firm hold on to oneself and go very slow if one was to presrvee any sense of proportion, but even so it was a very muddling time.

The Whitsun week-end, which began on Friday, the 10th of May, will perhaps serve as an example of what I mean. Auburn heard on the early morning wireless bulletin that the invasion of the Lowlands had begun and later on, during the day, the windows began to rattle faintly in their frames as they used to all the time when I was a child and there were big guns in Belgium before. The other things that happened during that day to us in the house (and the same sort of things were happening in every other house in the village) were these. Grog began to make careful preparations for the long delayed blitzkrieg. Then my young sister arrived on leave from the Wrens. She was just going to get her "Chief's" brass buttons and was at last a fully fledged wireless telegraphist, all set to do really useful work. This was a great delight to us even if the world was on fire. All army leave was cancelled and there were many disappointments in other homes besides ours, where we had been expecting P.Y.C. over. There was great excitement everywhere, naturally. Everybody came out into the street to talk. Invasion was in the wind and the advance air attack was expected every second.

I took the precaution of putting my only valuable, my manuscript (which represented, if nothing else, at least six solid months of my living time), in a biscuit tin, and Christine, who felt we ought to bury something, began to look about for some silver or some china we could hide. She gave this up in disgust in the end and was cool with me when I suggested we bought something for the purpose. I thought the sort of things which would be valuable if the worst happened were pails and blankets and tinned beans and soap, but none of these things seemed suitable for burying.

Norry came down to look at Beau, who was alone in the front meadow for the first time. This is always an anxious step in the upbringing of a young horse, in case he goes silly with loneliness and blunders out into the road and hurts himself. It seemed absurd to worry about him, or indeed about my manuscript, when the guns had begun and the Lowlands were fighting for their lives, but on the other hand we knew we might be very ridiculous if we did not attend to them. Mr. Churchill's appointment as Prime Minister came through on that day too and that was the most important thing of all, but one could do little except say "Thank God for that," realise fully what it meant, and then turn one's attention to the problem of the moment, which happened, I remember, to be the wretched dog Theobald, who had taken off the roof of a neighbour's toolshed in the exigencies of one of his appalling love affairs, and after that to return to the desk and the work of story-telling.

As the week-end went on the big drama obtruded more and more into our tight little lives. An order came through to Grog decreeing that all Wardens' Posts should be fully manned and that the men should patrol at dawn and dusk to keep a look out for parachute troops. Word was coming through from Holland that these were sometimes disguised as "nuns and other familiar figures." Now a nun is not a familiar figure in Auburn and the arrival of one by bus, much less by parachute, would have occasioned considerable interest, not to say suspicion, so the information had a touch of pure fantasy about it very hard to stomach at first. Moreover, the Wardens were and are completely unarmed, of course, and therefore the patrols sounded either mad if unnecessary or very unhealthy indeed if justified. However, all the Wardens went out dutifully in the grey times and scouted along the little green hedges as secretly as only the native can.

The rest of us in the house took turns at minding the telephone for raid warnings when they were out, and on my dawn watches I used to get on with my thriller and try not to see myself objectively for sanity's sake.

All through the days, which were green and luxuriant, Auburn looked and felt, save for the far-off mutter of the guns, just the same as usual in the Spring, and the familiar little jobs cropped up as usual. Tom, P.Y.C.'s old hunter, got into hot water once more for cribbing on the cricket-bat willows on the Hall land and tearing their barks off. Another collection of suicidal starlings nested deep in the hollow walls between the Queen Anne and Elizabethan parts of the house and had to be got out before the worst happened to them and we were let in again for the depressing dead rat hunt of previous years. An enquiry from my father's agents came in for an old serial story of his, written in the last war, which was somewhere among all the others packed away in an attic. All these were little but important things which had to be considered and attended to if life was to go on. It seemed vital that it *should* go on as much as possible just the same as if nothing untoward was about to happen. How

much of that was instinct and how much horse-sense I cannot
tell, but everybody appeared to have it.

It was the new jobs which seemed so melodramatic and
were yet somehow so reasonable. Grog turned the house
upside down looking for our only firearm. This was not very
impressive when he located it at last. It was a ·22 Winchester
dated about 1890 and we had no ammunition for it, which
I for one was glad about because the whole contraption
looked dangerous to me. Grog oiled it but without enthusiasm. I found an Arab sword, which William McFee had
given us, in an umbrella stand. It was about five feet long, for
use on camel back, and a bit rusty, and we discounted that
also. I was feeling that this weapon hunt was probably only
our personal exuberance when I discovered that we were
by no means alone. Ordinary people were thinking extraordinary thoughts just then and were preparing for extraordinary deeds, all in the same private half-ashamed
way.

I had a word on the telephone with each of the First
Aid Point Leaders in the ten villages in my inherited area.
Their complete confidence, coupled in many cases with
downright belligerency of outlook, gave one a great sense
of unity. The district is tiny but the people are not at all
the same, and if *we* were all alike it seemed reasonable to
suppose that most of the country was not very different.
The odd scraps of gossip I heard were enlightening. Some
of the tales might be thought ridiculous but all were gallant.
There were anecdotes of staunch elderly ladies setting aside
their shears and trowels and training their old gardeners
as stretcher-bearers or arranging trench refuges for the
children next door. There was no hint of panic: on the
contrary, rather a sort of grim enjoyment. Evidently we
were to have no streams of refugees in our lanes.

As far as I could hear each private castle was to be held
to the last, each sacred doorstep to be a Thermopylae.

The sophisticated view, as I very well knew, was to regard
all this sort of thing as pathetic, but the trouble with the
sophisticated view is that it never decides where foolishness

ends and staunchness begins. I began to wonder if the
sophisticated view had not been taken by the Danes.

Doubtless any well-armed parachutist could have killed
all these dear gallant people, but it was clear that he would
not be able to do much else with them, and it occurred
to me that while he was killing old Miss Jane, for instance,
there might be a very good chance for, say, Miss Ethel with
her rook rifle or a basin of lighted kerosene from the top
of the stairs. A man is only a man even if he has a tommy-
gun. The gangster's weapon does not make him superhuman.

That was the mood of the countryside round about Auburn
at the time, anyway. It was angry. Anger does alter people.

I had another telephone adventure during the day which
was enlightening too. I had had a business cable from Paul
Reynolds, Jr., in New York, concerning a story I had
written called "Black Plumes" which had been sold to *Collier's
Magazine*. The war had overtaken us all before publication
and the cable contained a request for my consent to the
story being altered to bring in a war background. It proved
not to be possible, as it happened, but I cabled back, using
the telephone. I said, "Plumes realise exceptional circumstances demand alteration plan. Trust Colliers not to ruin
construction."

Within twenty minutes I received an urgent call and a
suspicious voice demanded an instant explanation.

"Which colliers might ruin what construction, please?"
What sabotage was this? I had a most difficult ten minutes
explaining. *Collier's Magazine* could be checked but "construction" proved a difficult word. The technical side of
story writing is a mystery to many people and it appeared
to be an incomprehensible one to my questioner. I heard
myself saying helplessly, "It's a tale. I made it up. It's
fiction," and the voice at the other end said blankly, "Fiction?
Do you mean it's a lie?"

In the end I cleared myself, but the incident made the
solid world appear a little less so for the evening.

This sort of thing continued in a crescendo, and within
a few hours, it seemed, we heard the first tragic account

of the defeat of the Dutch Army. Of all the neutrals who went down fighting rather than side together I suppose the Dutch were probably the people we in Auburn respected most in our hearts. They, like us, are not primarily charming and entertaining like most foreigners. Moreover, they understand the same sea and beat us upon it once with a broom at their masthead. All along our Auburn and Flinthammock estuary coast there are Dutch names and Dutch blood. The DeWitts and the DeMussets of the island are family names of importance and much of the local severity, staunch independence, and hard bargaining powers come from the Lowlands.

We had hoped and expected that when it came to it they would hold out longer in their water fields, and the ruthless completeness of their conquest brought home to us for the first time the new Nazi septicaemia tactics by which they spread out and poison a land. The Queen of Holland spoke that night on the radio and showed us country people that she was a proper Queen who might easily have been a Queen of England speaking, to judge by her strength and royalty, and it was largely she, I think, who brought something else right home to many of us.

Courage was not going to be enough.

For the first time in probably all our history we were not going to get by, this time, with just courage and the improvisation it brings with it.

That is rather an alarming discovery when you have just unearthed courage, like Mac's sword, and are busily engaged in whetting it.

Queen Wilhelmina of The Netherlands,
Queen Regnant 1890-1948.
*(Library of Congress, Prints and Photographs
Division, FSA-OWI Collection)*

18

THE method of the German advance fascinated everybody. In the next few days it was discussed exhaustively by everyone who came in or whom we met in the square.

Gradually a very important and sobering fact emerged and crystallised. It was the same old growling Jerry, just as dirty in a fight, just as dogged, just as overbearing, and, God help us, just as strong if not stronger; but, and this was the new factor, so terrifying if one was in the mood to be terrified (which one was not, personal funk being out of fashion for the first time for a third of a lifetime), somehow or other in the twenty years' armistice Jerry had got himself some brains. They were just the kind of brains which suited him, a wonderfully sound machine but tricky and overcomplicated; no wisdom, no saving grace or instinct to let him tie up with the eternal in the universe and save himself and his conquests in the long run, but a wicked short-term rat intelligence. He would "think of anything." It looked as though we were going to have our work cut out.

P.Y.C. came home the following evening and he and I walked down to Mr. Sayer, the saddler. P.Y.C. had a genuine Second Lieutenant's trouble. He had been issued with a very large revolver and a very small holster to put it in, and, as he said, apart from the danger to morale there was always the chance that the perishing thing would fall out and crush his feet. Mr. Sayer was sympathetic and set about cutting out another holster at once. He would get it done next day, he said, and P.Y.C. promised to come over and get it if possible. We came back up the road and went into the garden to do our best to make some sort of personal arrangements in case of serious trouble, as doubtless everybody else was doing at the time. The position was peculiar because P.Y.C. was due to go back further inland, and therefore if invasion did come, which seemed very probable, to-morrow or the next day or to-night, the chances were that we in Auburn would see the enemy first. We considered our geographical position and decided that the real odds were that no actual landing from the sea would take place within a considerable distance, as English distances go, from us, and that the probability was that the fighting would take place behind us, our danger arising when the enemy fell back through us. It was very difficult to realise that we were not both playing the goat and being unduly melodramatic, and that the danger was real. Norry, who had come up to have a look at the hay crop, gave us a wave from the meadow.

There was no active course to pursue because there were so many possibilities. After all, a landing on our actual coast might be possible, and in that case, if they were going to turn the area into a battleground, P.Y.C. said that he thought the chances were that most of us would be bundled out of the way, if it could be managed in the time, and if not we should have to go to ground and they'd have to fight over us. Anyhow, the one thing which did emerge was that speculation was silly. The only thing to do was to keep one's boots and spare cash at hand and do exactly as one was told.

I said if I was ordered to leave I would put a note to say where I thought we were going under the sundial, if it was still there, so that if by chance he came back at any time he would have some clue, but all this sort of thing seemed very foolish. The awkward part was that you felt you ought to make some sort of arrangements in case you regretted it afterwards. If you went around saying it couldn't happen, you were behaving exactly like the Dutch, a few miles across the water, and where were they that evening? Finally we agreed that Malcolm's office in America was the only safe address in the world. If we got irrevocably split up we would get in touch through that, somehow, if we had to swim the Atlantic or wait ten years.

When P.Y.C. went off he said he would come back the next day if he could and I pottered about in the garden.

The situation made me feel self-conscious. I could not pick a few flowers for the house without wondering if it was a waste of time, or, worse, a gesture.

It is very difficult not to sound as if we were unbearably chilly and matter-of-fact, like English people in foreign plays, but the danger was so *close*, the appalling size of the smash-up so apparent, that the only thing to do was what everyone else was doing, keeping a steady eyes-front. Once you looked sideways, once you looked round, once you let your imagination out, you knew you might lose your head. Clearly the thing to do was to get yourself into a certain definite frame of mind and keep in it at all costs, even if it made you slightly stupid. Everyone I met in the village seemed to be doing this instinctively, but I have been trained to remark since I was seven and I must always be watching and noting and putting things into communicable form. It has become a second nature and is inescapable. The whole thing was a very peculiar experience, very distinctive, and I suddenly remembered that it had all happened to me before.

To explain this I suppose I had better touch on a delicate subject. This book seems to be full of delicate subjects but it is an attempt at a history of a delicate time and I do not see how I can avoid it if I am to tell the truth, which is my object. The basic root of the whole business lay in the answer to a very personal question. It was the same great question which was getting such different answers all over Europe and it had now presented itself to the private minds of ordinary British people like us. Naturally no one discussed it openly (except on the wireless, in the newspapers, and among the very young, all of whom are rather remote and unreal compared with one's own thoughts in the dark), but I had it presented to me at this time and, from what practically everybody has said since, I was one of a crowd.

It is one of those bald and awful questions. Would you rather die, perhaps horribly, than be controlled by a force of which you do not approve? Would you rather lose your right or your left leg? Sentiment, cant and heroics aside, would you personally rather go out here and now, leave

off living with all that entails or doesn't according to your
private beliefs, leave your home and your friends and your
family (and see *them* die) or settle down to make the best
of a life in which your country's soil, your own soul and
your children's children's souls are not yours or their own?
You could cheat, couldn't you? You could think one thing
and do another.

Whatever anyone likes to think afterwards, there is no
immediate "of course" about that question, or at least certainly not for people like me. When it cropped up in my
mind again any immediate attempt to answer it was side-
tracked by a shock of surprise as I remembered that it had
all happened before.

I must have been about ten or eleven and I remember
sitting at my desk and looking out of the window at the
green chestnut trees. It was one of those remarkably clear
days we get hereabouts, well washed and not quite dry and
cold in spite of the sun. The Old Doctor, who was an important person locally at that time and who was allowed to
wear uniform and a brass hat occasionally (Heaven knows
why, now I come to think of it, but he must have been on
one of the many tribunals of those days), had called to see
the grown-ups and there had been a hasty conference in
my father's study. I had gone nosing round, sniffing excitement in the wind, and had gathered from the muttering
in the kitchen that the threatened invasion, which had been
talked about for months, was actually upon us, and that
the "second warning," meaning "load up your farm waggons
for the road," had been given. (This was all part of the
false order I mentioned before.)

Every responsible person had duties at that time and I
was very much in the way while they made up their minds
what to do with us children, so I returned to my desk,
where I was at work on one of my interminable poems, and
was frightened stiff.

I was confronted by this same question: would *I* honestly
rather die than give in? To be sure there did not appear
to be much hope for me anyway at that time. In spite of

Mrs. Molesworth and my beloved *Nuremburg Stove*, as far as I could gather the Germans gave Herod points. That was the period when the entire country was seething with tales of German atrocities in Belgium. We get the same tales from Poland to-day and they still sicken but no longer astonish us as they did in that gentle age when our governess's trunk was still full of sugar hearts from Vienna.

I had heard about the Belgian cruelties from the girl who had come to look after the pony when Arthur Fletcher went to war. My impression always has been that little pinky books about these horrors were given away at the Post Office, but on looking at this statement in cold blood I can hardly believe it. (Northcliffe was "propaganda" then, wasn't he? Would he? I don't know.) Anyhow, what gave rise to it I cannot remember, but I did have in my mind, or on paper, a very vivid picture of a baby stuck to a stable door with a bayonet. In my imagination, of course, it was our coach-house door and our baby, my sister Joyce, born in 1913. I have kept it in my mind all these years because it explains why I have an otherwise insane dislike of coachhouse doors with harness pegs in them. However, Herod or no, there was a choice of sorts. At ten my problem resolved itself, I remember, into the simple question of whether I should sidle up to the first Hun who appeared and give him a meat patty which I had seen in the pantry, or whether I should get up into my secret hiding place, where the japonica and laburnum hung over the road, and drop a chunk of the broken stone pedestal from the Glebe garden on his head. The notion of doing nothing did not occur to me at that age. I cried miserably over my problem, mainly in terror, and partly no doubt at the piteous spectacle of a noble child deciding to be pinned to the coachhouse door, but after a bit, when I had sucked that mental orange and conquered my immediate funk, the question was still there and I knew then that with me it would be a question until circumstances forced the answer, and that then I should have to do something to my mind at the time or I should certainly go to pieces and choose the meat patty. I had no idea what to

do. The responsibility of making the choice reduced me to
a state of abject misery and when I heard that the grown-ups
had decided to bundle us children off to London there and
then with Cissie I was more relieved than ever in my life
before or since. To be honest, I do not believe it was entirely
because I was escaping from the actual danger, for my
anxiety for my father and mother, not to mention my
donkey, was almost unbearable, but at least I was escaping
from that mental hardening up. That responsibility was
gone, or at least postponed.

On this other evening twenty-five years later the problem
was very much the same. I was still the same person and
I still accepted that mental and moral slavery was worse
than death, and, which is important, not only for me but
for everybody. The chief addition to my personal make-up,
however, was that now this conviction was not merely
instinctive. When I was a child I just knew it. In the interim
I had acquired information to back my beliefs. In a very
happy if strenuous life I have had many moral and mental
adventures and during them I have found out, no doubt
with millions of others of my generation, that there is a way
of living, entailing constant effort, which leads to growth,
and another which leads to stagnation and then to rottenness, and finally to the death of one's powers of every kind.
There is an up-pull and a down-pull, a building and a
demolition, a fecundity and a sterility. That is true. That
is fact. Among all the chaos our lot were heirs to we have
found that. To be forced to leave the one and live in the
other, not to be free to follow one's own private hunch or
conscience, which is the only reliable flashlamp (far exceed-
ing the intellect in efficiency) I know of to show one where
on earth one's going, would clearly mean the end of growing
and the beginning of rotting. Indeed, in the twenty years
the problem had become blessedly matter-of-fact. It had
resolved into the one which is put so often to individuals
by their doctors in the most civilised of worlds: "Will you
have a dangerous operation now, which may easily kill you
but which may restore you, or will you just die by inches,

slowly and painfully, in a few months or years?" I am not pretending this is a pleasant question, but it is an ordinary one and nobody thinks the patient particularly peculiar or noble if he chooses the operation. Rather the wretched man is considered a howling funk if he doesn't.

Having settled that point beyond question—and at the time I did not realise that it was the first point of its kind which ever had been settled beyond *question* in all my adult life—I had to return to face the old responsibility of long ago. That was exactly the same. I still saw that if it came to it I and everybody else would somehow have to screw our courage to the sticking place, that is we should have to get into a resisting frame of mind and then go deaf and blind and obstinate and think without future or past. I thought maybe we'd be able to do it if we kept together and accepted the compensating enjoyment in it without feeling that that was wrong.

When I saw the others and heard them talking in the next day or two I saw they had all come to roughly the same conclusions, either by the same sort of mental process or by that combination of instincts and adult ideals which is probably the safer way.

They said things like "Looks like we'll have to stand up to 'em then," or "We'll have to get riddy of them, no mistake about it," or merely and most firmly, "We can't have *they* here, no no."

It was not a thing one could ask about, naturally. I wouldn't have thanked anybody to ask me. But as I came in from the garden I saw a familiar figure mucking about in our garage and I blurted out involuntarily, "Will you mind dying, Albert?"

He blushed, as if I had been indecent (as I had of course) and said, "Ain't keen on it," adding after a bit, "Har! we'll get two or three on 'em first."

"Har" is a sort of battlecry in Auburn and the surrounding district. It is deep-throated, two-syllabled, and not at all unlike the demon king's, now I come to think of it, if you substitute tremendous satisfaction for the traditional malice.

There is the same gusto, the same seriousness. "Har! now
we'll beat ye!" says Pontisbright, going in to bat after a
disastrous first innings. "Har! you've *proved* yourself a liar
and I'll tell ye why," says the man in the pub when you've
all but defeated him. "Har! that'll be a fine little old colt,"
says Mr. Saye, advancing on the prostrate mare.

So when Albert said, "Har, we'll get two or three on 'em
first" I knew that since he was a practical man the chances
were we might.

That evening seemed to have settled something definite.
It was not until a long time afterwards that I realised just
what a universal and tremendous thing it was. Independently and simultaneously, round about that time, Britain
must have decided to back growth and must in fact have
decided to live if it had to die to do it.

Right: 'The Old Doctor' — Dr J. H. Salter.

Below: Margery with her mother and
brother at Layer Breton Rectory before
the First World War.

19

THE next morning we were still not invaded. Still no German soldiers, with or without disguise, had dropped out of the sky, and I could not help hoping with Norry, who insisted "all this will pass," as if he were a stone or a tree, that it would never come. However, we knew it was criminal just to hope. Already the cry "wishful thinking" was being thrown at us bitterly as if we had originated the sin and we were inclined to resent it. (There is a tendency to take everything very personally in Auburn.) We had never been optimists about anything and had been called "defeatists" in our time.

Meanwhile the news was growing rapidly frightful. It was like a nightmare recollection of 1914, worse even than the reality of those terrible days. There was no sign of P.Y.C. and we wondered if his unit had been moved already. We were told not to use the telephone if we could help it and we felt cut off and very ignorant.

On Sunday morning I had to go over to Flinthammock to make up the First Aid equipment to full strength. The early morning bulletin had been more than merely bad. Uncle Beastly's death-voice had given out altogether and he had sounded human and shocked for once. The French were disturbingly quiet about Gamelin and the Maginot. However, with six million men under arms, it seemed to us that they must be able to hold Jerry somewhere while we backed up Belgium, which was known not to be very strong. Yet if we really had fallen back behind Brussels because of the break at Sedan it made one think twice. It made Mr. Parker think several times, so he said, as he and I sorted out the haversacks in the big back room behind Joyful's pub.

Mr. Parker is Flinthammock by adoption only. He comes from one of those parts of London which are as much villages as are Auburn and Pontisbright. It is one of the secret strengths of London, I fancy, that it is not a city at all but several thousand complete places, packed rather tight but each one as jealously insular as any other islet in this bursting nest of them. Mr. Parker's village is evidently a sporting place. He and his family have always been interested in the trotting horse and his old guv'nor had some champions. The family have always had shops, too, and when this Mr. Parker caught a packet in the last war he was recommended to go to a place near the sea but not too much on it, so he chose Flinthammock and he and his wife have two shops there.

There is nothing remarkable in a man from a London village choosing to come and live out here. We have always had associations with the places "up the road," as Norry calls it. In the great days of horse traffic there were many races along the highroad and the produce marketmen of London, than whom there are no more complete and insular cockneys, have many pals and clients in this district.

Mr. Parker was and is the leader of the Flinthammock Stretcher Party. In the last war he became a King's Corporal, which means that on one occasion he must have been the senior private who took charge when every rank over him had been killed. Those stripes are permanent. No one but the King himself can take them away.

In his leisure he is a great student of the last war and had read practically every book upon it. Of all the writers he is inclined to give Robert Graves first place as being the most sound and the best workman, although he has a warm regard for Edmund Blunden. I told him P.Y.C. had said he was interested in strategy.

"Strategy?" he said. "Lord Almighty, I was very nearly court-martialled for it once!"

He was very interested in the military situation, naturally, and we began to talk about the Meuse, which he knew well. If they could get over there they'd learnt a thing or two, he said, unless there was something we didn't know about the French.

That was the first time I ever heard anyone in the country

question the reliability of the French, although more informed circles in Town had been whispering about it
uneasily for months. Mr. Parker said he only hoped that
there was some sort of trap waiting somewhere, and that
in the past we had permitted dangerous advances for that
very purpose. Like the rest of us, he could not believe that
we could have been at war for six months and not have
had the main plan taped. It shook one's faith badly. Meanwhile, he said, it was a good thing the L.D.V.s had been
formed and that Flinthammock was getting a fine crowd
of them.

As I came back I realised that no one had said anything
against Mr. Chamberlain. Mr. Churchill was safe in the
saddle and so at any rate everything was all right now.
There were going to be no more stragetic withdrawals on
the moral front. It was going to be "do it or bust," and no
playing the goat. We'd do the blaming round the fire later,
when the books were written and we had the facts.

That Sunday evening Mr. Churchill made his most needed
speech and only part of it was addressed to the nation. The
rest was *for* the nation, and that high-pitched stallion
trumpet, than which there is no more fearful sound, was
far more martial than anything heard in Europe since Queen
Elizabeth noised it for her country at Tilbury.

To the country he gave what it had been needing so
badly since Munich time, trust. Incidentally, too, he gave
it authority to do the things it had already decided to do.
We could fight them on the beaches, on the roads, in the
lanes and in the cities, could we? That was fine. That was
grand. It was all right, then. The Miss Ethels and their
brothers were not incited but they were sanctioned, and
in Britain sanction makes a lot of difference. The speech
was also inspiring, but no man on earth can inspire a
country to make a stand like that. No rider whose horse
is not straining at the bit can speak with such supreme
defiance.

He *proved* his trust in the nation too, which was important
at that time when there had been so much secrecy and

going behind one's back. He gave everybody a broad but confidential hint, "If necessary for years, if necessary *alone*. . . ." Alone? Eh? Really? What's up with they little old Frenchies and their six million men? What did he find out when he went to Paris?

P.Y.C. came back for an hour or so the next day and we got the holster. There was an uneasy feeling in the air that the French war news was being broken gently. Weygand's appointment was very popular, however, for he was thought to be a stern hard man and that gave rise to the hope that there would be a great counter-offensive even if it was followed by hell's delight over here from the air.

It was my birthday and I was thirty-six. I noticed that I did not feel very brave but was oddly settled in my mind and relieved.

The muttering of the guns seemed nearer that day and only partly because of the clarity of the air. There were several "Yellow" or preliminary air-raid warnings, but nothing developed. The L.D.V.s were forming up fast under Mr. James and Doey and Mr. Hart at the station. Grog said rather bitterly that it was nice that someone was going to get a rifle and it was a great relief when they took over the patrols and let the Wardens go back to their own work.

In the next two or three days the weather was good and the atmosphere absurdly peaceful on the surface. Just below it was by no means so smooth. We were finding out things fast. It is all very well to summon your courage one day, but to keep it sword-bright for a week, or a month, or a year, if no sign of danger materialises is quite another matter.

There were other disturbing things also. For instance, it was odd not to be able to make any conceivable sort of arrangement for any day in the future; never to know if the letter you were writing would get to its destination before something happened, or if the things you were saying in it would matter in the least when it did. I did all the silly things one is liable to do, I observed. For instance I drew out eighty pounds and had the notes in a thick envelope.

I had no idea where to hide these, for it seemed important that they should not be lying around in the bureau, and yet be fairly close at hand. Finally I put them down the side of the old granny chair I bought at old Mrs. Seabrook's sale, but they fell through among the springs and I had to undo the canvas under the seat to get them out. I felt like Pepys with his money in the garden at the Great Fire of London. I had always felt him a blithering old fool for that business but I began to sympathise with him heartily, poor chap. Since then we have decided not to keep any money around. It seems to be safer where it is.

Meanwhile there was always my thriller, which was desperately late anyway. It was impossible not to keep wondering if there was any point in going on with it, but a blessed instinct for self-preservation insisted I put in the usual hours. Everyone else appeared to have been bitten by the same urge. Sam worked like a black and so did everyone you saw, harder even than usual; indeed, it seemed to get more important every day that one should get on with one's normal routine. Things like doing the washing up and weeding the vegetables and making the beds and cleaning the house seemed vital. It appeared urgent that the meals should be to time and the clocks wound up and even the flowers kept fresh. I cannot explain quite how strong this feeling was except by saying that it was violent and involuntary, like remembering to hold your breath under water or turning up your big toe for the cramp. It was *the thing to do* for the emergency.

The instincts in the blood were very apparent just then. They gave you the comfortable feeling of being more rooted than you thought you were. For myself, I suddenly became very much aware of past heads of the family. I found this so astonishing and so salutary that I venture to mention it, especially as it seems to have been a fairly common experience at the time.

In my case all the old family sayings came back. There was Great-grandfather's cheerful boast, "Give me *time* and I'll pay the National Debt." He was born in 1800 and was

left ten thousand pounds and the injunction that "no gentleman ever works." He devoted his considerable powers to
laying out his money judiciously and lived like a rich man.
We great-grandchildren have a double dose of him since
our parents were cousins. There was Grandfather's sly "Be
a bundle of sticks; one by one they'll break us, together
we'll smash their thighs." The neutrals would have driven
him crazy. And then Dad's own savagely confident "He'll
break his teeth on England," first about the Kaiser and
later, when it seemed a bit unnecessary, about Mussolini
and the new German Chancellor. Odd things to come into
one's head but all reassuring and all peculiarly and personally one's own inheritance, as if the old boys would have
liked to have been in it, and what there was of them in
oneself was handing out the family weapons to one eagerly.
I am not given to this sort of fancy, preferring not to be
beholden, and it was all the more impressive to me because
I felt it was out of character in me to go and think such
a thing.

On the Wednesday night the B.B.C. published a brief
résumé of the Government's powers under the new Bill. They
are impressive. A conquered country could not give up much
more of its freedom. Those three old men (or three young
men) would have had something to think about there, yet
I don't think any of them would have been wholly appalled.
Great-grandfather would have to have shaken off one great
shackle and gone to work. From what I hear of him he
would not have minded much. The annihilating bondage
of never being able to work like anyone else of one's ability
without losing something irreparable must have irked him
as it would me. Never being able to do anything constructive
is a monstrous sort of restriction. Grandpa would have been
looking for a way round it. Dad would have laughed at the
excitement of it, at the gigantic changing panorama, and
would have banged me between the shoulders and said
explosively, "So we go on!"

In Auburn I seemed to be one of the few people who
noticed the bill at all. The folk who would fight for a Church

School took the news without blinking. Few people even discussed it. I see a great foreigner said the other day that there is no democracy left in England. I can't help feeling that that is as dangerous as an assumption that every woman whose husband is not at her side is a widow. I doubt if democracy is not stronger here now than ever in the whole of our history.

Who made these temporary new laws for our protection? *We* did. That's why we did not even have to discuss them. If you are putting the grandfather clock in the furnace and are prepared to put everything else in, including your boots, to keep the turbines going, you don't discuss each item. Why should you? There isn't the time. All you've got to know is that it *is* you who are doing it. You've got to be in it: it's got to be your show. In fact you've got to be so absolutely certain of democracy that you can treat her like a trusted wife and not a goddess who may prove fickle and leave you any time. The unity of instinct and the universal belief in freedom for the individual which is the backbone of democracy is a very real thing in Britain to-day. We are not only fighting for it: it is our greatest weapon.

Most people thought that the powers under the new Bill were greater than they were, as it happened. For instance, in the matter of commandeering property. In actual fact there was only one man in each wide area who was the person appointed to commandeer, and everything ought to have been done through him, but so general was the belief that the military or Government could take all that many young Army officers commandeered all kinds of property in those few months and nobody questioned or protested, as far as I could hear. The main reason for this smoothness was that the habits of the human animal remained civilised. The social codes held. This may be a weakness in the matter of speed but its value in morale is beyond price.

Our own case was one in point. The following afternoon I was working as usual up in the studio when Sam came up in a high state of cheerful excitement and insisted that

I came down at once. I went down the garden stairs
and found P.C. Me on the lawn behind the house. He
also was highly delighted. He had with him two exquisite
young Scots officers, who looked very apologetic. P.C. Me
said in apparent rapture, "They're going to commandeer
the house."

"No, no," said the Major in a tone a doctor uses when
he says, "I'm going to 'operate,' not 'cut open.' "

Being naturally slow to change my mind from one subject
to another, my first thought was that I was only on chapter
twenty and here was the invasion, and so I said cautiously,
"Come and have a drink."

In the bar it emerged to my relief that there was no
question of turning the family out and that all they wanted
us to do was to put up five officers in the house and a couple
of hundred men in the cricket meadow. That seemed quite
simple to me. I took it I was wrong about the invasion and
gradually an entirely comic situation developed. Looking
back, I see I was still worrying about getting my work done
and was the complete mug, the real old lady out of *Punch*.
As we talked I could not for the life of me understand what
I took to be quite incomprehensible idiosyncrasies on their
part. For instance, I insisted they slept on the spare beds
in the spare bedroom and not on their palliasses on the
floor. The Captain, who was a delightful person, more like
the gallant Regular Army officer than I had thought possible, had quite an argument with me about it. We also
gave them a bathroom, naturally, and their reluctance to
accept it, while yet obviously being very pleased at the
prospect, was very bewildering.

In the other part of the house Margaret seemed to be
having the same sort of trouble with the batmen. They
wanted to camp in the place and she wanted them to have
the big back hall and put up some beds there like Christians.
She also told them to put their bayonets away in case they
hurt each other.

My one anxiety, I remember, was the hay crop. If we
were invaded, of course, we should lose it, but meanwhile

until we were I had a hunch that hay was important and we had a good thick crop coming up. I saw the Major giving me a curious look as I was telling him all this, but I also saw that he was just an ordinary chap, probably younger than I was, and I remembered how P.Y.C. had gained in authority when he put on uniform. Also I wanted my hay.

He was charming about it, in spite of his faintly sad expression. The men would only have a strip of the meadow, he said, and they'd wire off the bit they wanted. I walked down to the paddock with him to see what he had in mind. They were a famous regiment and very splendid. I was impressed by their smartness and, wishing to say something complimentary and yet anxious not to say the wrong thing, which I suspected might be easy, I said that the village would be delighted that they were Scots since the Scotch were very popular. The Major was pleased. His men were wife and child to him and he became entirely human. He was so glad, he said shyly, because they'd naturally feel a bit strange as they were raw troops and this was the first time they'd ever been in the front line.

I had turned back before the last words sunk in and I stopped and looked at him.

I said, "What?"

"Well yes," he said nicely. "What do you think there is between you and the enemy?"

I thought "The Navy, I hope to God!" but it was not an aspect of the situation I had considered quite so baldly before, and when they'd gone off to complete their arrangements and I went back to my thriller I wondered if I really could be as ridiculous as I saw I was. Still, young men read thrillers when they're flying out to bomb Kiel and so maybe it was all right for middle-aged ladies to write them at such a time. Besides, I did not see what else I could possibly do. First Aid arrangements were made and in Auburn we were as ready for anything as we could be. All the same, I saw the soldiers' difficulty over the beds and the bath. They had come to fight and there was I insisting on treating

them as if they'd come down for the cricket. It seemed to
me that exactly the right deportment for the honest civilian,
midway between nonchalance and gallantly concealed terror,
was going to be very difficult to maintain.

We may have taken refuge in laughter, for another frankly
comic situation developed when P.Y.C. raced over in an
hour he had got off to say goodbye. His crowd were moving
and he did not know where. As a mere subaltern, a non-
army man, and anyway a member of the R.A.S.C., army
etiquette decreed that he was barely permitted to breathe
the same air as our visitors, who on the other hand were
slightly younger men and all very much of the same
Tory kind as himself. They were a little at sea too,
being in his house, while he was astounded to see them,
a genuinely awkward social situation, and yet all the
time the whole thing was absurd because, as everybody
knew, the Jerry might arrive in some form or other at any
moment.

Grog and I, who were the only free agents in the entire
party, were inclined to laugh, which was fatal because the
one thing you must not do in the army is to laugh at it.
It is not funny seen from inside.

I said, "Well, thank God he's got a commission, anyway,"
aside to one youngster in an effort to lighten a social situation which I saw was beyond me, and the fervency of his
agreement set me back on my heels.

P.Y.C. and I went off presently and I told him he was
like a shady terrier who had come back to his kennel to
find it bursting with dozens of apologetic prize St. Bernards.
He agreed absently.

"You look out," he said. "That kind of chap suddenly
decides to shoot the women."

"Why?" I demanded, falling for it.

"To save 'em from being shot by a cad," he said and
laughed at me.

So we parted cheerful. Grog and I felt rather lonely when
he went. Our own world had hardly solidified. However,
our visitors were no trouble to us and we grew to like them

and to respect them, although they kept us in a constant state of astonishment.

The village was delighted with their smartness and out in the kitchen the formal Caledonian politeness of the eighteen- and nineteen-year-olds was greatly admired.

As soon as they arrived things began to look like real business at last. Up went the barricades. Every road out of the village was blocked with old farm wagons (there was a big blue wain by the pond which was complete Constable), rolls of barbed wire, and bars of steel from Norry's store. We were fortified all right and I think every civilian looked himself out a weapon, if only a pitchfork, to defend himself when attacked. From the stories pouring through from Holland it was clear that to be a docile civilian was to be a shield for an enemy soldier. It appeared they held you in front of them and fired round you or through you, so there was no more point in appealing to their humanity than to the humanity of a railway engine. Jerry's father had not been very human, but he seemed, by all accounts, to have begotten a robot. One of the Scots officers was wild to get hold of a tommy-gun, and as we saw his great gaunt figure melting away into the landscape we could not help feeling what a pity and how infuriating it was that he should not have one. That was the first time we in Auburn realised what lack of equipment meant. It was heartbreaking. We could have done without cars and buses and hot-water systems these last ten years easily had we realised.

Meanwhile, round about this time, maybe a day or so later, odd news was beginning to creep in from Flinthammock and all along the coast. Unexpected people mentioned it, many of whom did not at first see its terrifying significance. The Government were collecting little boats and men to man them. What for? Things were as bad as that, were they? What a sporting chance, though! What a move! How like old Churchill! How tragically make-shift, but how traditional! How fine! Bad news, terrible news, but news with a lift to it. Tremendous times. Our turn next, most likely. Horrible, but we can't have *they* here, no no.

It was wonderfully good weather, King's weather, warm with a slight mist, a moon just past the full. Grog and I made discreet inspections of the fortifications and noticed that our house had evidently been selected not for its comfort, as we had innocently supposed, but for its strategic position in the dead centre of the four road blocks. That sobered us considerably. I took my biscuit tin to bed with me again and I put my money in it as well as the manuscript. As far as I could see the entire village was as calm as a fish and I could not help wondering if I was the only funk. Auburn is very down on windiness, descrying it in the most unlikely people, and I was secretly very much afraid of disgracing myself. It was very difficult to imagine what the moment would be like when it came or to gauge at all how it would take you. Christine, Margaret, and young Ralph who helped them, simply would not bother their heads about the Germans. They had the British Army to look after. The officers were not eating with us, but the yard was a sort of troop's club and washhouse.

The four batmen, who were very young indeed, were disconcerting at first. They were so regimental that they trotted up and down our back stairs, which consist of a series of companionways just conceivable in a ship of the old Victory class, at the double and sometimes in pairs, a manœuvre only possible because of their extreme slenderness. They made a clatter like the end of the world and in times of stress carried rifles, sometimes with, we discovered with respect, "one up the spout."

It was very good for us. It broke us into the idea gradually and was also very comforting. There is something very nerveracking about waiting for an attack in a night so still that you can hear a dog-fox bark two miles away.

The King made a speech on the air one night, a very fine, sincere and simple one which crystallised the moment. The whole tenour of life had altered and had become simpler and in a way much easier. There was more than a touch of the address before Agincourt in the air, a secret satisfaction that if it was coming we were to be the chosen, we few,

we happy few, and all the other happy few round the coast
of an impregnable island. All this looks childish written down
but it was a direct, childish time, quite different but more
entirely satisfying than any other piece of life which I at least
have ever experienced. It was big enough and sound enough
to fill you, and if it went to your head a bit the luckier you.

I had been asleep about two hours when the motor-bikes
woke me. I had the shutters closed because of the black-out,
but the windows were wide. There was a staggering din going
on and my old four-poster was vibrating like a truck. Our
front door has great iron latches on it and makes a noise
like dungeons if you bang it. It banged several times and
I could hear the rather high-pitched Scottish voices, then
a noise as though an army was charging the stairs, and then
the unmistakable chill noise of steel. I sat up in bed listening,
my hair on end and feeling sick. Out of the rumble on the
other side of the door came the Captain's voice, delightfully
nonchalant. It said:

"Well, then, fetch me a couple of rifles."

I slid out of bed, put on a dressing-gown, and, sneaking
over to the door, opened it very cautiously, an insane thing
to do which might well have got me shot. (When your own
side is running around the house with loaded rifles the one
thing to avoid is secretive movement.) There were several
people on the landing when I looked out, including the
Captain in an Indian full-dress pink silk coat by way of
a dressing-gown. It made him look an astonishing but even
more martial figure than usual. Standing stiffly with his
back to me was a Scottie, his bayonet towering over our
heads. I was within six inches of him and I said very softly
in his ear, "What's up?"

He shot in the air, poor chap, as well he might with me
creeping about on the thick carpet, but controlled himself
and gave me a severe stare.

"They're heerr, Ma'am," he said.

It always shocks me to find that I do by instinct just what
any other old fool does in an emergency and that I respond
to my training rather than to my mind. On this occasion

I said, "Oh dear, I'd better make some tea, then," a remark guaranteed to irritate any man facing invasion. However, he let me by and I went down to the kitchen quaking and yet very excited and made some farmer's tea, a rather frightful beverage believed in Pontisbright to be just the thing for any sort of upheaval in the night. It is one part black tea, one part whisky, flavoured with milk and lots of sugar, and is drunk boiling. "That keeps out the cold and the ghosts," they say.

I felt better for it and most people drank it without grumbling. There was some sort of conference going on round the phone with Grog, who had been on duty by it, and despatch riders were coming and going. I gathered that a parachute landing (a false alarm, as it transpired afterwards) had taken place several counties away and that others were expected, possibly near us.

I could not help wondering why none of the neighbours had come in. Somebody usually turns up when something is afoot and P.C. Me is invariably about. However, putting my head out in the yard, the first thing I saw was a Bren gun and it began to dawn on me that a quiet stroll through Auburn that night might not be too healthy for anyone.

I found Grog, who was secretly tickled by it all in spite of the gravity of the situation. As a family we have always laughed at the etiquette and formality of the Featherstones, as we privately dub the Regular Army, and to see them in the flesh doing and saying all the things we had said they did was an experience. However, for the first time we began to see the sense of it. It made the whole thing possible. If there had not been this rigorous code of manner and thought everybody might have been dithering hopelessly, however brave he was, and although that might have been more natural it would not have been so sound by any means. The idea was to win not to be clever.

The Captain admired the enemy's efficiency from a purely professional point of view. You had to hand it to that feller Hitler, he said. He knew how to get a move on.

In a very short time all the necessary arrangements had been made according to the book of the words and the house settled down again. Those men who had a few hours' sleep due to them were instructed to take them. As civilians it was presumed that we had our own affairs to see to. Grog returned to his telephone. Christine was away at home at Pontisbright that week-end, which left Margaret and me with nothing to do. We went back to bed. I put my clothes ready, found my biscuit tin, which I had entirely forgotten, and then I got into bed. It was extraordinary how easy it was to sleep. I had no responsibility. I simply had to do what I was told. I was less frightened than I had been for months. My principal emotions, as I remember them, were fury and astonishment, the two things I knew it was quite illogical to feel. It was not until twenty-four later that we knew the island was still unviolated and by that time the news was so depressing that it seemed scarcely of interest.

Two of the ships that set off for Dunkirk:
Left: SB. *Tollesbury. (www.adls.org.uk)*
Below: fishing smack *Iris Mary. (Mark Wakefield)*

20

AUBURN first heard the news of the abrupt and un-heralded capitulation of the Belgian Army on the direct order of King Leopold on the midday wireless bulletin on the Tuesday after its own midnight adventure. Of all the blows in the wind, and there have been many, this I think was the most sudden and annihilating. The late King Albert of the Belgians must have had the King Edward the Seventh touch, for all over this district—and therefore no doubt over all other country districts, for we can hardly be peculiar in this respect—you come across men who speak of him as "a very nice gentleman" in that particular affectionate way which means that he had the squire's gift for making the ordinary chap feel he has a grand friend who knows him as well as anybody else and who likes him for personal virtues, instantly descried, just as anyone else might, but who yet retains all his grandeur.

The desertion of his son, therefore—and at that time it did look like a desertion—was exquisitely and personally painful to an enormous amount of people. It got right under the skin. Leopold, the handsome and the tragic, had been one of the popular heroes for years. People thought of his children in the same breath almost as they thought of the little British Princesses.

The A.R.P. Sergeant from Fishling, who is a great friend and ally of ours and a pillar of strength in the area, came in that afternoon looking as if he had had a private disaster. It was not the danger to the island, not the situation. Like the rest of the country he expected a fight, had decided on it, was not above looking forward to it, and had given up worrying about it. The fight was settled. It was coming. That was all "laid on." The blow had come from the young King, the son of a hero. He talked about King Albert all the afternoon, and you got a very vivid picture of the man. Our own picture in the bar did not help matters. It was a coloured reproduction of Sir Bernard Partridge's famous *Punch* cartoon showing Albert and William the Second standing in a battlefield. The German is saying, "So, you see, you've lost everything," and the Belgian is replying, "Not my soul." The Old Doctor must have bought it in the last war, because we found it still unwrapped when we moved in, and we hung it in the bar as a suitable period piece. The bombast and high-falutin sentiment in the drawing, Albert so handsome and William so depraved, had struck us as delightfully overdone; but on that afternoon it did not look so funny. It upset the Sergeant badly, and it made me feel rather frightened, for I wondered if the young King had ever seen it and had ever been faintly amused. Our generation has had a curious history of hot and cold, and it made one suddenly afraid of what the effect on the essential fibre of us all might have been. The danger now, obviously, was of swinging back to the same place and breeding the same disillusioned children; but the middle course is very hard to steer. Somehow or other it looked as though our lot had got to stick to its habit of testing and trying, and it seemed that weakness would have to be faced as squarely and curiously as strength, fear questioned as minutely and suspiciously as confidence. Belgium was a great personal disaster, though, very damaging at the time.

Hard on the heels of Belgium came the news of Dunkirk. I always suspected Auburn of being a little jealous of Flinthammock's part in Dunkirk, for Auburn has no boats.

Every man approached in Flinthammock went off without question in any old craft. "Di'nt get no further than Ramsgate. Old boats fell to pieces," said Auburn spitefully and libellously under my window one morning, and I did not recognise the voice.

Auburn had fine men there, however, and it lost the Major from the Court there, who went down gallantly beside his men.

Albert Clover came through unscathed, and his comment when invited by his family to give his impressions of one of

the most gruelling experiences of all time was unusual even
in a race with a partiality for understatement.

"Har, there were plenty to occupy your mind," he is
reputed to have said. "That weren't *slow*."

The soldiers in the house had tremendous tales from their
friends, all passed on in the same restrained colours. Old
so-and-so had picked up a dinghy and rowed himself across.
That was considered a "pretty fair effort." It made them
very anxious to begin over here though, and they thought it
must come soon. They almost apologised for the falseness of
the first alarm. Any night now, they said.

The batmen in the kitchen kept their "wee swords," as
they called their bayonets, very much in their minds and
were clearly itching to fix them. To blunder into the back
hall to find a smooth-faced fair-headed child sleeping sweetly
on the camp bed Margaret had produced, his rifle clasped
in his arms like a toy, was one of those things you could
have wished not to have seen until you remembered how
lucky it was for you that there were children to do it, and
that if you had had any sense there would be your children
growing up to take their place.

In the village the reaction to the defeat was everywhere
the same. It hardened everybody up at once. A lot has
been written about this natural characteristic, but the only
person who ever put it into words for me was the Old Doctor
long ago. He was probably the most uncomplicated, un-
compromisingly English man who ever lived, and he said
that one of the great joys of bare-knuckle prizefighting (he
went back to that) was the agony when you first felt the
other fellow's fist in your face, and every sinew and essence
in your body tightened and boiled up in splendid rage as
you plunged in to give him one better. I don't know how
many of us felt "the splendid rage," but there was a general
feeling that now, if ever, was the time to get a move on.
There was never any hint or question of capitulation
anywhere then or later. The possibility, I swear, did not
occur to anybody that I saw, and when I got a letter from
America suggesting sorrowfully that it might conceivably

happen, I must say I was astounded. Like everybody else,
I felt we had not started.

Men were joining up everywhere. Phil phoned me that
he was sending me all his possessions, and that I was to fling
them in the shed until he came back. He had volunteered
as a driver and was away to camp.

Meanwhile there was ordinary life to attend to still.
Preparations for invasion and death were all very well, but
it was also important to continue the usual preparations for
going on living. If these were strenuous, as they always are
in Auburn, one's mental stability needed watching if one
was to survive.

On my part the completion of my thriller was a vital
necessity; no question about that. My part in the family
war effort was to keep the home going and pay the taxes,
and there were times when I wished I had been 'prenticed
to a different trade. My tale was about a man with amnesia
and required a mental contortionist with uninterrupted
leisure to write the blessed thing. I was putting in about
seven hours a day on it, and it had got to be good. It was
an odd life. I was always hoping that the end of one thriller
would not overtake me before I had finished the other.

There were other aspects of living to be considered too.
We still had one or two evacuees to attend to, although by
this time we were a Defence Area, and meanwhile there
was the question of war-time economy. Margaret and I
decided that the rationing of food was being done remarkably well and quite differently to most Government measures,
which are very often inclined to be unimaginative. There
were as yet no real hardships, and the prices of most things
were being kept down. We had no big store cupboard. The
early advice to housewives to lay in reserves had been
followed by awful warnings against hoarding, which suggested that one must not overdo it. The happy mean was
difficult to fix. We came to the conclusion that a supply
sufficient to last the household for three weeks was probably
about right, and we arranged for that. Soap we always had
bought in bulk, and we got in the usual year's supply. The

spring had been bad for the garden, but the vegetables were coming along fairly well and the hay was very promising, the soldiers keeping rigorously to their appointed strip of meadow.

Meanwhile, what with the growth of the Home Guard, as the L.D.V.s were now called, and the floods of amazing stories coming over the water with the troops, the whole place was becoming very military minded. Fifth Column excitement was mounting to fever pitch.

Whoever thought of the simple measure by which Fifth Column activity was stamped out in Britain was one of those elementary geniuses whose gift lay in knowing the country. It simply became generally known that any private suspicion whatever would be treated with great sympathy by the police. If you thought anything or anyone was a bit funny or a bit queer, you could go and talk about them to your heart's content to the local bobby, who would put the magnificent machinery of the C.I.D. in motion. Anything promising meant that M.I.5 would turn up, and even though you heard no more about it you could rest assured that all had been gone into. Well, what a chance! What an opportunity! What a picnic! Under a mask of indifference the average village Briton, be his home in the city or the country, is the elephant's child reborn. His insatiable curiosity is boundless. Also he never takes anybody on trust. In Mudlarking, down on the marsh, you are a stranger for fourteen years, and then at a public drinking party you are sworn in as a true Mudlarker. In Auburn there is no such ceremony, and I should think the period of probation was considerably longer. In fact, unless your life is an open book, you can be a mystery family for generations, exciting the curiosity of your neighbours by almost everything you do. So what happened here, and no doubt in other places, was, it is my private belief, that pretty nearly the entire population was considered discreetly at some time or other by the police.

To our secret regret we never got a single spy. "Soil di'nt suit 'em," as Sam said. But there were one or two good false alarms. A young woman in the Flinthammock bus sat behind two small boys, one of whom she recognised. The other, an eager child, was confiding in an undertone to his friend that he had been playing in the yard of a certain farm near the sea wall and had stumbled, falling against a stack. He put out his hand, he said, and felt something hard. Investigation had shown that it was not a stack at all, but a "great pile o' guns."

The young woman went to the lady in whose house she worked and told her story. The lady had a son stationed at Bastion, and she telephoned to him. Within a few hours the Flinthammock P.C. was confronted by two personages. They sought out the known boy, who promptly sacrificed his friend in the country's interest. Confronted by so much officialdom, the second child gave way. He was sorry, he said; he had read it all in his weekly comic paper.

However, this sort of adventure was evidently unfortunate, because the stories coming in from the troops, and especially those from Holland, showed that the weekly comic papers had nothing on the new Jerry in the matter of invention. Startled soldiers told you extraordinary tales of trickery, among them stories of fierce long-haired women in Belgian farms who turned out to be stalwart Nazis carrying disguise to the point of farce. It seemed to us that an entire mental readjustment was going to be necessary, and that was not easy. Of all the fixed things in the mind the point of the ridiculous is the most secure. When at last we had adjusted ourselves to the new one—and it took some time, because the tales were many and varied—it made us peculiarly angry and brought home to me at any rate, more quickly than anything else could have done, the real purport of the new fighting. Working at home here and listening to all the tales, it became clear that the Jerry was just being thorough as usual. In his backing of the down-pull and the certain road to chaos he was doing the thing properly. The lie or the double-lie was to be always best, the twist to be always better than the straight, the white flag must always hide a gun, the outstretched hand always wear the poisoned ring.

Destruction was to be complete. Last time he cut down the
fruit trees as he retreated: this time he was going to poison
the minds of the children as well. Nothing which could stand
true was to remain. No God and man-constructed foothold,
mental or moral, was to be left unbroken.

Against this sort of thing mere Christianity seemed to me
to be helpless. The occupied territory in which Christ lived
was not ruled by men whose ideal of government was a
mixture of carefully weighed lies knit together by considered
acts of violence, and a system of proselytising all children
by force to a religion which fanatically substitutes evil for
good. This new-old notion of living of Jerry's was considered
obsolete and uncivilised long before the time of Christ. Man
had found it did not work centuries before that. It was this
element of Nazism which was so difficult to comprehend.
Few people can see God, and it seems it takes an even
bolder mind to see the Devil. Active evil is more incomprehensible in this two-part-perfect world than active good,
and so it ought to be, Heaven knows, after all the effort
towards universal improvement which has been put in on it
these two thousand years.

However, at that time, with the enemy showing his hand,
it did for the first time seem elementarily obvious to ordinary
people that the Nazi doctrine has no aim save slavery and
methods which are lies and violence and broken promises,
and yet, most terrible of all, a force which is fanatical and
spiritual. For the first time in my life I felt exasperated with
mental niceties, with all the Gothic tracery of little doubts
and tolerancies. This was big and clear and as obvious as
a hole in the road. This was plain elementary wrong. This
was the worship of the other god.

Apart from the distant guns, the soldiers and the barricades, there were other active signs of imminent danger in
Auburn. Two of them which were most apparent were the
habit of the wireless announcers of mentioning their names
before a bulletin (so that we should get to recognise their
voices and not be taken in by false speakers) and the silence
of the church bells. Little things, but very significant because

they kept cropping up so constantly. Church bells are a
great part of normal life in the country. When anyone dies
from the village the passing bell is tolled for him. It is
sometimes the first indication that death has occurred, and
often a man would straighten in the fields and say, "She's
gone then, poor little old girl," or, "Who's that for?" The
Sunday bells ring out from all the churches three times in
the day, and it was very strange without them. The realisa-
tion that when they did sound again it would be to ring
a clarion which would mark the beginning of the great fight
was another thing which became very clearly embedded in
the mind, and it was impossible not to think of them every
now and again, imagining them jangling horribly in the
night or in the clear air of the dawn.

When the French decided not to defend Paris there was
no criticism on the wireless or in the Press, naturally.
Officially, I think, we were deeply sympathetic with the
decision of our great ally; but in a countryside like ours,
ignorant at that time of the power of the enemy machine,
the decision seemed to be terrible beyond thought. To our
minds, on land France was still the boss. We thought we
were to look after the seas and keep the channels of supply
open. We also thought we should have to get hold of the
money somehow because France never seems to have much,
and we were prepared to pour every man into the Continent
when they were needed; but France was the boss of that.
Now she had an army of six million men in the field, and
she was not going to fight for Paris.

In a place like Auburn it is not easy to visualise great
distances, and this story of the German advance seemed
either incredible, or it made France seem far smaller than
she is. We began to wonder if the shakiness at Sedan might
not go all through the administration. Many of us had
acquaintances in France, not very important people but
ordinary folk like ourselves. There was Virginie in her pub
in the Pas de Calais, who is so like Vic, Norry's sister. Paul,
très serieux, who might be another Albert and who drove
P.Y.C. and me all round the Alpes Maritimes. The nice

people at St. Malo, who still always showed their youngsters with the old proud "another son for France." They were all all right. They would fight to the death, just as we expected we would; but there was something very funny about a High Command which would not defend Paris with six million men. Everybody mentioned it in the same half-astounded, half-frightened way.

It was about this time that the subject of America first cropped up in Auburn. Albert said something about that country when he came past one morning when I was having breakfast in the conservatory and was snuffling over *The Times*. We agreed that the war news was really "worse than dull," and he said, "What about the Americans?" and mentioned that the papers had said something about them. I asked him what he thought, and he shook his head. He said there was "something behind to be got over." Albert is often rather cryptic, and I had to get him to explain. He said he thought the Americans did not want to be caught twice, and that *The Past* was behind. I agreed with him, and we remained depressed.

During the war there had been a strong inclination not to think too much about America. Since that time, last summer (1940), Mr. Roosevelt, who has "wonderful long eyes" (as we say when we mean a man sees far), has mentioned the garden hose. Just then Albert and I were both thinking of the equivalent of the garden hose, and we both had the same misgivings. It seemed to us that we had borrowed America's garden hose once before and had done it in. Worse than that, regarding her as more or less of a relation, we had not got round to replacing it, and had consequently never heard the last of it. Now the perishing place was on fire again.

This feeling that America is a close relation is to my mind one of Auburn's biggest mistakes. You can see how it has arisen. Sons and brothers have gone to America from Auburn and have become Americans. When they come back on a visit they are still sons and brothers and still Americans; but what Auburn does not and will not see is that exactly the same sort of process has taken place in every village in Europe too. Also there is the question of size. Auburn must know that America is bigger than England, but I very much doubt if it realises it. Then there are the language, the ideals and the movies (which last seem to be all about our better-looking summer visitors). Even Christine, who of all of us has actually been to the country and worked in Washington, says "Foreigners? Oh no, they're just like English, only easier to get on with. You could not call them foreigners. Foreigners are funny."

Some of the rest of us have even wilder ideas. When Malcolm came over I actually heard Norry enquire if he had seen a relation of the family who went to America twenty years ago wearing a brown suit and looking unmistakably like himself and Jack. It is not that we are daft, or even particularly ignorant. It is that we are insular. We cannot imagine an Auburn man becoming half Auburn and half something new, and his son being entirely new. We are wrong, and now at last we are beginning to understand that two men may have the same language, the same ideals, the same way of living and even the same great-grandparents, and yet owe different allegiances and have different axes to grind.

However, right up to last year we had not got that idea quite clear in our minds, and the "relation we had offended" was still the most popular picture. The simplicity with which we saw our offence was typical of Auburn. We had not paid the bill. The real reason, we suspected, was because America was a relation and would not sue us. That is a situation common enough in Auburn, and no one on earth understands the trouble it can brew better than we do.

As an example of what I mean by this feeling of close relationship, consider the children. At this time of peril, when Albert and I were talking in the greenhouse, there was a strong feeling everywhere that if we could only bundle every child in the island over the Atlantic to Canada or the U.S.A. we could clear the decks and get down to it and fight to a finish, and if not an English soul were left alive at the end of it, it would still not be defeat. To Canada or the United States: you see the feeling. Parents don't just send their babies to a strong country. A nation does not want to put its entire living future in a box. Children are not bags of gold. You would not trust them to the vaults of a bank or to strangers, however admired. When it is a question of blood instinctively you think of blood, whatever the family row has been. I know when my mother sent us off to London on that famous occasion in the last war, she and my aunt, her sister, had been having a period of distinct coolness and were not on speaking terms. Mother had lots of friends in London, but she sent us to Aunt. I am certain the same sort of feeling moved everybody this time. Had the position been fantastically reversed, I do not think the ordinary people would have been so eager to send their children to France, Belgium or Holland, whatever the danger from the West, and yet our admiration and affection for those countries is considerable.

We were wrong, of course. Not in sending the children, God knows, for that kindness in America has done as much to cement the friendship between the two countries as any other material help; but in thinking in terms of blood, for we who are as a rule so good and punctilious with foreigners (as we are in private life with friends) are often very bad indeed with wealthy relations. It is probably something to do with the laws of inheritance, which are so old that they have coloured our instincts. I firmly believe that if only America had seemed as foreign to us as France we would have paid the debt somehow, if it broke us and the world. The politicians and the economists may know better. They think they arrange these things. So they do, in a way; but it is we, the common people, ignorant and muddle-headed and governed by the heart and not the head, who are really responsible for everything in the long run, and we know it. If we disobey our principles, we get into difficulties at once, and always have done. That is why they *are* principles.

So there, as Albert and I saw it that morning, lay the trouble. We had been in the wrong. Old Lady America was riled, and we would most likely have to suffer for it. Meanwhile the fire was taking hold.

In the interim, naturally, a great change has occurred. The careful, kindly explanations on the wireless of Mr. Swing, who of all American commentators has the necessary patience to realise that he is not speaking in quite the same language his listeners use and will go on explaining until he is quite clear, has done much to get it into country minds that America is more foreign than, say, Lancashire, and more strong and more like Britain in ideals than France.

Meanwhile Mr. Roosevelt has emerged as a great statesman. It is that quality in him which has probably done more to impress the Auburn kind of person in Britain than even his great kindliness and sympathy towards us. The statesman touch on the reins is unmistakable, and we have come to see him as a great rider astride *another horse*. That is a tremendous step forward for us. That means, I think, that at last we are getting the right idea.

America, too, seems to have a great wealth of big men. When people like Mr. Willkie and Mr. Winant come over here they behave like big men with personalities and not like ordinary foreign diplomats, who very seldom emerge as real people save to those close to them.

L to R: Robert St. John Cooper ('Coop'), P.Y.C., T. E. B. ('Tibby') Clarke, Sir Henry Rushbury ('Rush').

21

THE capitulation of France was a blow on a numbed head. Fortunately Auburn (and it would seem the country) does not appear to go by the head. The reflex actions were still all right. At home it was the usual announcement on the wireless, the familiar crunch in the belly and the immediate instinct to get down to work again quick, but Christine produced the most vivid account of its effect on the countryside that I heard. She was out in the pea-fields. Christine is funny that way. She is close on my age, a way-up professional housemaid, has travelled all over America and seen good service in London. Her professional dignity is enormous, but on her holiday she likes to go home to Pontisbright and spend her time pea-picking. There is no freedom in the world like it, she says, and you are making money as well. She and her sister were up in the broad fields on the hill of Ney, the little village above the Pontisbright valley, and the picking was good. The Ney people, who are "old-fashioned," which means roughly that they are Puritanical and simple and a bit pessimistic, went home for every news and came back at last, pale and horrified. "Now we're alone. Now they'll be over here in no time," they said.

"We wondered," said Christine, "if it was worth while making any more money."

"Did you stop picking?" I asked.

"Oh no," she said. "We went on picking harder than ever. We had to get the peas in. We only wondered."

This, I believe, is basic. I know Fred, who used to work for us at Pontisbright, cleared off one morning and put in a day for the farmer next door. We protested about this to him and found he had accepted no money from the man. "It was the *hay*," he said patiently. "We had to get the hay in before that rained." It was not Fred's hay or our hay, but he could not see what that point had to do with it and discounted all our arguments, which he clearly thought immoral. "Must get the *hay* in," he said.

Norry is always doing the same sort of thing. If a mare is foaling she must be properly fed, whose ever animal she is and whose ever food. The allegiance is to the ground and the life upon it and the things that must be done.

I do not think this is purely country either. It is in the blood of a certain type of Briton. You find it in all the crafts and even in the kind of people who post forgotten mail for the office next door even though they do not like the folk who work there much. It is not even kindness of heart but loyalty to life, and largely accounts, I fancy, for our national reputation for being old busybodies.

One very general reaction to the fall of France, in Auburn especially, was the genuine satisfaction at getting the boys back in the country and taking the job on ourselves. There was, not unnaturally, a new mistrust of foreign generalship. Both our flanks had been uncovered. "Har, we'll get on better alone," said Norry. "Much better have the boys over here," said the women. "We shan't have anyone else to blame but ourselves now, anyway," said the pessimists among us.

Gradually the value of the situation became apparent. To feel alone is only terrifying if you are naturally gregarious. If you are naturally insular it gives you an added strength. You feel untrammelled and safer. Besides, we had the Colonial boys, most of them in Bastion it seemed. They were a tough happy lot. They reduced every young woman in the place to a state of giggling excitement and every senior Regular Army officer to a turkeycock. However, whatever they got up to, they were never foreign. The day they swapped every baby in the pram park behind Woolworth's they made the mothers wild, but there was no one in Auburn who did not laugh. It was a simple, very British sort of joke; not very funny to a foreigner.

We also began to realise that we had a lot of friends. You saw Poles and Belgians and Czechs and Free French and Dutch as soon as you set foot in a town. The island was very full and good and ready. In Auburn itself the various defensive organisations became so many that once or twice

it looked as if they might tread on each others toes. The
Home Guard were patrolling regularly and efficiently. David,
from the farm, had an ecstatic story about himself and three
other guards up on the church tower one night being mistaken by a newcomer to the village for parachutists who
had come down. The idea of them all landing neatly
together in the square box of the thirteenth-century tower
tickled the locals' sense of humour and there was a lot of
chaffing all round.

Parachute nights continued in earnest for a long time and
there was nothing fanciful any more in stealing out on to
the flat roof in the grey dawn, to peer out over the leafy
country and watch for any faint movement anywhere.

Our first Scots soldiers were moved on, to our regret, for
we had grown to admire and like them, and a new contingent from an equally famous regiment took their place.
The new Captain was a martinet, newly returned to sol-
diering from a spell of private life between wars. He had
a row of ribbons, the M.M. and the Mons among them.
His soldiers belonged to the new army and also to a very
old one. They were rougher and not quite so smart as the
first lot had been with their wee swords and parade ground
manners, but they were tough enough and were itching to
get at an enemy. There was three days' coolness between
the village and the army and then it suddenly percolated
that the newcomers were real country folk from a coast even
wilder and more barren than our own. Fraternisation set
in and a Border–East Anglian entente was set up. They
had habits and etiquettes as settled and obstinate as our
own, we discovered, and the two companies settled down
together in that amicable near-silence which in Auburn is
an indication that a complete understanding has been
reached.

However, in the interim two days after the collapse of
France, we had our first genuine air raid. It was a clear
still night with a moon as big as the dining-room table and
the whole place lit up as bright as day. Our fiery Captain
was horror-stricken to find startled people scurrying up and

down his well guarded territory "blawing wee whustles" and kicking up the devil of a noise generally.

The faithful Wardens, on the other hand, who had been keeping patient guard throughout close on ten months of silent nights, without encouragement or reward, in order to blow their whistles among other duties, and who felt pretty silly doing it anyway, were irritated by his contempt. Since they were all in the same house it might have been difficult, but there was a real raid and that took everyone's attention.

That was the period of what the Jerry called "armed reconnaissances." These were a series of raids directed mainly at searchlights and were also, in Auburn's opinion, an attempt to get his hand in by practising on us. It was the first time we heard the curious broken rumble of the bombers. Christine says they sound like lions growling and once that idea has been put in your head it is very difficult to get it out. There is the same hollow lamp-glass note in them.

All the Wardens appeared, Grog and Cliff and Reg and Sam and Johnny and Herbert, and for the first time we saw the searchlights, apparently helpless against the blazing moon, feeling about the sky like "an old 'ooman looking for fleas in a blanket."

Over the meadow, behind the elms, in the direction of the county town, there were odd lights in the sky, coloured fireworks dropping like one used to see them over Bastion on carnival nights. Once or twice the growling came very close but passed away overhead. And then, still between the elms and too far away to be anything but breath-takingly exciting, the rattle of a giant typewriter, sparks, and finally a great blaze much further away still. It flared in the sky, dropped to the ground and set up a flame like a heath fire. It was a plane, Grog insisted : first blood to us.

Later on in the night there was another chase and the bomber sped out over the house, above the lawn, and away to the sea with a fighter after him, the tracer bullets making new stars in the sky.

They got seven down that evening; one of the highest
totals for some time to come, but we were not to know that
then. It was not at all the kind of raiding we expected,
either. We were right as it happened; that was an unusually
good night, the sky so clear and the moon so strong, two
days from midsummer.

There were no bombs that night. None of us had heard
any then. Two nights later we had our first experience. I
was out on the far lawn watching the searchlights crossing
and recrossing each other and making the sky look like a
shot-silk plaid skirt. There were planes everywhere, or it
seemed like it. I saw the flash away over the meadows and
like a complete fool had no idea what it signified, so that
the noise ten seconds later frightened me out of my wits.
There were twelve bombs, not very big but of the kind they
call anti-personnel because the bits fly out so far and go
through anything, almost. I only heard one noise and at
the risk of being ridiculous I must say it reminded me
of the night a burglar kicked a pile of washing-up bowls
down the back stairs on to the stone floor underneath
my bedroom when I was a child, a monstrous and awful
noise.

However, Herbert, standing out with the others in the
yard, had heard everything. He too knew nothing about
bombs but he can hear a rabbit walking underground and
can see a hawk's prey at the other end of a field. He said
definitely that there were twelve bangs, about two miles
away, and that some of them had fallen in water, for he
had heard the splashes and the widgeon getting up. He
seemed astounded we had not heard them too. He was
quite right. The bombs had come down in a sheep meadow
and in the water adjoining it not so far from where a Zepp
had grounded in the last war. Anti-personnel or no, they
had certainly been bad for the sheep.

Our Captain was still exasperated by the "whustling," and
we had a job to convince him that it was not private enterprise on our part inspired by fright. He pointed out how
ridiculous it was and privately we agreed, but, as Grog said,

if you had said you would do a thing you had got to do it, and if people wanted to know when a raid was on and you were appointed to tell them you must carry out your obligations however much of a fool you look. The Captain still thought it was insane until we were inspired to put it to him in a military way. We suggested that his sentries must feel pretty foolish guarding an old farm cart in the middle of a road while everybody in the village went through the back gardens to avoid them, but they could hardly lay off because of that. Extraordinarily enough, once he saw that the order really did come from a higher authority, he had nothing but the greatest sympathy and consideration for us and we grew to like him very much. He had a lot to try him. Front line or no front line, Auburn was still under civil control, and one day a great lorry full of sandbags arrived and the two men with them built an enormous and obvious stockade round the maypole more suitable to the Zulu War than to anything in this century. I never did find out which exact authority was responsible for the erection, but the grass grew over it in time and it became a sort of clubroom in the windy autumn. In the early days the Captain used to pass it bristling.

"Put a wee flag on it," he used to say bitterly to anyone he thought might conceivably have something to do with it.

The Captain knew a great deal about fighting and, had the invasion come in his time in Auburn, the village would have been defended magnificently. The new tactics delighted and fascinated him and after a bit it occurred to me that his interest in the windows of our house might easily be professional. I had finished my thriller at last and, having given up work for a week or two, had more time for imagining, and I began to feel that some sort of retreat might be advisable if the house suddenly became a strong point. In this kind of war, in this kind of country, it is no use thinking of real safety. There is none and to think about it is to ask for trouble. But it is very natural to feel that you would like an alternative roof over your head if someone is going to

have a battle in the house. I thought something of the
sort would be a good idea, if only for our morale, for the
one thing we really had learnt was that we had to keep off
the roads at all costs. I also felt that in view of the tremendous enthusiasm of our own men one should if possible be
able to get out of sight. Concrete was pretty well unobtain-
able at that time and anyhow Albert was busy, so on Sam's
advice I bought a couple of ton of baled straw and we filled
in the quarrelling place, leaving a space in the middle. I
have never regretted this because the straw has been so
useful this winter and I should never have got a stock in
otherwise, but at the time it made a neat little summerhouse,
not much of a target and anyway a hiding place. I came
in for a lot of chaff.

P.Y.C., who came over one day to see us, was appalled
by it and forbade me pointblank ever to go anywhere near
it in an emergency, but I was obstinately and illogically
glad of it, and I think there is a lot of that in this new world.
If you feel happier in a third-grade tin hat, which would
not keep off an acorn, there is no reason at all why you
should not wear one. A real one is not guaranteed to save
your life.

To my despair the Captain was attracted by the little
house and I had an uncomfortable impression that his
interest in it might be professional too. He was very obliging.
He got a rifle and fired at it to see if the machine-pressed
straw would keep out a bullet. It would not. The bullet
went through the straw, a dustbin lid on the back of a chair,
and in my opinion through a second bale, hitting a building
half a mile away, but I have no proof of that. Anyhow the
Captain lost interest and I retained my little shed, and we
never found the bullet.

The greatest strain at this time, still, was this never being
able to plan ahead with any degree of certainty. While I
had been working very hard I had not noticed it so much,
but now it became irksome for a while until, miraculously,
we got used to it. We seem to get used to things very quickly
in Auburn, much as plants do, and we go on much the

same as usual now except for a mental *d.v.* when anything is planned.

There were many scares just then and many false alarms, and gradually we became more and more used to hearing the lions growling in the sky.

Left: Cartoon of Winston Churchill
(*Topfoto*)

Below: 'When Hitler Missed the Bus' by Leslie Illingworth. Cartoon published in the *Daily Mail*, 7th May 1940.
(*Associated Newspapers*)

22

As I mentioned before, seen from Auburn's ringside position (just under the canvas) the war did not present itself in quite the same order as it came in actual fact. For instance, the Battle of Britain did not appear to us to coincide with the worst shock of the invasion threat. By the time the Battle of Britain was in full swing our Scottish soldiers had moved on to the next village, Auburn was defended by its own Home Guard like any other place and was prepared in mind and body for anything. This was an alarming but somehow a cosy time, full of tremendous mental adventure and a thing I can only call a doggy old gallantry, very good in spite of the worry and the not knowing from one minute to the next what was coming down the road or out of the sky. I think everybody privately wished they were a year or two younger (most of our young folks were away by this time), but the general health improved considerably and it was a rejuvenating time.

I had never wished my father alive again before this, since he had a most exasperating life, but at that time if I could have disturbed his eternal meditation and tweaked his sleeve and said, "Come on. England, Scotland and half Ireland are alone in Europe, *Churchill's* in charge and we're just going in. Do you want to miss it?" I think I would have done so.

We had constant daylight air-raid warnings and night bombing began as well for us at that time, which was not the case further inland. The ominous growling of the planes, which is very close and personal when there is no other sound in the world, became fairly constant and for some people nerve-racking. I found out one thing very early, which was that you could never tell how fright was going to take you and that I at any rate was not at all consistent in the matter. I was going to bed one night and listening to a plane overhead rather absently, having heard a great many by that time, and I was thinking idly, "Yes, my girl, one of these days you'll be pottering about like this and you'll hear '*whee-e-e*' and then what?"

At that precise moment I did hear the "*whee-e-e*," an horrific noise, quite different from anything else in the world, and then the curtains billowed in spite of the shutters and the house grunted as if it were alive and had been winded. I heard no crash at all, having been apparently rendered stone deaf by terror. However, I heard the next "*whee-e-e*" all right and it was much closer, and I shot under the four-poster like a rabbit, but there were so many hat-boxes under it as well as a great cedar coffin which I had had made for some furs that I could not get in, and I felt the old ship's timbers of which our floors are made crunch together as I lay on the mat laughing. So I was hysterical, intermittently deaf, and craven on that occasion, and also peculiarly angry. The noise was so spiteful, so viciously against one, that it was infuriating in the way that a bang on the nose is enraging. Yet as soon as it was over I was delirious with pleasure to find I had not been hurt. It was the most purely animal reaction I ever remember having and when I got downstairs, which was almost immediately, I found that everybody else appeared to be in the same mood. No one could have called us expansive people, but had we gone about shouting, "Not dead! Not dead!" we could hardly have expressed our satisfaction more obviously. Thinking it over, most of us behaved like any other country creature startled out of its wits, first rigid and then ecstatic.

It did not last of course and we in the house were lucky because we had something definite to do. As the main body of Wardens came hurrying up, the real problem of very rural A.R.P. presented itself for the first time, and solving that absorbed everybody's attention. As soon as one put one's head outside the door this difficulty loomed up so large and obvious that it seemed incredible that we should not have seen it from the beginning. The Wardens were confronted by a black and silent night, miles and miles and miles of it. There were no searchlights because of the low cloud and at first I thought there was not a sound, not a breath. But soon, as one's ears got used to the quiet, I could hear all the animals and birds kicking and rustling and chirruping, not I think so much in anger as in relief. Now they get angry when they first hear the heavy planes, but at that time I think by the sound of them they were with us, delighted at a danger past. Beau was lumbering about in his box over in the meadow and I heard birds I did not recognise, and cows snorting and stamping a long way off. There was no way of telling where the things had come down. No one had actually seen the flashes and so the craters might be absolutely anywhere; just behind us or half a mile away.

Grog and the others went off to look for them and left me to mind the telephone. Margaret got some hot water ready and cast an eye over the First Aid Point. Gradually it seemed that half the village dropped in, all looking for information and all of us, as far as I could see, grinning with satisfaction at being still alive. There was a lot of talking, for us. Our local accent has a distinct quack in it and there was a deal of Donald Duck noise going on. P.C. Me had been in a ditch full of stinging nettles and was being teased and was laughing at himself, his familiar bellow echoing all over the house.

Finally Ernie Chaplin, Doey's assistant butcher, in Home Guard uniform, turned up with the necessary information and a rabbit. It was the only casualty and was earnestly examined for wounds on the kitchen table by candlelight, the crashing having fused our house current. It had none at all that I could see and must have died of astonishment.

Ernie had brought some bits of the grey-yellow bomb casing we got so used to afterwards and Norry pounced on some of it to take over to the forge and examine on the morrow. It was very good metal, he said the next day. Lovely metal. As good as any in his shop.

Grog kept impressing on him earnestly not to go putting *anything* that came down from the air slap into the forge fire and we thought he was being a bit over-explicit until we found out later what some people will do.

There are few things more irritating to the bombed than tales of other bombs which just missed somebody else, and within the first week of serious raiding the word "bomb-bore" was in constant use. However, vast numbers of various kinds of bombs did fall in and around Auburn all through this period and right up until Christmas, and P.Y.C.'s old bomb map, which had been so innocent-looking for so long, gradually became pitted all over with a plague of black flags. The same thing was true of all the other villages between us and Fishling, and in all that period, in all that area, there were no serious human casualties. It began to look miraculous, and some people think that it was (for, as Granny says so seriously, if not a sparrow falls without *Him* knowing, how much more so a bomb?) but, be that as it may, under Divine protection or not, even so it was not pleasant. The effect was to make one feel like the knife-thrower's assistant with a new, unskilled and insane employer; but some guardian angel did look after Auburn folk.

Johnny's mother and Auntie, who live up by the church-yard, had a stick of bombs fall beside their house on two separate occasions, the actual bomb-path being identical. The first incident occurred at night and that one blew all the windows in and took all the hinges off the doors, a startling experience for all concerned. Then, just when Johnny had finished putting it all straight, another great procession of craters appeared at about half-past ten one morning, with no plane in sight or earshot, the Jerry was flying so high. There were several astounding escapes on that occasion, chief among them Mr. Eve's. He was turning the churchyard corner in his car when a large crater opened just in front of him and another just behind him. They could not have been more than twenty-five yards apart and he was in the middle. His car was smothered with mud and gravel but that was all, although the wall of the moat round his house two hundred and fifty yards away was considerably damaged and we heard pebbles and stuff coming down on us by the square.

Johnny's aunt was in the kitchen on the corner and the

windows blew all over her, but she clapped a washbowl over her face and was not hurt.

Both Norry and Mr. Eaton, who were in the group on the green triangle up there afterwards, were appalled by the nearness of the craters to the churchyard.

"All those little old dears might have been shaken out of their graves," said Mr. Eaton and Norry reeled off a list of his relations who lay there to me and Cooee, who was home on leave from her lorry-driving. "That would not have been at all nice, them to be disturbed," he said.

He was right. It would not and the fact that even worse things were happening, and were about to happen all round us, did not really make it any nicer, I thought. The material damage of this anti-morale air attack on a civil population is appalling but the damage to other less visible but equally vital things is enormous too. Our lives, relations and friends, houses and barns are desperately important to us, but so is light and the sanctuary of our own hedged fields and proper dignity and privacy and the respect of the hearth and our parents' graves. Auburn tends to notice one lot of things quite as much as the other and I am inclined to feel that this is not so visionary even as it sounds when one is looking at material wreckage. It has taken us all a long time to get all these dear possessions, longer than it took this generation to grow, or yet to build the houses.

The first civilian casualties of the war occurred on 1st May 1940 at Clacton-on-Sea. Margery heard the explosion.

Above: Victoria Road, Clacton.
(ww2today.com)

Right: The remains of the Heinkel.
(www.historyofwar.org)

23

AUBURN's amazing luck, or Divine protection, went on holding throughout the Autumn. Mr. Withers and his neighbours, just outside the parish, had an extraordinary experience. His is one of two or three bungalows set side by side, with about a house space between them. Their stick of bombs fell neatly between the bungalows, one bungalow one crater and so on. They were big bombs too. The lips of the craters touched the roofs on both sides.

In the actual spot where Mr. Withers's own bomb fell he had a shed containing a pony and trap, a cat, some budgerigars, a jackdaw and a ton of coal. They got the pony out from under the trap in the crater and held it up for a minute or two until, to everyone's amazement, it wandered off and began to eat. The cat ran away for nearly a fortnight. The budgerigars were none the worse. Most of the coal was retrieved, and the jackdaw died three days later more from rage than anything else, Mr. Withers said. No one in the houses was hurt, but it shocked them considerably and made a dreadful mess of their homes. Mr. Withers came down one morning soon after and, finding us all in the kitchen, where we have come to hold a general council about eleven o'clock, he had a cup of tea with us. He had got over his initial rage and was grimly cheerful.

"Three cups, one saucer and two plates left between the three of us, God save the King," he said.

The "God save the King," by the way, in that sense is not lese-majesty nor yet *Heil Führer*, but a sort of "God bless my soul, what a set-out! What a life! What a picnic! That's what being an Englishman does for you, and why the hell not? Why shouldn't it? I like it" remark, very difficult to justify or make logical, but which is very common.

"That's finished my gardening," he said, but he underestimated himself, for the crater is now in full cultivation.

Meanwhile, interlarded with these night excitements there

227

were continuous battles and patrols going on overhead in
the day. The wireless gave up being dull or even sober and
became a blessed tale of triumph for a change. Twenty,
thirty, forty German planes down by six o'clock. Fifty, sixty,
eighty by nine, and the century up by midnight. The little
old boys were getting them. But even then most of us did
not quite realise how very small our Air Force was. That
was made plain later and the blazing heroism of those few
was fully understood.

At that time the news was so good that at first some
people doubted the wireless for the first time, but not for
long. German planes began to strew the countryside. Lorry-
loads of bits of them appeared on the roads and nearly
everyone had seen someone baling out.

A rather silly little tale went round our district at this
time about a startled elderly gentleman nearby who sat
spellbound in his car watching a pilot descend by parachute.
He did nothing whatever but sat looking at the boy, who
came down on the verge within a few feet of him. The boy
said nothing either but recovered himself very slowly, un-
harnessed, and stood up, pulling in his parachute. When
he had got it in a bundle he looked full at the old man,
who felt that he ought, he *must*, at all costs, say something,
so he said explosively and in a great bellow, as one's voice
does come sometimes in moments of stress:

"How far have you come down?"

The young man shook a sad head at him and said earnestly:
"A hell of a way."

The whole war at that time was a bit like that. From the
ground you could only see the planes with great difficulty,
for they flew very high. It was golden, glorious weather and
the world hummed with planes all day like bees in a lime
tree. The only way to see them was to do the thing you were
warned not to and lie on your back in the grass and look
up. Christine said they looked like little white lice, which
was unpoetic but unpleasantly true. They had an impersonal,
transparent appearance at that distance. To see a Spitfire
attack a formation at that height was like watching tiny

creatures in a pond, and it was only when suddenly a plane would come hurtling through the eddying blue, growing larger and larger and disappearing over one's immediate horizon that it came home to one with unbearable vividness that they were real machines with real men in them.

Auburn again was very lucky here. Very few bits came down over it, although there were times when Sam preferred to go out and collect his vegetables in a tin hat.

Goldenhind next door, on the other hand, was a place for planes. A burnt-out aeroplane on the ground has a very corpselike look. It is very much a dead big creature just as the men by it are dead little creatures, and there is something pathetic in the wrecked machine.

German planes, we discovered, had a curious and distinctive smell. It is very pungent and very clinging. One of the police sergeants dropped in to see Grog one evening fresh from an investigation of a crash down the road, and P.Y.C., who had seen several and who was home on leave and with me in another room, suddenly sat up, sniffing in incredulous astonishment.

"Jerry plane in the house," he said, his eyes popping.

On investigation it proved to be the sergeant's boots. It was a peculiar smell, rather like very rank white vinegar.

The most impressive war sight I have yet seen in the sky in daylight was just before the beginning of the big London blitz in September. It was about five in the evening, I think, and I was ironing on a big table out in the yard. The hum of planes, which by this time had become a commonplace, was in the air but I was not taking much notice of it until it grew and grew until I felt it rather than heard it beating on my eardrums. Then I looked up and saw in the mid-sky over the apple-store seventy-five Junkers bombers in formation. They came sailing along, low enough to see and apparently very slowly. It was an incredibly menacing sight. Christine came running out and Margaret, and I could hear Grog shouting from the lawn. There were a few high clouds in the sky and against their goose-breasts the planes looked black and enormous. I shouted to Cliff, who had paused by the gate on one of his trips up the village, and he said, "No, no, they're ours. Must be." I said, "I don't think we've got that many, have we?" for I had not done counting and was frightened and therefore irritated with him.

I saw two little planes darting in and out amongst them, moving up and down like a woman sewing, for quite a while, or it seemed a while, until they began to break formation, and then I realised who and what the little ones were. It did not look real, any of it. And then, over the house (everything in the sky seems either over the house or over the elms or over the church) the whole armada of them slowly swung round and sailed out to sea again. Grog said they'd seen the barrage, which was more than I had.

When it was all over and the last drone of the engines had died, Christine brought me a tin hat and made me wear it while I finished the ironing. It was very heavy and made me feel silly.

I am very much aware that I am not describing the emotional aspect of all this but it is not easy. Fear is a funny thing. Once you have got it into your head that you or anybody else may die to-morrow, or in half an hour (which is after all true in the best of times), fear of death and physical injury seems to become largely subject to health or what you happen to have been thinking of last when the thing that frightened you happened or so it seems to me.

I was wakened by the first of a near stick one night when I had been sleeping very heavily. I lay cowering in my bed until they had all come down and then decided in an owlish fashion that they were miles away. I turned over and began to be aware of acute and frightful discomfort. It got worse and worse and I suddenly thought "My God, I'm gassed," and I shot out of bed and took a deep and gasping breath, suicidal had I been right. This woke me completely and I found I was better and that I must have caught my breath on the first crash, which half woke me, and not had the sense to go on breathing again.

Other people say they noticed the same sort of phenomena,

and the main thing we are all agreed on is that you can never be sure how it is going to take you.

Some people just go on sleeping upstairs, whatever happens. Some bring their mattresses under the stairs, some have a chair in a certain spot in which they feel safe, and many like to be together. The one dangerous state is when you begin to fidget and need to hustle round the house without settling. But I think most people have a deep self-preservative instinct that that is unwise.

The animals vary too. Sometimes they get angry and sometimes they sleep through far worse noises. Theobald, who is an old dog and very humanised through long association with us, behaves like a completely unselfconscious human. The first bomb of the night infuriates him and makes him bark, but a bad night of them merely makes him sulk and gives him a nervous hangover next day. Out of doors he takes cover like anyone else. Sam threw himself in a ditch one night when a scrap developed overhead while he was cycling round blowing the whistle, and he was almost winded by Theobald charging in on top of him to lie flat as well.

The fighting and stray countryside bombing went on so long without us having any local casualties that at one time there was almost a danger that we would get too used to it, but then one morning Mr. Eaton came in with the milk and the news that the crump we had heard on the night before (apart from that one the evening had been quiet) had been a bomb falling on the house of the Mayor of the county town, which had killed him and all the family. Everybody knew the Mayor and his wife and they were both liked and deeply respected. The aim could not have been deliberate as the house was one of many in a big residential district.

The complete finality and ruthless completeness of the tragedy brought most people to an abrupt halt. Life, wife, son, grandchildren, house, possessions, all gone as savagely as if a giant had trodden on them.

Mr. Eaton had had his own farm straddled twice and had

been abed each time and had heard the crashes coming
nearer and nearer and then mercifully go on the other side
of him, so he could sympathise very vividly with the news
he brought of an old friend.

Above: J. O. Thompson, Mayor of Chelmsford and Editor of the
Essex Chronicle seated centre. *(The Essex Chronicle)*

Below: Mr & Mrs Thompson, their son, his two children and
Alice Emery, domestic servant, died when their house, Brierly
Place, was bombed on 13th October 1940. *(The Essex Chronicle)*

24

SAM and Ralph and Mr. Jack Saye went to London after the first big night raid on the city without realising what had happened up there. They went on my behalf very early in the morning before the first news. With a characteristic gift for the inapt I had chosen that precise date to deposit a small lorryload of furniture in a top-floor flat that we have next to the British Museum. P.Y.C. had been moved up north and we were hoping to have seven days in London on his next leave. We had heard and seen a great deal of activity during the night, but when one's horizon is as confined as Auburn's it is very difficult to guess at night where exactly in the misty world outside an attack is taking place. The difference, for instance, between the glare of a basketful of incendiaries two miles away and a thundering great fire forty miles away is very difficult to be sure about until you are experienced, especially when there is a good deal of banging and flashing going on locally. There is also, of course, an idiotic tendency to assume that any stream of planes going over your own head is the only one coming in over the island, which is ridiculous. At that time, too, there had not been any concentrated attack on any one target in our area.

The three from Auburn went to London by the best early morning route, which is straight through the East End. They were back by lunch time, having delivered their load and fled, as far as I could gather from Sam, whose powers of description had temporarily deserted him. Their horror was far more impressive to us at home than any mere recital on the wireless, or even the photographs in the newspapers. The unfortunate Ralph, who had never seen London at all before, went about looking petrified for days.

For some little time Auburn was rather like the child left outside the pub while the fight takes place inside. Occasionally the swing-doors burst open and missiles and casualties shot out, but for the most part there was just

233

ominous sound, ominous sights, mystery, and no way of knowing how the rest of the family was faring.

At the same time there was plenty to occupy one's mind on one's own account. This was the first period of the heavy bombs, the oil bombs, the time bombs and all the other odd things that were coming down all round the coast.

Our own personal preoccupation, apart from the many gatherings and conferences on the mornings after local "incidents," was the arrival of Granny, who had been persuaded at last to leave her home on a mud island in the Thames Estuary and come and stay with us. She is eighty-eight and fortunately extremely active, and her reactions to the upheaval are still Victorian, as are also, as far as I can see, those of the vast bulk of the older generation. Her refuge is in manners and in God. Whatever else the Victorian conventions were, they did impose an iron personal discipline, and a long history of iron personal discipline seems to be just about what one needs most to weather a storm like this. Some of her actual concrete and visible defences are exasperating because of the obviousness of the outmoded social machinery producing them, but even so they keep out the draught of fear and that is something. Better a shield covered with an antimacassar than no shield at all.

An example of this is her insistence that one should count one's blessings at all costs and in any circumstances. Two or three days after her arrival the now familiar evening raid seemed more localised even than usual. She had had considerable experience of bombing on her island and after every particularly loud crump, which had rocked her chair and drained the colour out of her face, she would say firmly: "Quite quarter of a mile away."

This had gone on intermittently for several hours and it was getting on my nerves (I found I had become twice as frightened since her arrival), when she smiled at the fire in the bright room with palpably false complacence and said quite seriously: "But for the *noise* you wouldn't know there was a war on, would you?"

Later on that night I could stand the stoic let's-pretend-it's-not-happening no longer. One cannot spend a lifetime, I found, in getting out of that way of mind and then suddenly be able to pop back into it as soon as one needs its protection. I put a mattress on the flat platform under our stairs and persuaded poor Granny to get into the cavity. Margaret had left us by this time to be night operator at the Post Office exchange, but Christine was about and I got her to join Granny. With them if not perfectly safe at least as safe as maybe, I felt almost lighthearted with relief and went out to join the others in the road outside. There is a great comfort to a person of my temperament in being able to see what is going on. I found the crashes were not so violent if you could see the flashes and count, and I decided the worst of the noise was made by our old house grunting and protesting and shivering in its shoes. Half an hour later, feeling very guilty, I went back and Granny scrambled out to meet me.

"If you're not so frightened now I'll go back upstairs to bed," she said.

"I'm not frightened," I protested indignantly.

She said, "Well! You didn't think *I* was, did you? I only came down to be with you and the girl if you were nervous."

After that she kept to her bed at night whatever happened and only protested once when I for one imagined the end really had come at last. Even then, still sticking to the convention that the complaint must never be personal, she simply said: "This is very bad for the foundations."

I discovered her main secret later and I was glad to know it because I could not believe that mere convention could produce such an extraordinary evenness of control.

About this time we began to get lingering planes. A wave of bombers would go over on its way to London, entailing at least an hour of steady roaring overhead, and when it had passed we would discover that one or two planes had been left behind. These would hang about, altering height, circling and coming back over the house again and again.

Sometimes they seemed almost on top of one in the blackness (as the winter went on the raiders seemed to prefer
thick nights) and the effect was very nerve-racking because
almost invariably, after ten to twenty minutes, these strays
would drop something and bolt away as if a pack of fighters
were after them. Auburn had all sorts of theories about this.
One of the most popular was that they were the frightened
pilots who "had to make their *pedometers* tally with the rest."
Another school thought they were Italians who wanted to
go home and say they had been over London, and others
thought that they were "young'uns practising." However,
whoever they were, they got on people's nerves at first,
although they worried the folk indoors far more than those
outside. I hated them myself and, since Granny would not
come downstairs, I said: "Look, if you really do feel like
this about it, wouldn't you like to bung your ears up with
cotton-wool and then you could go to sleep?" But she said
no, she liked to hear them because when she judged that
the plane was directly overhead she could put up a brief
prayer to Almighty God to call His attention to the fact. "If
He *means* me to go I shall go, of course," she said, and in
that much she was fatalistic. However, being human, she
was evidently prepared to take certain precautions against
Divine Inadvertence.

I think far more people in Britain than one is normally
aware must share her particular kind of faith which is, as
I have seen with my own eyes, the perfect answer to anti-
morale measures directed against a civil population. Simply
speaking, the idea of any kind of purely anti-morale measure
against a defenceless people is a spiritually destructive idea,
so that it would seem obvious that the real protection from
it should be a spiritually constructive one. They are neither
of them intellectual affairs, but I can never see that the
intellect is any more important than any other part of one's
make-up. The myth about it being so is one of the more
untrue theories upon which I was fed when I was young
and it has taken me thirty years of noticing things to find
it out a lie. The intellect is a vital thing, but it is not the

only vital thing. Indeed, alone it is one of the most hopeless crutches on which to try to get through a three-dimensional world. Still, maybe it is just another of the half-gods who, as gods, are scuttling away so fast.

One or two people from London came down to Auburn for a rest but they did not stay. They hated the lingering planes even worse than we did, which was natural because they had seen worse damage. They did not like our absence of visible shelter, either. Auburn's shelter, which lies in its space, in the enormous chances against anything hitting the one minute spot on which we are standing, in our absence of anti-aircraft guns to drop shrapnel on us, in the fact that we are no sort of target and are not being directly attacked, is a different sort of shelter to their cellars. Ours is immeasurably safer, but you must either have all your wits about you to realise it or else have the country animal instinct which says, "Get down in the grass and the chances are you'll get by." Some folk came to stay with Sam and, after a night of comparative quiet on which they had been making the country cousins' hair stand on end with tales of the city, there was a very bad night in Auburn.

" 'Where do we git?' says he," said Sam, describing the conversation with his guest. " 'Har, we don't git,' says I. 'There's no place to git to. That's the difference.' "

There is a great deal more to it than that, though, as the tales of the casualties tell. Auburn has better chances than most.

With everybody else Auburn had its share of time-bombs. When you come to think of it the time-bomb is a refinement. It is in the second degree and it is important because it supplies the evidence that the mind behind it is working for the down-pull—which is only to say that it is just out of the normal "true" with decent human anger. There is nothing new in this, of course, but I venture to mention it because its modern clothes are very concealing. From an Auburn point of view the time-bomb is one of the many modern expressions of that ancient evil which, stirring in weary agony, says heavily, "Ah, but I cannot bear that you should *only* die. I *hate* you. Oh, oh, my hungry vitals! There is not enough to fill me in your simple dying."

Modern talking can clean this up and re-dress it until it appears reasonable and even wise. "Destruction of civilian morale." "Nuisance value." "Disorganisation of supply." All these sound reasonable adjuncts of war, but nevertheless, beneath this civilised trousering the shiny boot has a funny and an ancient shape, and Auburn who, bless your heart, has seen that shape since the beginning of history, cannot be deceived.

"Har, they're wonderful dirty," says Auburn.

However, in this remarkable equilibrium of a world the down-pull sets up its own antidote, and behind Officialdom's exquisitely simple announcement, "Time-bombs may be removed," there is something fundamental and constructive belonging to the up-pull. That any man alive should walk up to a time-bomb and "remove it" voluntarily is another piece of evidence and *for the other case.*

Since the mind (or just my Auburn mind perhaps) is always suspicious, there is a temptation to wonder if lack of imagination, stupidity or even bravado might not explain or counteract this evidence in some cases, but every now and again something happens to correct that sort of thinking.

One day I had an occasion to direct a man who was going to remove a time-bomb. He was the sort of good-looking, lazy-eyed lad one would normally expect to find lying on his back under an old sports car. I told him where the thing was and that it was thought to be of considerable size. He thanked me kindly and I offered him a drink. He said he did not think he would at the moment, if I didn't mind, because he'd like to be absolutely clearheaded for a bit. At that moment I suddenly realised quite clearly and in precise terms what he must have known all along and it was a vivid and awe-inspiring knowledge. I said involuntarily and idiotically, "Oh, be careful." He laughed like a child at me and went off chuckling.

This Courage, which my generation is discovering in the

world so late and which our elders threw away in disgust
with the bath-water of Sir Bernard Partridge's fine decora-
tive but fundamentally unreal cartoon of Albert and William
and the lie of the recruiting sergeant's ribbons, is emerging
naked and adult and shocking and very beautiful indeed.
Also she is most gloriously alive. It is this last quality about
her which is so comforting, for it proves that she really is
immortal in a race. Twenty years underground has not
weakened her, much less killed her. It has only taken away
her clothes. Please God we shall not dress her up in fustian
again, nor yet put her on such a false eminence that our
children find her either untrue or inadequate and throw
her away again. That is obviously what must have happened last time. If we can keep Courage as it were a wife,
an ordinary well-appreciated darling helpmeet, as she is
to-day, we shall at least have got one great sound thing,
but if we make either a remote all-powerful goddess of her
or a false little strumpet of her to parade and grow sick
of, we shall forsake her again. The lesson of the last war
seems to have been the same as that of this war in that one
respect.   Against this enemy of ours, this short-sighted,
thick-headed force for chaos, armed with all the heritage
of mankind's inventions and all the vices (and all the virtues
too save the one vital sense of direction, the one essential
sense for construction, for going on and not under, up and
not down, towards growth and not death), against him
Courage, as the Greeks have shown us, is not by herself
enough. She cannot stand alone. She is a part, not a whole,
a wife, not a man and wife. Somehow or other we must
make a full man of ourselves and get hold of the rest to
support her and let her triumph. Our enemy has Courage,
even if he makes a harridan and a slut of her.

Of course there were people who approached time-bombs
in other ways than did my visitor, whose attitude towards
them was so unassumingly and intelligently brave. There
was the old man in the orchard at Goldenhind who went
on picking his apples while one of the wickedest-looking
holes in creation lay at his feet, for, as he said, he wanted

the apples, and if death came he didn't know but that he
hadn't been knocking around long enough.

And there were other people too, but their adventures
and what they did or did not do in the leafy secrecy of
Auburn is for telling after the war, when there should be
a great deal of talk on the benches outside the pubs or on
the sea-wall when the skies are clear again.

Left: Margery,
Maud Hughes
and Granny.

Right: Christina Carter.

25

THE countryman's tendency to wander around at night and see what is going on became very noticeable in Auburn during the early winter. There was always a dark figure or two in the club-room dug-out by the maypole and many fathers of families formed the habit of standing outside their homes, like bears before their caves, watching the sky and the blazing barrage over London. At any nearish flash they would shout reassurance or warning to the family within, their voices sounding a second or so before the crump. Sometimes, of course, they dived inside with an admonitory "Git down!"

The London barrage was a sight to see. P.Y.C. predicted that it would be the "end of fireworks in our time," and I think he may be right. In Auburn we have seen fireworks now.

London took our imagination. These were the villages who could take it all right. The old villages in the East End took it first, but the central ones had it too, and the tale of the great buildings going in two's and three's continued week by week. We in Auburn could tell the size of the raid, or thought we could, by the degree of lateness of the letters and the papers, but they always came along during the day and our link with the main world was never broken even for twenty-four hours.

The spirit of the London villagers was epitomised for us at home by the family of the Corporal. The Corporal was frequently on duty at the telephone at the local searchlight post and, as his headquarters was as importunate as Grog's at Fishling for the exact location of each crater in the twenty-five square miles of open country near us the moment the noise of the explosion had died away, we got in the habit of pooling our information whenever possible. He told us one night that he had never considered himself a disgraceful funk, but that one week's leave at home in London had

put the "wind-up him good and proper." He said his mother
had got really wild with him for falling on his face about
the place whenever the furniture slid from the walls at one
moment and back the next, and had finally told him that
he'd better get back to the army in the country if he couldn't
behave himself.

"Come out from under the table, do," she would say,
he said. "A great boy like you in khaki."

In fact his picture (which he fully appreciated, being a
natural comedian) of the gallant young soldier son returning
to the old home to find it suddenly inhabited by all the
familiar characters startlingly transformed into iron front-
line troops was one of the most remarkable, tragic and
absurd aspects of a frightful yet magnificent situation.

His father, said the Corporal, gave him the creeps. The
old man used to stand on the doorstep, Auburn fashion, his
pipe going and his cap very flat on his head, and watch
the raid. One night he called his son persistently and the
youngster ventured out without great enthusiasm. "Searchlights, tracers, star-shells, lumme it was a how-d'ye-do!"
he said. "It made me feel sick."

The old man nodded to a flare slowly descending from
the enemy circling above.

"*Now* you're going to see something," he said with satisfaction. "That's the powder mill just over there."

The corporal said Jerry missed it but that he was glad
to get back to his field, which only had three craters in it
so far. He also said that he was certain that at the end of
the war it would take everybody a week, if not a month,
to locate their relations.

"I went to see my auntie," he said, "and I couldn't find
her bloody street."

By the side of this sort of thing Auburn's rural alarums
seemed rather small beer. We had this brought home to
us very forcibly one night when we called out the Flinthammock Fire Brigade—the funeral parlour one—to attend
to a shower of incendiaries which spread out over our fields
to the astonishing length of two miles. It was the first time

we had heard them coming down and the noise on a still dark night is awe-inspiring. "Like a great flight of tin widgeon," said Mr. Read and there is something in that but not enough. I know the entire village on this occasion appears to have crouched for a moment waiting for the greatest explosion of all time to follow, and then cautiously put its head out only to find, as someone put it so sweetly, "we was in fairyland."

The whole countryside was lit up with a thousand thermite flares and a stack of baled straw (so much for Sam's other theory about baled straw) was making a fountain of glory in the night. It was the fact of this stack-fire which called out the Fire Brigade: the fairy lamps are theoretically a job for ourselves.

The Fire Brigade was polite but unimpressed. It was fresh from a fulldress fight and this, as it said nicely but firmly, was scarcely worth worrying about.

The Fire Brigade became our knights errant. It was they who paused in a Sunday morning practice run and put Mr. Dice's bungalow roof on for him (as from one old friend to another), and before the proper authority could arrive with the official tarpaulins. This was when a continuation of the unexplained blitz on that remote corner of windswept heath and plough had blown most of it off.

No one quite understood that brutal attack on nothing, except Mr. Dice. There is a big empty field up there next to his lonely bungalow, called, for some equally strange reason, "Mexico." Mexico was always in trouble. The famous H.E.s fell up there too and so did one of the messy and destructive oil bombs.

Mr. Read had one of the most unpleasant experiences of all with an oil bomb. He was riding on a truck on the other side of Fishling when one oil bomb and one high-explosive fell together just beside it. The truck was blown in half and Mr. Read happened to be in the half which stayed on the road. His mate was not so lucky. He dislocated his neck. However, he was saved. A walk of three-quarters of a mile to the nearest house. which should have killed him. did

much to ensure his cure (so Mr. Read says), and at any rate
by all reports he is back at work again now. The experience
was a harrowing one for Mr. Read, for he had to put out
the fire bomb, which he did with the equipment they happened to be carrying in the back of the truck, and after
that to persuade the folk barricaded in their lonely cottage
nearly a mile down the road that he and his mate were
locals and not parachute troops. Once they were sure of
that, as he says, "*of course* they could not do too much."

Mr. Read did not volunteer this story. I heard of it first
from young red-headed Basil, Bill's son, who remarked one
night when we were all out watching the barrage that Mr.
Read was "setting wonderfully quiet" since he had been
bombed the day before.

Setting out to visit London at this period was an adventure comparable with the same journey when I was a child.
The early morning bus, lit with ghostly blue because it was
still dark, was full the first time I went up after the opening
of the blitz. There were soldiers and sailors going back from
leave, the regulars, strays like me, children, factory folk,
a sack of shrimps and parcels of all descriptions for any
destination along the road. Ken was driving, conducting,
and leading the conversation with an efficiency and a professional charm and ease of manner which would have made
a fortune for him in peace time on a liner, had he preferred
the life.

There is something very shiplike about all that family's
buses. They are waterside folk and all the large family has
the aristocratic independence allied to charm which salt
water seems to breed so often.

Half-way there Ken said something which made me sit
up. (He talks over his shoulder from the wheel, sounds his
horn in greeting to every friend on the road, and remembers
everybody's destination, family history, luggage and exact
fare.) He was talking about the air-raid tragedies in the
county town and about a friend of his who had been engaged
on rescue work there. What had particularly impressed his
pal, he said, was a child of about six who, on being dragged

out of the wreckage of her home, had insisted that she was perfectly all right and would they please go and get Mummy out. When the mother had been released it was discovered that the child had a broken shoulder and was in agony.

"She was so young, you see," said Ken, "*so they knew it could not be bravado.*"

Bravado. Ye gods! thought I; this is a Sparta we're coming into.

I had chosen a day on which there was one of the comparatively few daylight attacks on the city and there were aerial battles going on over the line as we travelled up. These dogfights high up in a blue sky are very beautiful; there is no other word for it; for the white trails which the aeroplanes leave behind them hang about like bridal veils in long graceful festoons. We had seen a great many on the coast and I did not join the excited gang in the corridor because I had so many odds and ends to carry that once I got settled I thought I would stay where I was.

When we steamed away from the fight the other occupants of the carriage came back and I recognised them at once. They were some of the business executives who live out some way since they need not get to their offices before ten-thirty or so in the morning. They are grey, middle-aged men most of them, well-to-do, fathers of families and owners of businesses in the city. I had not seen any of them for about a year, perhaps, and they did not recognise me, naturally, for I have never spoken to them, and whereas I travel to Town perhaps six times a year in peace time they go every day. However, I have seen most of them on this same train and nowhere else on and off for ten years or so. They had not changed much, I noticed, except that they all looked a trifle older. They were apparently delighted at the fight and came in grinning and a trifle flushed.

They agreed among themselves that it was one of the best and I began to wish I had seen it, for it sounded as though they too had had experience. They took no notice of me, of course (a fact that always astonishes me for the

first two or three hours I spend in urban life again after
the family atmosphere of Auburn), but went on talking as
freely and formally amongst themselves as train acquaintances of perhaps twenty years' standing do talk.

They still chatted in exactly the same peculiar train-
journey way but about new things. In peace time they used
to discuss cricket, mainly. A man in the corner would throw
out an opinion on a score or an average coming through
from Australia. One of the others would remark on it and
then they would relapse into easy silence for a while until
someone added a third comment. And so it would go on
for an hour and a half. No one said anything much of value
and the subjects were all completely public and impersonal,
but there was great familiarity and understanding among
the speakers, so that unless you knew a little about the
subjects too it might easily have been one of those incomprehensible family conversations, all obscure words and
cross-references.

Now they were talking about bombs and bombing and
the black-out, but in exactly the same way.

"What time was the warning last night? Exactly seven
o'clock, wasn't it? I thought I heard the sirens just as I
got in my car."

"Was it? I didn't hear a thing last night. Too tired."

"Do you *want* to know the time of the warning?" This
was a third man, putting down his paper. "I think I can
tell you exactly. I've got it in my little book here somewhere." He took out a neat pocket-book, turned over the
pages and nodded contentedly. "Yes, here you are. Nineteen-
oh-seven hours. That's seven minutes past seven, isn't it?
You must have been late getting in. Stopped to have one,
I suppose."

"Nineteen-oh-what-oh? You a Warden?"

"Part-time only. Very part-time, I'm afraid. There's a
lot to do one way and another. We have to duplicate everything now, you know."

And so on and so on. They discussed the night's noises,
as we had done on the bus, but more impersonally. We had

been interested in so-and-so's daughter's father-in-law's house, and so-and-so's field, but they were talking about "Wychwood way" or "over by Green's Heath." They did not talk about the London damage at all, but as they got in closer they looked out of the window and commented, still impersonally but very grimly, on anything they thought might be new.

London has always shown the most draggled hem of her underskirts to us as we come upon her up the line and I was prepared for horrors, but at that period the view from the train at that distance, and at the pace we were travelling, was very like itself only much worse. The slums had never seemed more immense or more grimly indestructible. There was still washing on the lines, still flapping curtains and ragged wireless aerials, still a few children screaming and laughing and waving at the train, but every now and again there were whole areas where the ancient blackened pantiles on the shark's-mouth roofs had every one of them slipped, so that brick-red ribbons had appeared in the soot like awful red gums showing above blackened teeth.

The station was as I remembered it in childhood in the last war, dark and cold and blacked-out overhead My first port of call was on the top floor of a big block of offices not far from St. Paul's, and I arrived with the sirens. Gillie and Mashie began to grumble and collect their work.

"If the roof-spotters whistle we have to go down," they said, and indicated a couple of tin-hatted men on the fire-escape. They whistled as I watched and Gillie began to curse mildly as she collected her bag, the proofs she was correcting, some lay-out sheets and a bundle of "stills." Then we clattered away on high heels to the marble stairs.

"Bad enough going down," they said. "Wait till we start trotting up."

I completed my business with their chief, who came and joined us almost at once in the neat air-raid shelter under the building. The firm is an old one which publishes many magazines. My entire family has done work for it over a period of forty years and I have known it since babyhood.

It seemed absurd to nod to all the well-known editors and their staffs as they sat grouped round different tables set out in the low-roofed concrete catacomb. The period of self-consciousness, for I suppose there must have been such a period, had evidently passed. Now everybody was extra-ordinarily normal and affable but a little bit irritable under the surface. The atmosphere reminded me very much of something I had been in before and it worried me all day until I remembered that it was a rainstorm at a big garden party, when everybody had been annoyed but of course not with anybody in particular.

As I left the All-clear sounded and to my surprise I found a cab outside without any difficulty. London taxicab drivers are natural villagers and will talk like any other small-place men. The cabdriver told me he hadn't had any glass in his house, or a roof over his bedroom, since the first night of the blitz. It was going to be "a bit parky" in the real winter, he remarked, and advised me to stay in the country and wrap myself up.

"There's a bomb or two fell this morning somewhere about," he said. "I don't know what they think they're up to, coming over here in the daylight."

I was going to drop in at Madame Caporelli's, who had a little shop opposite the flat where we all lived on the actual city borders when we were students. She used to specialise in a certain sort of Dutch toffee and I had promised to bring some back if I could, but I did not have time just then for I wanted to catch Nerney before lunch.

Once again I arrived with the sirens and I began to find this stormy-petrel role embarrassing. Nerney, ever hospitable —bless her—asked me if I'd like to see the cellar, but I was not anxious and we stayed up talking for a bit until the local guns began to bark. It was different from a day-light raid in Auburn. Down on the coast we have the wide sky to watch, the enemy fairly visible, and far fewer bricks to fall on our heads when a bomb does come down. On the other hand, of course, we have less between us and trouble.

The cellar, however, did frighten me. It was leased by

a very good old firm of surgical boot and artificial limb manufacturers, and the walls were completely lined from floor to ceiling with such a scarifying collection of lasts that I dreamed about them for nights afterwards. I was afraid I was going to become utterly demoralised by them at the time, for a leather bunion nailed to a grotesque wooden foot with no heel has a visual horror which has to be seen to be appreciated, and I begged Nerney and Vi to come out and lunch with me without any further ado.

They came meekly, but the first place I suggested just down the road was no more, they said, and we walked on to the next possible restaurant. I had not seen much damage from my taxicab and was unprepared for the scene when we turned the corner out of Nerney's street into the main thoroughfare.

Do you remember those old German films of the *Nibelungen* and *The Golem* and *Faust* which we used to admire long ago? There was a trick they had in those to denote the passage of a year, which was very Teutonic, and, now I have seen what I have seen, no longer very pretty as an idea. They would present a little apple-tree covered with blossom and leaves, with flowers at its foot, and then show it blown by a great wind which swept away the blossom, withered and destroyed the leaves, scoured the twigs and made barren the earth around it. That is exactly what had happened to the corner I knew so well. I could see the very old church I was married at down the road much more plainly than I ever remembered seeing it before, and was trying to decide which little pub or shoeshop had gone when Nerney pulled me on out of the traffic among which I had paused to stare.

The restaurant we were making for was still, I was glad to see, exactly where it had been when the head waiter of the period lifted me into a specially high chair a very long time before, but it was peculiarly deserted. The dance floor, which is an innovation anyway and not usually uncovered at lunch time, was bare in the centre of the room. I found the table I have always eaten at on a visit to London (it

is the same one at which I heard my uncle describing my
grandfather's funeral to my mother, at which we once had
a falsely gay Christmas dinner in the last war, at which
my father bought me an ice to celebrate my first printed
work, at which P.Y.C. and Grog and I ate on our decision
to return to the country to live; at which so many family
things had been discussed and celebrated, in fact, that it
might be in our own house). It was almost on the edge of
the dance floor and I noticed the others were not drawn
to it. However, I sat down and when we had settled ourselves the All-clear sounded and everyone brightened up
and the orchestra climbed up into its box.

"Isn't that nice?" said Vi, referring to the siren and
looking up with unconscious relief.

I followed her glance and saw for the first time that we
were sitting under one of the few very large ornamental
glass domes in all London. Considering so few places in the
entire world can be called safe in these days, it seems foolish
that the discovery that that one might be very dangerous
should have shaken me so. No one talked about it, though,
and we chatted on about other things.

On my way back to the station late in the afternoon I
remembered Madame Caporelli again and decided I had
time to walk down the street to her.

I had been prepared for damage along the way but I had
not envisaged anything so local or so complete. Here was
no winter apple-tree. The whole plant had been tugged
up by the roots and cut into firewood. Whole sections of
the not very beautiful but very familiar façade were exactly
as usual, and then, where there should have been a restaurant
or a bookshop or a tailor's or a sports outfitters, there
was suddenly just a great clean-sided hole with chaos
in its mouth. The inside walls of these cavities were like
those adjoining buildings demolished in any other way.
There were few untidinesses, little of the jagged look I had imagined. Rather, complete smooth annihilation. The only
oddities were ornaments left on mantel shelves, a towel
rail still on the wall, pictures, and sometimes even a rag

on a hook, but few wrenched-out beams, few holes and rents.

The craters themselves were another matter but here again there was not the sort of wreckage I had imagined, all scraps and pieces of familiar things, but rather a dreadful grey uniformity as the dust and fine-powdered plaster had made a decent pall over all.

I went on towards the shop and stopped on the pavement. Madame's business had gone and with it the tobacconist's beside it, and the chemist's with the weighing machine outside. There was still a certain amount of activity about the wreckage and I gathered it was one of the morning's incidents, the work of one of the two or three bombs which my taximan had said were somewhere about.

A policeman told me that and had no other information for me, so I never knew what had happened to Madame. Further on down the street London was miraculously as usual, just as dirty and just as busy.

"Cheer up. It'll take 'em a 'ell of a time to knock it all down, dear," said the old lady from whom I bought a paper, and she had been standing on her corner all day.

The train was on time and the bus waiting when I got off it, but someone in front of me was telling a friend how London was in utter ruins nearly all the way back to Auburn, which itself was still happy and intact.

Right: St. Paul's Cathedral
surrounded by smoke.
(U.S. National Archive)

26

ONE cold wet morning the King came to Auburn. To be exact he came through Auburn on his way to Flinthammock, but he did look in at the Auburn Observer Corps post (thereby terrifying the Corporal in the next field who was in the dirtiest of undress and thought he had developed hallucinations out there in the wilds), and he did look out at Auburn through the windows of his car. The arrival of two or three military policemen in the square half an hour earlier gave the village the first intimation that something highly unusual was afoot and then the rumour sped through the place like a bird. What happened in our house was probably fairly typical. Grog put his head in the room where I was working and said, "Oh, the King's coming." I said "What king?" and he said, "*The* King. The real King. Buck up and look out of the window if you want to see him."

I bustled out to tell Christine and then up to Granny and everybody looked out of the window at once except young Ralph, who ran out in the road and was caught and made to stand to attention by Mr. Eaton, who was outside the back gate beside his milk-float, waiting to uncover in the rain. There was not much cheering, only expansive smiles, not because the King was any less the King than the day on which he was crowned and the staidest old maiden lady I ever knew climbed up a lamp-post to wave her hat at him, but because there was a vague feeling that he might be going along in a semi-private capacity and would prefer not to be shouted at. Auburn has much natural grace in such matters and so for the most part it stood in the wet and beamed from ear to ear.

Charlie and Mr. Moore, who were on duty at the Observer Corps post, were spoken to by the King and they spoke back to him successfully, and there was a photograph of them in the evening paper some days later with the King between them which was such a satisfactory but unexpected

thing to happen that hardly anybody in Auburn recognised
them, although they were clear enough, until it was pointed
out.

There was not as much talk about the King's visit as one
might have supposed. Auburn was just pleased and I wondered if I could set down what it is that impresses me so
strongly about the Auburn attitude towards the Crown, so
oddly aristocratic and ancient and possessive and which
goes so deep. The same thing is apparent in the London
city-villages too and must be the same, I think, in other
places, especially the Colonies. The principal obvious thing
about it is that it is entirely devoid of snobbery and almost
solely idealistic, which explains much.

It seems to me that the King is different. As soon as he
puts on the crown he becomes, by ancient custom very like
ancient magic, the only human being to whom a decent
British Auburnite can be really subservient without feeling
he is sucking up and disgracing himself. There is something
very old and peculiar in most of us ordinary British country-
people which desires to have some human being like that
in the world, someone who can have all the things not only
that we would like to have, but that we would like to *want*
to have, and who will always behave towards them as we
would like to want to behave if we were the sort of people
we feel we, or our children, might be if we could really get
around to arranging it and breeding it. Once again time
does not seem to be taken much into consideration.

I advanced this whole theory to a caller at the house
one day and he said, "Don't you simply mean that the
King sets the standard of the English gentleman?" and I
thought, "No, I don't only mean that. I don't believe it is
a question of setting a standard so much as of maintaining
a slowly rising one as our standard of living goes up." I
mean that the King is also the ideal English sport and the
ideal English squire, that he has the ideal wife, the ideal
children, the ideal houses, the ideal clothes, the ideal way
of meeting people, of spending his holidays, of choosing his
friends, the ideal memory, the ideal dogs. When his best

house was bombed it was not an ideal thing to happen but
it gave him the opportunity to behave in the ideal way,
and in view of what was happening to all his neighbours
the fact that his house was bombed too put him in an ideal
position to sympathise. These are far more exacting requirements than could be asked of an ideal gentleman. These are
the attributes of an unreal person altogether, a man who,
though in no way strange or unnatural, is yet ideal in every
particular. In simple elementary language, in character and
in manner and in possessions, the best man of all, the King.

I suppose this need of a visible material King is a highly
primitive instinct in those of us who possess it so deeply,
but I also venture to think that those intellectuals among
us (nearly all of them of foreign extraction) who find the
idea so monstrous in us, are probably really only not quite
intellectual enough. The intellect is not in itself better than
instinctive idealism. It is only a machine for understanding
it and other things and doing something about them if
necessary. The flashlamp and the spade are not *better* than
the path.

After the King's visit the nights grew longer as Christmas
came slowly nearer, and it was a noisy bomb-filled winter.
The enemy, who had never shown much discrimination in
his bombing, now sailed high over the clouds and appeared
to drop anything he thought he would through them whenever he judged he was somewhere over the island. The raids
began about seven at night and ended round about eight
or nine the next morning. Auburn settled in and "bopped
down" and escaped with a shaking or two. The wild nights
were probably the most disconcerting. A good stormy night
can shake up our unprotected coast considerably without
help, and the howling of the wind is eerie enough, but when
the wailing drowned the noise of the plane engines at intervals and made it sound as though the pilot had suddenly cut
out just overhead, it was very upsetting to the nerves.

The panels started shaking out of our heavy old door
in the Wardens' Post and at times the assortment of noises
was unbelievable.

Food became more of a problem but it was never really short in Auburn, even though Auburn folk cannot supplement their rations by eating out. Nor did the price of it become exorbitant. The worst that could be said about food at that time was that it was plain and dull and required more thought in preparation than before.

The animals' food was more difficult and I was very thankful that we had braved the Major's kindly smile and had preserved the hay crop. The straw fort came in very useful too, or the straw did, even if it was no protection from anything but the cold.

There were absurd little incidents, of course. Pauline and I each gave the other some Earl Grey China tea at Christmas. We had each saved up to surprise the other and the gifts passed on the road.

This was the time of the first main strain. The excitement and the stimulation were wearing off and the village, in common no doubt with the rest of the country, seemed to be settling down to the long pull. The war had ceased to be a series of shocks. We had seen the size and the depth of the enemy and knew what we were up against, and it was a real war again, siege and men going overseas. America was considering helping us. The question of the hose was being faced. And meanwhile there was work, night vigils, the cold, and in the cities tragedy and heroism.

Of the family, Phil had already gone overseas to the Middle East, P.Y.C. was due home on embarkation leave, Cooee was driving her lorry in all weathers, Joyce was stationed at Dover and wrote to say that news of the shelling sounded worse than it was, which was a relief to us. Our new neighbour's Spitfire and bomber sons brought home great tales. Young Alec used to come in on his leaves and speak with an enthusiasm we had not realised was in him for the men he served as a member of the ground staff of a fighter station. News came in of other boys in the village, of Pontisbright boys, and news of old student friends in new uniforms. A great war, the greatest civil war of all time, was slowly rolling on to full tide and Auburn was in it all right, swimming strong but feeling it and taking the strain.

The enemy was still the Jerry, hated only at times and in the main treated as an evil thing like a plague or a volcano rather than as a person, a brilliantly organised force for death and mayhem rather than a reasonably warring nation.

The magnificent Greeks were the Finns all over again, and as they surpassed their own history they lifted the whole scale and standard of the war, giving the world again what they always have given it, it seems, a touch of the sublime.

The Italians were not to be thought about. It is very difficult to put this down, but I honestly believe that the ordinary chap rather likes the Eye-ties normally but is frankly embarrassed by and ashamed of them in war. ("They ought not to *go* to war," says Sam.) In peace they make us happy, and always have done so since the birth of the harlequinade; in war, nowadays at any rate, they make us blush whichever side they are on.

Of course in individual cases this is not true. We have all good cause to hate the Italians, but in the main, speaking in the broadest terms and about people who feel first and think second, I fancy that is not far out. The spectacle of a hokey-pokey car with a placard on it saying *"Entirely British"* made every other man who passed it burst out laughing, as I saw with my own eyes one day at the end of the summer.

With the re-election of President Roosevelt interest in America grew enormously, naturally, and it was noted with private satisfaction that the Old British Charity was not being mentioned so much and also that the American nation, never thought to be shortsighted, was taking a serious look round at all the other neutrals who had preferred to be broken one by one by the ever-growing Jerry. ("This Herr Hitler, he's an ambitious bloke," said one of the Wardens. "Doesn't mind taking things on, does he?")

Gradually America's generosity and growing interest began to dawn on Auburn, who is never quick on the uptake but who now started to look towards her hopefully as the planes actually began to arrive and American types of aircraft began to be seen in the sky actually over Auburn.

However, the thing which finally transformed the village's entire attitude towards the States, I think, was the tone of the American Press towards the heroism of the bombed Londoners. This was personal. This was the *people*. It was not a question of government. There was "nothing sarcastic" in it, nothing grudging, no sting, no fighting to the last Frenchman. This was honest praise of something both nations understood perfectly, luxuriant but honourable praise poured out in glorious buckets, and Auburn, who in my adult lifetime at any rate, has heard very little praise of anything British from any foreign commentator and not a lot from her own, lapped it up like a thirsty pup. For the first time that vitalising warmth which is America's peculiar and individual attribute came through to the public as well as to the man with a personal American friend. It arrived opportunely too because it was a grim, hard, cold time, lightened rather than darkened by the bomb alarums I have recorded.

Norry had relations at Coventry and others at Portsmouth, but they all came through in spite of some narrow shaves.

"The old 'uns took it better than the young 'uns," said Norry.

However, other friends were not so lucky with their families.

There were compensations but they were austere ones. At Christmas P.Y.C. came home on embarkation leave before going off to the Middle East. There were other men home on the same holiday and it was not much of a time for rejoicing.

The new values were becoming apparent everywhere. Money was so earmarked, so arranged for, that it was losing much of its old interest. There was going to be no spare money for anybody and as far as anyone could see there never would be ever any more. The odd thing was that that really seemed to settle it to a large extent. Ordinary

people were more interested in other things, I thought, than
I had ever known them before. It was almost as though
they had been released from a lot of worry by facing death
and real straitness of circumstances, and the effect had been
to give them a sort of balance. It was not a general reaction
which I had envisaged at all, so I do not think I can possibly
have imagined it.

Everybody I met seemed to have got a little younger,
more serious, and far more decided. That flaccid middle-
aged spread of the mind, which had been so depressing just
before the war, had largely disappeared. Also, which did
seem amazing, nervous trouble seemed to have vanished.
There was too, I noticed, a growing tendency towards a
far stricter code. Sophisticated drivel was going out of
fashion fast.

An odd example of this cropped up one day when P.Y.C.
and I had gone into Bastion and were lunching at the local
hotel. The entire place was filled with khaki and I was
sitting in the lounge chatting to a charming army lady while
our menfolk were joining the other boys at the bar. We
scarcely knew each other and she was evidently searching
round in her mind to keep the ball rolling and I was doing
the same. She said suddenly:

"Oh, I must tell you the wildestly funny thing. A friend
of mine just spent eighty pounds, far more than she could
afford, getting a divorce from her husband and the idiot
got himself killed next day. Wasn't it maddening?"

As soon as she had spoken the utter tastelessness of the
story in our situation occurred to her so violently that she
gaped at me in horror as I smiled politely, and I suddenly
saw that not only did she not think the tale funny herself
then but that never in her whole life could she ever have
thought it really funny. It was only a formula to her and
never had been anything else, and now not only would it
not work but it had let her down badly.

That was the kind of thing which kept on happening to
people. There were no sudden changes of heart, of course,
no miracles, but most folk did seem to give up pretending

they did not love their husbands or wives, or that their
children were mentally defective nuisances. That phase
appeared to have passed. *Making* trouble for yourself was
out of fashion at last.

London was a little more knocked about, I found when
we paid a flying visit on Christmas Eve. P.Y.C. himself was
happily unchanged. I went to the tailor's with him and
sat in a most pathetic dusty travesty of the usually so chaste
little shop and heard him chattering away to the fitter in
a further fastness.

"My dear chap, I *know* it's a battledress, but my belly
is liable to retract with fear, not to expand seven or eight
inches. I won't go into battle, or anywhere else, looking
like a blasted kangaroo."

When we came away little Mr. Billum said sadly to me
as he showed us to the door and out into the exclusive little
street strewn with dust, its gutters full of powdered glass:
"This is a depressed area now, you know."

None of the shops was crowded, but they were still doing
business at a price. I never heard so much foreign language
in the West End before. The turban-and-trouser fashion
was still in vogue among the women and the whole place
had a smart-woollen-pyjama-party-on-the-arctic-beach look,
which was unexpected and not at all without gaiety. There
were people camping in the Tubes by tea time and it was
the same sight as the one in our schoolroom at the beginning
of the war, only much worse, but I don't think they represented a fifth of the population. In town, as in Auburn, folk,
I discovered, had their own individual dislikes and pre-
ferences. Aunt moved into a hotel in Piccadilly Circus at
the beginning of the war as soon as the black-out became
complete.

"Better be bombed," she said, "than keep falling over
getting home from the office."

Someone had a nice story about that hotel but I do not
vouch for it. They say an incendiary bomb fell through the
cupola over the crowded central lounge and lay burning
on the marble, and that everybody drew their chairs away

from it while a man in a tin hat rushed forward with a
shovel and a bucket of sand and scooped it up and took it
away "as if a dog had done it." That is probably an exag-
geration, but I do know that when Aunt's windows were
blown all over her room when she was downstairs one day,
and no piece of glass larger than a sixpence was found anywhere in it, she moved into the one next door and is still
there. Yet, as she has always insisted, she is not a brave
woman. What else *can* one do? she says.

The next time I saw the city, however, there was a change.
It was the day after the fire. P.Y.C.'s leave ended, as leaves
do, and I went to town again at the end of the week to
see him off on his adventures. We knew there had been a
raid the night before, naturally, but thought it had been
soon over. The papers had not arrived and we missed the
early bulletins in the excitement of packing. The train was
on time and we sat in a compartment with a grimly handsome Squadron Leader and two old gentlemen who did not
know each other. Some way outside the city, the approach
to which was beginning to look most pathetically like Marie
Lloyd's famous song, the train stopped for two hours. We
sat in complete silence for those hours, the notices behind
our heads saying "Careless talk costs lives." Had we been
all civilians I think we might have chatted, but, having
had one awful experience in a railway carriage at the height
of the anti-talk campaign, when I inadvertently remarked
that the harvest was good and got myself vigorously ssh-ed
by a young subaltern, I have become rather afraid of
opening my mouth in public places and no doubt I am
not alone, which is obviously a good thing. The Germans
are the great disciplinarians, but I doubt if their organisations can compare with our public opinion, which in a
matter like this transforms almost everyone instantly into
a government agent.

Suddenly, at the end of the two hours, the Squadron
Leader got up and said abruptly that he was going to walk
and everybody else's patience became exhausted at the same
moment. We had got the carriage door open when an old

railway worker appeared on the line, waving at us to stay where we were. He was not very clear, but we gathered that there had been an unexploded something or other nearby which had now been removed. It simply seemed a good thing at the time, for the habit of looking dead ahead and not allowing the imagination to wander had become universal I think by this time.

The train moved and we arrived soon afterwards to find no light in the station and a very curious smell everywhere. I said to a porter, "It's a fire, isn't it?" and he gave me that pitying glance in which the Cockney excels and said, "Yes, dear, it's a fire." He found us a cab, though, which did not seem as extraordinary then as it does now, and the driver kept saying it would cost us seven-and-six. We still had no idea of the situation at all and said all right, if he felt like that. We just wanted to get across the city, that was all. He said he couldn't take us *across* the city—whatever did we expect? We were very preoccupied by P.Y.C.'s departure and were very slow-witted and inclined to be irritable, so we said, "Take us round it, then." Take us where he liked.

We sat in complete silence on that drive. I do not know where we went but I saw "*Sheba Street*" up once and it took us two hours' hard going to get to the British Museum. There were no crowds and few hold-ups. The roads were very wet and charred scraps of wood floated in little rivulets down them. The police looked tired and preoccupied and the first constable who held us up had a face like a stage butler. He said very pedantically and with exaggerated patience:

"Think what you like, but across 'ere you do not come."

Our taxidriver swung round on what felt like a swivel under the back axle and said over his shoulder to us:

"Perlite, isn't 'e? 'E's been up all night *and* he knows it *and* he's not the only one."

He drove us off at great speed and we attempted this road and that, leaping the hoses and skidding in the water, our driver chattering to policemen and every other cab driver he passed.

"So-and-so is closed now. Try So-and-so street. Cut through So-and-so and it'll take you into So-and-so."

He was wild with excitement like a child on an adventure.

I remember seeing auxiliary ambulances like ours at home, little fire wagons and mobile canteens, and whenever we came to a main thoroughfare the familiar traffic going on as usual, or nearly as usual. We went all round the mean streets, past rows of surface shelters, in and out alleys devastated by past raids, and across squares, moving all the time very fast and erratically as our driver guessed, felt and diagnosed his way. The place was not a ruin but it was ravaged and the residential parts seemed to have got it worst. There was miles and miles of it sound still, but amongst the solid bits were great areas of complete desolation. Half a church and a quarter of a garage, the front door of a pub, a shop—or had it been a cinema? There were hundreds of scenes like this.

There was not much more smoke than usual but the awful stink of fire was everywhere, very alarming to the country nose.

P.Y.C. would not let me go to the other station with him because of Noel Coward's *Cavalcade*. It made us laugh at ourselves, but there it was. It was our outlook and it could not be cured or ignored. I said a nice background of burning London was rather better, I thought. There was a sense of utter awfulness in the air just for a little while. Rome must have burned like this and all the other dear ancient sophistries last time the barbarians got really out of hand.

However, after P.Y.C. had gone and I had to find my way home again I walked for a bit, and it occurred to me that London in this dreadful visible trouble was yet not so terrifying as I had known her. I was alone in London throughout the General Strike, and that, as far as I was concerned at any rate, had been far more frightening. The atmosphere now was intensely friendly and busy and tired, almost the atmosphere of a moving day or a spring-cleaning, or at any rate of a big domestic upheaval which had not involved a row. It was "the day after we had a fire," in fact; very different from "the day Dad and his brother had a fight."

The General Strike was another great crisis and in some ways the two were alike. There was the same quiet stoicism and the same spontaneous gallantry, but in the strike there was menace and danger and, if I may say such an odd-sounding thing, evil in the air, hatred and anger, which I certainly did not feel at the fire. In fact this felt like unity and the other felt like a row.

All the same, as I went along and I saw the damage done by the water as well as the fire, I wondered if the Londoners really would be able to stand months of it until we got enough planes to keep the Hun off.

I joined one or two groups and listened, as one is apt to, and wandered on, and, as I realised I'd have to hurry to get my train, it dawned on me that there was something very familiar in the expression of the majority of people I passed. It is a funny look and you can see it in the photographs which are being printed now of the crowds all over the country staring at badly bombed buildings they know. It is a grim but conserved sort of look and it reminded me of a rather absurd incident which may possibly explain what I think lies behind it better than any other description I could give.

It was years ago when we were all in our very early twenties. We got let in for a Christmas afternoon party composed entirely of relations. One of them, who was north country, who had better be called Aunt Halifax, was a relative by marriage to another relative by marriage and she was a bit tired of P.Y.C. and Phil and me. We were the little cleversides at that time. We were the smarties. We got our tales in the magazines and our pictures in the R.A. Everybody else thought we were pretty hot. Aunt Halifax thought we were "reet stook oop."

It was a difficult party and my father, who was a man who could be bored and for all his tolerance would not stand that, suddenly commanded us in sultanic fashion to perform for the entertainment of the gathering. It was either annoying him or complying, and, not having a recitation by us (as P.Y.C. said, unfortunately) we did a silly old trick we used to do as children. It is simplicity itself. One person goes outside and finds two broomsticks and a sheet. He puts his shoes on the broomsticks and holds them out in front of him, his head thrown back. His assistant then arranges the sheet over the broomsticks in such a way that all is hidden save the shoes and the performer's head.

Meanwhile the third member of the troupe acts as a barker and introduces "the human miracle. The greatest experiment in levitation the world has ever known" and so on, to taste. The door is then slowly opened and, feet foremost, the broomstick man floats into the room, the trailing sheet and the swinging door hiding, between them, his real body and legs. The whole beauty of the performance is, of course, that after the first shock it does not deceive anybody.

Everyone was amused on this occasion except Aunt Halifax, who sat grimly in the best position, near to the door and a little behind it. She looked at us very steadily when we all returned and said:

"You seem very pleased with yourselves."

She did not add that at any rate she was not impressed, but that was the idea that got around.

However, later on, when I was upstairs, she came into my bedroom and stood looking at me for a bit and then she said grudgingly:

"Thaat was quite interesting, maaking your yoong man flo-at in the air. How did you do it?—not that I want to know."

She left me helpless. I saw as far as she was concerned *we had performed a miracle* and still she had not been impressed.

The people I met in London that day reminded me vividly of Aunt Halifax when she said, "You seem very pleased with yourselves." They had her grim, withdrawn, conserved look. They were not going to be impressed. Jerry could do what he liked. He was not going to startle them or put one over on them.

I came home to Auburn feeling very proud to belong to the same race as they did, and it seemed to me too that although as a nation we were losing so much we were also getting something utterly indestructible back out of it. I got something that day, anyway, which will last as long as I do.

There is something very good in pride of race if you can be satisfied in your heart that it is absolutely genuine and is based on things you have seen and heard and felt rather than on those you have read.

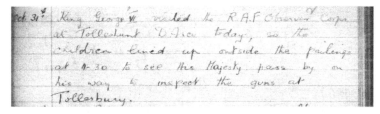

Above: School log October 3rd 1940.
(St. Nicholas Primary School)

Right: King George VI, Arthur Moore and Charlie Flack.
(Meg Bunting)

27

JOYCE was the next whom we got ready in the house to go to sea, as other families in Auburn and Flinthammock and all the other country places were doing for their younger ones. She was off to Singapore, to the naval station, and was dying to go. We got her kit together in Granny's bathroom, which is also a family sewing room, and as we read the official list, so like a boarding school list, and sorted out her clothes, Granny began on the subject of wars. She is close on eighty-nine now and has never been anything but what she calls "a muff." However, her experience of wars, from the personal and private point of view of the muff, that is of the ordinary uninformed, unimportant civilian, is comprehensive to say the least of it. Her father remembered the Battle of Waterloo without any difficulty, being very nearly old enough to have fought at it, and considered Napoleon a personal enemy who, he was happy to see, got his deserts, and the present map of Europe would not have surprised him as much as it does me.

Granny's first recollection of war was Austrian prisoners being brought into Godesberg when she was at school there. She did not bother to leave Germany and come home for that war. "Handsome fellows they were," she said. "Our servants were up praying all night." But whether this was for victory or the prisoners she is not able to determine at this distance. She remembers, however, that the Austrians wore white uniforms.

Joyce and I found her attitude towards great men educational.

"When Julia used to read *The Times* to Pa, that General MacMahon was all the go," she remarked. "Now *he* could have helped General Gamelin if he hadn't died long ago. He knew a great deal about that Sedan."

Other wars came nearer to her. "When dear Hattie came over from New York (she bought such a beautiful night-

266

dress in Paris: it was all gophered and fitted at the back)
she had her new husband with her. We never saw her first.
He was killed, poor fellow, in that war they had over there."

"Independence," suggested Joyce, who was growing
visionary.

"No, no, I think it was the Civil War. Very cruel."

Then she got on to the last war again when Uncle Wallie,
her only son, was killed with the Canadians at Ypres, and
then this war and the letter she was writing to Phil in Libya,
and then Joyce.

"I shall cut out everything I read in the paper about
Singapore for you to keep when you come home."

We asked her what great-grandfather would have thought
of the present show, which was a silly question and got the
reply it deserved. She laughed at us.

"He'd keep us women reading *The Times* to him all day,"
she said.

She is a great newspaper reader herself and the stories
of the bombing infuriate her.

"Oh, isn't it *wicked*!" she says, throwing down the paper.
"Isn't it *naughty*! You'd think almost . . ."

"What?" I say.

"Well, dear, I was going to say almost . . . you'd think
Gord would do something."

"Drop a brick on him?"

"Or smite him," says Granny brightly. "All those poor
nurses. Let me read you this bit about the hospital ship."

Since that conversation many things have happened, and
yet it is scarcely more than a couple of months ago. Greece
has fallen and Thermopylae has been held and lost as
gloriously as once it was. The Germans have recaptured
Libya. Haile Selassie is back on his throne. London has
been bombed and bombed again and the Parliament must
sit in another room.

Auburn is as it always was, save that the fathers of the
families still stand on the doorstep at night and food is not
so easy to come by and will be shorter in spite of Mr. Ford's
pig club and the preparations in Mrs. Eve's kitchen for the

Women's Institute to make the season's fruit into jam. Eggs
are twopence each, even at this time of year, and we are
lucky to get them. Christine is putting them down in waterglass. Vic refused to take the money for a chicken she let
us have, but accepted some tea I had saved in exchange.
There are still a few sweets to be had every so often in
Albert's father's old shop. Jose's mother rations them roughly
and sees no one gets an unfair share. Reg does the same
with other luxuries. Three oranges arrived the other day
as our portion and Christine promptly collared them and
made a pound of orange curd.

Sam has got me to invest in two small rabbits at one
shilling each and confidently expects several generations
before the end of the summer. The two geese we acquired
last winter are still wandering round the front meadow like
highbrows at a private view, honking at anything which
displeases them. They have shown no disposition to become
domestic, and my suggestion that they may be both ganders
has begun to irritate Sam. Norry and I are quarrelling about
Beau. Soon he must be broken, and I say he must go in
a dogcart and earn his keep. Norry cannot bear it. "Wait,"
he says. "Wait. Those lovely pasterns. That narrow little
old head." Poor Beau. No gentleman ever works. Poor Norry.
I hope he never has to eat him.

There was the annual entertainment at the school not
so very long ago. Granny and I went and there was a "Red"
on, but nobody takes any notice of them in daylight, thanks
to our neighbour's Spitfire son and his pals. The children
were in form. Roy, Sam's eldest, was very much to the fore
and so was young Jose with one tooth out in front, and all
the other kids were magnificent too, of course. Marg, dressed
up as a cross between Britannia and the Fairy Queen, stood
in the middle as she was the tallest, and recited, "*Where are
you going to, all you big steamers?*" with a stark brutality in
her raucous young voice which made my blood run cold.
"*And if anything hinders our coming . . . you'll starve!*" Oh, my
God! Lay off, Marg! Have a heart.

Still, we're a long way off 1917 yet.

The Spring is late this year, which is all to the good. The planting is done and the flowers, left to themselves, look better than ever to my mind. The weathercock on the maypole shines gold against the blue, still the best bird in the sky, still very much cock of the roost.

The hay is late but the crowns are good and strong. The papers were late too after the big raid the other night, but they came all right by lunch time and reported some of it in the Stop Press. There are still plenty of advertisements in *The Times* for London flats. "Unique chance . . . well furnished . . . third floor . . . 5½ gns. p.w."

Mr. Parker came over with the others for a First Aid conference. His London village has got it very badly and his family have suffered. He says there's a new slogan up there which has taken everybody's fancy. It is uttered with a great bellow of that slightly fierce laughter which underlies all British primitive wit.

"I wouldn't be dead for a pound!"

That's London. It's getting angry. That's not so far away from the terrifying *"I know where he is, I know where he is. He's hanging on the old barbed wire."*

Auburn is still Auburn. Cliff has just come in. He and Herbert are going to put our old pig court into commission once again for the club. Mr. Saye has some fine young ones nearly ready to leave the sow.

I have not mentioned our defences. There is a reason for that. Sufficient to say they are so much better than last year that Miss Ethel and the kerosene will not be needed, and if she is shot it will be as a non-combatant.

Our old ·22 rifle from the fun-fair has been turned in. We are civilians, unless as the Cabinet Minister has told us, we are attacked in our homes, in which case we are at liberty to defend ourselves with anything that comes to hand, the breadknife or the Meissen vase.

A cable has arrived at last from P.Y.C. *"Sans origine. Am well. Good trip."* A p.c. from Joyce from the Cape. *"As good as a cruise but nicer passengers."* Letter two months old from Phil, now a corporal. *"We may go to . . . (*a word of six letters

heavily blue-pencilled)." Grog says he will be in the Air
Force in a few weeks now. Norry in the kitchen. They've
heard from the nephew who went to Canada under the air
training scheme. He's all right, having a good time. The
London wires are clear for ordinary calls again, Nerney
coming through brightly from the capital. "Yes, yes, all's
well. Isn't it *grand*? No, not a scratch. No, thank you. Nothing
to see from here."

Thank God for that. Thank God for rather a lot.

A line in a letter from a troopship. "*All my chaps write
screeds which paraphrase 'Oh to be in England.' Fancy they must
all be gardeners. Feel a bit like that myself.*" Letters from
America. "*We look on in amazement. . . .*" "*We're on your
side.*" "*If the Atlantic is now in danger we must fight for it, however
we feel about England. That note of self-interest, questionable under
other circumstances, is really valuable now.*"

All the other thoughts. Mine. Other peoples'. Things I've
noticed.

What *are* your war aims, Mrs. Carter? To keep this soul
I've got alive. To keep my spirit unenslaved. To say what
I like and feel what I like . . . and the same for you, my
neighbours, whether you like it or not. I believe with all
my heart that we must *all* be free. There is only one stable
thing in the whole world, the character of the steadfast
individual, and he must be protected and allowed to grow.

Your peace aims, then? The same. The same, but trans-
lated into the little difficult ways of peace. The same for
Auburn. Peace without suffocation. Room to grow in,
spiritually, mentally and physically. Something to grow
towards and a fair start for everybody. None of us can
possibly have much money or other possessions at the end
of this conflagration although we shall have all our normal
potential wealth between us, so that fair start ought to be
possible to arrange if we keep our heads, keep our sense of
values, feel the way as well as think it, and avoid all schemes
which are based solely on theory. There seem to be too
many pitfalls in pure theory. For instance, if only the farmers
in the last war had been paid the subsidy on what they

actually grew and delivered, quality being taken into account, instead of on the acreage they put under the plough, we would never have spoiled a good crop not only of grain but of men. That was an elementary mistake, so easy on paper but almost impossible to anyone who thinks in terms of human nature, I should have thought. Man is obviously the main crop and to grow him one needs great experience as well as good theory. If the Government only sticks to that main crop, as our great and great-great-grandfathers did, and does not leave it all to the parsons, as our fathers suddenly seem to have decided to, I think we shall get by and get the seed in for a better world.

Will Britain go Red? No.

Socialist then? Only inasmuch as she always has been socialist. It looks to me as if the unprofessional British sort of socialism is now, as it ever was, nothing more or less than an honest attempt at practical Christianity without bringing in Jesus, since religion was found to make for trouble in the Government. So far, after a lot of muddling about and backsliding and going on again, we have achieved democracy. This is bald, Auburn kind of talk, but plain thinking leads to plain talking and will perhaps be forgiven.

Why are you so certain of this? You are a free country person. No one in the world can force an opinion on you. How do you *know*? How dare you say this with such confidence? Because I am so free the answer must be careful, I see that. I must only speak from what I have seen personally.

Well, in my life I have heard a great many British people say to one another, in effect, "*I am as good as you are*," but I cannot think of more than two who have said in my hearing "*you're no better than I am*," and the two statements are not at all the same, are they? Besides, when a Briton "gets on," as they say, he hardly ever stays a rich member of the jolly proletariat, nor does he as a rule go in for Roman orgies or indulge in other excesses. On the contrary, he is much more likely to submit himself and his family at once, and instinctively almost, to all the discomforts and uniforms of a way of life which he thinks is better and grander than his old one. This is not mere snobbery. As an ordinary chap he is far more likely to make friends with a "nob." He does not want "nob" friendship; he wants to *be* a "nob." He wants to be equal to what he thinks, rightly or wrongly, to be the best. Also he prefers "the nobs" not to be less nobbish but if possible more so than they are naturally, and is irritated with them if they let down his ideal. He expects them to keep the code of behaviour, possessions and manners *up*, so that his ascent may be the higher. His sacrifices for this climb are colossal, for he knows the journey may take a generation or two, and he evidently considers it worth it or why on earth does he keep on doing it? How many of our best families are very old? The misleading element I fancy, and with respect, lies in the brains of the country. Real brains allied to all the other virtues and a grasp of the essential up-pull can do the journey in a lifetime and raise the standard higher, as is shown every year or two. Brains without the rest cannot do this and it is they, it seems to me, who get so angry with the two-generation clause and who cry out for instant equality to be given them by a lowering of the standard instead of achieving it in the time-honoured way. They create a lot of confusion, but they do not prevent the slow natural process from taking place everywhere and all the time, and I do not think they ever will. In print there is a great deal of "down with the old school tie" and "blast the public schools," but if, as I firmly believe will come (if somebody only has the sense to arrange it now when there is a chance), it is possible, or even compulsory, for every child to go to a public school, say, of the Christ's Hospital type, with all its traditions, its magnificent discipline and its blessed swank, which gives a youngster a pride in belonging to something his own, something sound and fine and proud which can destroy in a great measure any social inferiority complex he may be cursed with, which will give him a fair chance in fact, I do not think many parents would stand in the way, especially not those in the country.

As for Red propaganda, we had an example of that in Auburn. A man came to the village some while ago and his method was the time-honoured one, as used on the Continent. He got into conversation with the various chaps privately and asked each outright how much he earned a week. On being told, whatever the figure, he expressed complete bewilderment and horror. "Thirty-five bob! You and a wife and child on thirty-five bob! This is criminal. This is frightful. Don't you know what your employer gets? Why should you put up with it? He is no better than you, is he? Thirty-five bob!"

I only know what answers he got in two cases and both these stories were told me casually and as a bit of a laugh. Albert, who had given his earnings as a slightly larger sum, was intensely interested. "I thought," he said, "that as he fancied three quid was nothing he must be pulling in five or six, so I sent the bill in at once." Sam was more loquacious. He was a bit embarrassed, he said, and did not know how to turn it off until he remembered a tale of a pal of his called Lefty, which he seems to have told at length and with gusto. "Lefty was *courting* a girl up at Heath. *Told* her he was earning *four pounds*. She *married* him. Come the Friday, he walks in and puts *twenty-three bob* on the kitchen *table*. She *stares* at it. Thought you was earning *four pounds*? says she. So I *am*, says Lefty. I'm a-*earning* four pounds but I only *gits* twenty-three bob." There must be many men who have not the essential grasp on the cold facts of earning a livelihood which these two possess, but on the other hand they cannot be unique. One of Sam's relations earning forty-five bob has to pay two shillings of this in income-tax now. Someone suggested he married to get out of it but he was appalled. "Har, I 'on't saddle myself with a wife for the sake of two bob," he said. "No, no, I'm not balmy."

Can we stand ten years of this war? I think we could in Auburn.

Twenty? We'll wait and see.

Suppose we fail? Suppose we don't get the machines in time? Suppose our delays and the machinations of our enemies, who saw our soft spot of over-deliberation and went for it, have made us just too late? Suppose down the road and out of the sky the thick grey men come swarming on us? What then? *Give me time and I'll pay the National Debt. Be a bundle of sticks. . . . He'll break his teeth on England. Courage is vital but not enough. Work for the freedom which means life. Pray for it, fight for it, die for it if you have to, live for it if you can. It's worth it.*

That's my contribution to the little family store of conviction. After a lifetime of *"it's all very difficult"* I can now say honestly, *"It's worth it"* and *"I wouldn't be dead for a pound."*

The conviction is mine but the seed of it is Auburn's. Auburn may die, but it will come up again all right, whatever happens, in the Spring, some Spring, when Spring comes

Auburn is a right thing and will survive all wrong things. Whatever happens, what *ever* happens, at some future date, if life lasts on earth, Auburn will be here again as like itself as makes no real difference. I am as sure of that as I am that the sun will rise to-morrow.

Well, there it is This picture is done. I have struggled to paint it very truthfully, yet it may be a little false inasmuch as the things I have left out have been in the main the less interesting ones, the small jealousies, the smaller spites, the minute unkindnesses and the fleeting despondencies. However, in the past few years all these things have been put down very carefully by writers who began with the false premise which our disillusioned elders left to my generation, the theory that only the unpleasant can be realism, a belief so widely held in the last few years that the very phrase "village life" has come to suggest the casebook of a small mental hospital for less dangerous patients. It is because they have done all this, and that side of the simple life has been firmly impressed upon everybody's mind, that I have not bothered my head trying to remember all the little odds and ends of things which have upset us here during the time under review There have been less of them than usual because we have been so busy. Let me see. Somebody complained about the quality of the knitting of the comforts. Somebody else thought the pig club must be a twist. Somebody refused to take in evacuees. Somebody said we were cowards to retreat at Dunkirk and ought to have gone on and beaten up everybody. Somebody said they would rather let their fruit rot than let the Women's Institute lay hands on it. And so on. Now I come to look at it, nobody *did* anything unco-operative It was all talk and we are fighting to say what we like. Unimportant remarks all of them and the devil's own job to remember after a month or two, as I can testify this very minute.

The main thing about Auburn, curled round the maypole, is that it is ordinary country, no better and no worse than anywhere else. So there you are. This, I really believe, is sweet Auburn. I love it as one does love one's home, and if that has made me give it perhaps a very slightly prettier face than some would see at first glance (although I would not admit this), you must discount that much, please, but not more I beg you, for remember only the really lovable is beloved for long.

I hear the Wardens stumping about down the passage getting their coats. Soon the phone will ring and then there will be lions in the sky once more. If I die to-night, and I don't see why I should, I shall have been sorry to have missed the finish, but I shall still count myself very lucky to have seen so much.

Later. I have been correcting this, and a white tin hat with a black stripe down it has just come round the door. The Wardens having missed the midnight news have been listening-in to one of our overseas broadcasts.

"I say, this is rather extraordinary. They've got Hess in Glasgow. He's turned up alone in a Messerschmitt 110."

Grog says it's a trap. Keep him away from Churchill. Sam says, "Har, it's the beginning of the great crack-up" coming, as he always said it would, suddenly. Doug, the Home Guard, frankly does not believe his own ears. George

never heard such a tale in all his life. Nor have I . . .
never.

Wait. Wait. We must be careful. "Judge not in a hurry."
Yet. . . . If one really chooses every friend, every employee,
every under-leader for what is false in him, if one's scheme
of progress is based *literally* on what is worst in man, on
Hess's theory that one is God, on Petain's tragic vanity, on
Quisling's self-importance, then why not? Why not a general
rat? Why not a slow irrevocable procession of double-
crossing rottenness and death? What true thing remains
to stop it?

It will be a lark if we get the whole gang of Frankensteins
over here in the end, one by one, each coming simply
because Britain is the one safe spot in Europe for the individual. I wonder, what has anyone of that gang that he
would die for willingly? What has death got to offer them?
There is nothing in them *certain* to come up again.

What a period! What an age to have been alive in!

Oh, thank God I was born when I was.

Left: Margery in her garden.

Clockwise from top left: Joyce Allingham, W.R.N.S., A. J. Gregory ('Grog'), R.A.F., Pip Youngman Carter ('P.Y.C.'), R.A.S.C. and Phil Allingham, R.A.S.C.

Top left: Anthony Seabrook circa 1938. *(Julia Seabrook)*

Top right: Jimmy Burmby. *(Nora Curtis)*

Upper left: Harold Curtis on a German 'Tiger' tank. *(Nora Curtis)*

Lower left: Reg South and Arthur Moore taking observations. *(Meg Bunting).*

Bottom: Edward Terrell, with his prototype 'Disney' bomb. *(Guided Rockets and Missiles, T. Burakowski & A. Sala)*

Appendix I

The People of *The Oaken Heart*

These notes are intended to give a slightly fuller picture of the Tolleshunt D'Arcy people mentioned in the text of *The Oaken Heart* – where they lived and what they did. Addresses in Tolleshunt D'Arcy then are not quite the same as now and one of the features revealed by the billeting map is the number of houses where adult brothers and sisters were living together or where families had rented a room to a lodger. Many of the families were, and still are, related to one another. The entries are arranged in arranged in the approximate order of appearance.

The Smith family. Albert and Charlotte Smith lived in 1, Council Cottages (also known as Coronation Cottages). Albert was builder, electrician and general handyman. He couldn't join the Army because of a twisted arm but, as the war progressed, he served as an electrician on the local airfields first at Boxted, near Colchester, and then at Wormingford, a village on the Suffolk border. At first he used to cycle there and back every day, a distance of about fifteen miles each way, often being called on to return to work when he had only just reached home. His oldest son, Alan, was ten years old at the outbreak of war and in his last year as a pupil at St Nicholas School. He remembers looking out of his window, hearing the flashes and bangs, the night that bombs fell on the Tolleshunt D'Arcy cemetery and across the fields to Hall Farm (p. 226). He also remembers the school bus to Maldon having to stop during air raid warnings. His cousin, John Houlding, who was about the same age, remembers one day that this happened. The bus stopped and the children were expected to take shelter in the ditch. Instead they all ran home. Alan Smith never liked having to shelter in the corridors of the Secondary School during air raids. One day, when machine gun fire hit some gas canisters outside the school, the glass blew in, despite the criss-

279

crossing tape that was intended to protect against blast. Later special air raid shelters were provided. John Houlding hated them. 'They were like the black hole of Calcutta'.

Alfred Smith, father of Albert, Olive and Clara, built and then re-built the existing shop in the Square with his brother, a builder from Maldon. He and his wife worked in the shop then sold it to Ernest and Edith Bore. It was a newsagent, as it still is today, and also sold groceries and sweets. Dorothy Houlding (Blyth) who was evacuated to the village went to work in the shop as a teenager and remembers her first job as counting the coupons. She worked there for many years afterwards. Alfred served as a Special Constable both before and during WW2. Olive married Fred Nevill and lived in Goldhanger. Clara married one of the soldiers who were stationed in D'Arcy early in the war. They had a week's honeymoon and then he was sent to Egypt with his battalion. Two weeks later he was killed when he kicked open the door of a booby-trapped house. Later Clara married again and lived until she was almost 90.

'The Old Doctor': Dr J.H. Salter, former owner of D'Arcy House, died 1932. He had been a dominant figure in the area for almost seventy years – notable as a shooting man, gardener and pugilist as well as a G.P. and leading Freemason. Margery Allingham remembered him from her WW1 childhood (and also gave him a walk-on part as Dr Bouverie in her 1936 novel *Dancers in Mourning*).

Robert (Bobby) Graves was the former vicar of Tolleshunt D'Arcy. Meg Bunting (Moore) remembers him as 'a friend to everyone, how vicars used to be'. His first wife had been an invalid and was pushed around the village in an invalid carriage by her devoted nurse Pauline who became the second Mrs Graves. At the outbreak of war Rev Graves had retired and lived with his wife Pauline, in D'Arcy Cottage near the Church. Pauline remained in the village after Rev Graves's death and married her neighbour Johnny Reynolds.

The Emeny family. These were the six children of Abraham Emeny. The two brothers, Jack and Norry ran the Thatcher's Arms, on the corner of Chapel Road and the blacksmith's shop in the Square. Norry had served in WW1. Sisters Susannah and Victoria lived at the Thatcher's Arms while Eugenie and Beatrice lived nearby at Alder (or Elder) House nearby. At least three of the sisters had been away in domestic service. They managed the Cyclist's Rest café.

Reginald and Dorothy Hammond ran a general store in the Square. This sold some groceries but mainly haberdashery and hardware, including agricultural supplies.

Arthur and Ismay Moore lived in the School House as she was the Headmistress. She is remembered as utterly dedicated to teaching and as fearsomely strict. Arthur Moore had been gassed in WW1 and was a leading member of the Observer Corps in WW2. They had one child, Meg, who was a teenager in WW2. Ill-health prevented her from undertaking direct war service so she worked as a junior matron in Endsleigh House, Colchester (where Margery Allingham had been a boarder during WW1) and as a children's nurse. She explains that one of the reasons for her mother's strictness was that, when she took over as head teacher at Tolleshunt D'Arcy, several of the older boys had become used to truanting. When they heard that a young woman was their new headmistress they returned to school ready to play her up. On her first day she placed a cane on her desk and had no more trouble. She could achieve very high standards with her pupils. Meg remembers her mother and Margery Allingham going round the village in the evening checking the evacuee children for head lice. Meg later married a member of a local farming family, the Buntings (as did Betty James, also from Tolleshunt D'Arcy). She remembered Margery Allingham as a striking figure in her long dresses but also as warm, kind and quite laid back. In those days she didn't know that Margery was a novelist. 'I just knew her as Mother's friend.'

Mrs Gager, assistant teacher, lived in Tollesbury at that time. There were other Gagers in Tollesbury. Margery Allingham met 'little Peter Gager' who she described as 'a child who will get on'. Peter's sister, Helen, is among those who contributed her memories to the BBC *People's War* project under the title 'We couldn't afford meat so we ate lobster'. She tells how people in a fishing village were able to supplement their wartime rations. She also remembers the visit of King George VI (p. 252) (www.bbc.co.uk/ ww2peopleswar/stories/57/a7921857.shtml).

Sam and Vera Taylor lived in Spring Crescent on the Tollesbury Road with Sam's father and with their children Roy, Barry and Barbara. Sam worked as the D'Arcy House gardener. There are five other families of Taylors on the 1939 electoral roll for Tolleshunt D'Arcy.

Margaret Nicklin lived in Pansy Cottage, West Street, with her aunts. She was working as a cook at D'Arcy House when war broke out but later left to work at the post office.

John and Kathleen Doe lived in North Street. He ran the local butcher's shop and was also the billeting officer with Margery Allingham.

Edward Terrell Q.C. (1902-1979) lived in Laburnham Cottage and also in the Middle Temple. He was Recorder of Newbury 1936-1971. Wartime service in the R.N.V.R. Invented protective plastic armour for ships and may have been involved in the Shingle Street experiments.

Charles Flack was the Tolleshunt D'Arcy postman and lived in 5, Spring Crescent with Mr & Mrs Fred South. He had been wounded in WW1 and volunteered for the Observer Corps in WW2.

Joan Barker and Cynthia Tatchell were daughters of Mr and Mrs Hortin who lived in Messing but also owned the Guisnes Court Estate. Major Gerald Tatchell, Cynthia's husband was killed at Dunkirk and she later remarried. Their brother, Captain Julian Hortin, died gallantly at Tobruk in June 1942.

Mr and Mrs Carrington Seabrook were members of an established local farming family. He, however, was a bank manager
and lived in West Street. Three Seabrook brothers, Anthony,
Francis and Brian had grown up at Wycke Farm. Francis and
Brian stayed in agriculture but Tony served on the *Rawalpindi*, an
armed merchant ship which was torpedoed southeast of Iceland
with great loss of life, Tony Seabrook amongst them. An account
of the sinking can be found on the *People's War* site
(www.bbc.co.uk/ww2peopleswar/stories/84/a7068684.shtml).

Clifford Otway lived in a bungalow in the Tollesbury Road with
his brothers Leonard and Charles. He was chauffeur/valet to Rev
Graves and for many years took a leading part organising village
events such as whist drives.

Albert, Sam and Mary Clover lived at Marshgate, Station Road.
Albert Clover was already in the Army and his brother Sam a re-
servist. There were other families of Clovers in Tolleshunt D'Arcy
and nearby Oxley Hill.

The Cornell family lived in 5, Council Cottages (Coronation
Cottages). Basil Cornell joined the Anglian Regiment and drove
an ammunition lorry throughout the war. 'Smiler' and 'Tiddles'
Cornell worked as delivery boys in Reg Hammond's shop until
they both joined up.

The Unwin family lived in West Street. Ralph Unwin worked
as the odd-job boy for D'Arcy House. Bob Cross did a similar
part-time job in the 1960s and remembers how friendly Margery
Allingham was.

Basil and Jessie Golding, members of a local farming family,
lived at Tolleshunts Farm, Maldon Road. The Goldings owned
Hyde Farm which had a narrow escape later in the war when a
rocket fell right beside the farmhouse.

William Cottis was an ex-serviceman and thatcher. He lived at
the Vinery, Kelvedon Road, with his son Basil who often drove
their lorry.

Weston and Dorothy Eve lived at D'Arcy Hall, next to the

Church. He was a miller and a 'gentleman farmer'.

Mr Saye has not been individually identified. He was a member of a large local family at various different addresses both in Tolleshunt D'Arcy and Tollesbury.

Alec Coker probably lived in Spring Terrace. He worked with Albert Smith then joined up.

Herbert Bullard had been Dr Salter's gardener. He, his wife, his brother and other family members lived in South Street in a cottage called 'Alstroemeria' after new strain of those flowers bred by Dr Salter.

Henry Driffield Smyth lived in North Street and owned an orchard in Goldhanger. His sister Beatrice was a nurse. The District Nurse possibly lived near D'Arcy House. Later this was Nurse Harker.

Johnny Reynolds, Tolleshunt D'Arcy resident, builder. Lived at Pound Cottage near the Church with his mother and aunt. Theirs was the only house in the village to suffer direct bomb damage.

Members of the Spooner family lived at three different addresses in Tolleshunt D'Arcy. One of these was Spring Farm, which was made available to 'Mama' and her large family (p. 131) as the tenant, Sidney Spooner, was already in the Forces, as was his relative Arthur Spooner. The Mr Spooner mentioned in the Oaken Heart lived in Tollesbury Road and was a baker before he joined up.

Jessie Bacon lived in Salter Lodge, South Street. She had been Dr Salter's housekeeper for many years and had assisted him with minor operations, such as tooth-pulling, which he had carried out in D'Arcy House.

Mr and Mrs A.C. Eaton lived at Frame Farm on the Beckenham Road. He had the local milk round and employed local boys to help. One Sunday morning, later in the war, a friend of Alan Smith's was doing this job when he saw a plane coming down and had to dive into the ditch to save himself. An American pilot was killed when his parachute failed to open and he came down on the clubhouse of the old golf course. His plane crashed on the twelfth green.

Mr and Mrs Foster probably lived on the corner of Station Road and Chapel Street. She was a member of the Seabrook family. He was in the Home Guard. Other members of the Seabrook family lived next door with Mrs Tuohy, a widow. She had a son serving in the B.E.F. (British Expeditionary Force).

Sidney Whipps and his nephew George Whipps owned and worked a threshing machine. One is remembered as having kicked the machine and lost his foot in the resulting accident. They lived at 7, Spring Crescent.

George Read lived at 9, Spring Crescent and worked for the council as a road mender. The day that his lorry was hit by a bomb (p. 226) is recorded in a letter dated 19.10.1940 in the incident book in the Essex Record Office. The driver, Mr Thurgood, had been blown right out of his cab and was later found to have a broken neck. George Read had been nearer the bomb but had seen the flash and saved himself by ducking just in time. He picked up the injured man, carried him to a cottage, persuaded them to give shelter to his companion, then walked on across the fields to find somewhere where he could telephone for help. He then returned to work and finished his shift.

Martha Cracknell and other members of her family lived in one of the cottages beside the bakery, next door to the Bouttells.

Mr and Mrs Lingley ('Tiff and Mrs Tiff') lived in North Street. He was a wheelwright and a carpenter and did odd jobs for Margery for many years after the war.

The Houlding family. Dick Houlding was an undertaker and a knackerman and a member of one of the largest families in Tolleshunt D'Arcy and the surrounding area. His nephew, John Houlding, who was a child during the war, has been an astonishingly rich source of information. John's wife, Dorothy (née Blyth), arrived in the village with her family as a private evacuation. They had lived in Clacton, moved away to an industrial area in the North, which was heavily bombed, then returned to Essex to live in Tolleshunt D'Arcy. Florence and Herbert Houlding who lived at 14, Spring Crescent, Tollesbury Road, looked after their evacuee, ten-year-old Doreen Pearson from Barking, so well that she too has remained in the area for the rest of her life. Margery mentions Doreen in her diary as 'the only child' (out of 225) to fill a whole page of her form. Another member of the Houlding family, Ruby Houlding, met her husband when he was billeted briefly at Guisnes Court, married him before he was sent abroad and moved to live in Manchester with him after the war. Reg Houlding, from Tollesbury, contributed to the *People's War* website. One of his memories is of a Dad's Army style incident when the local Home Guard mistook a newly purchased white carthorse for an enemy parachutist in the deceptive dawn light (www.bbc.co.uk/ww2peopleswar/stories/73/a7924773.shtml).

Thomas and Emma Bouttell lived in North Street, Tolleshunt D'Arcy, next to the bakery. Their son George joined up and served in India.

Joe Pudney lived with his parents at White House Cottages, The Wyck, Tollesbury Road and joined the Guards. Later he married Miss Smith who had been his neighbour in the Wyck and who had who served in the W.A.A.F.

The Goody family occupied several different houses in Tolleshunt D'Arcy. Alf Goody, who lived at Church Villa, Maldon Road, was a roadman and A.R.P. warden before he joined up. His brother Stan joined the R.A.F., survived the war, but did not return to Tolleshunt D'Arcy.

Geoffrey Townsend lived with his family at 1, Spring Crescent. He joined the R.A.F.

The Ford family were newcomers to Tolleshunt D'Arcy and lived in North Street. Both sons were in the R.A.F. – one flying fighter planes, the other in bombers. One of the sons died.

Fred Braddy had a cobbler's shop next to the Forge. He was

living with his parents before he joined up.

Harry and Jessie Hart lived at the Station House as Harry was the stationmaster. He volunteered for the Home Guard and is remembered as having 'done a lot of the shouting'. Their son, Frank Hart, married in 1940 and then joined up. After the war he worked in a garage.

Harold and Nora Curtis (née Hull) were married in 1940 when she was aged 18. He joined the Royal Engineers and later served with the British Army of the Rhine. Before that he assisted with rescue operations and clearing up during the London Blitz. His daughter, Ann, still has the coins he picked up on the night of the St Paul's fire. They had been fused together by the intensity of the heat. Nora did not wait to be called up herself. She volunteered to join the N.A.A.F.I and cooked for the troops stationed at Bicester. Her parents, who had a smallholding in Tolleshunt Knights had a narrow escape from an unexploded bomb and their neighbour's house was damaged when a German plane came down. The two dead airmen are buried in Maldon Cemetery. Nora and other young wives appealed successfully to the local council for new homes for their returning husbands. Harold Curtis was the long-term chairman of Tolleshunt Knights Parish Council and Nora has worked many years for the British Legion.

Johnny (correct name Jimmy) Burmby lived on the Kelvedon Road and became a Chief Petty Officer. He served in *HMS Belfast* and *HMS Victory* among many other postings.

Mr Todd and his wife Lilian lived at Sycamore Cottages Kelvedon Road. He died with the submarine *Thistle* was sunk by a U-boat off Utsira (www.naval-history.net/WW2CampaignsBritish-Subs.htm). The child, Marg, who performs 'Where are you going to all you big steamers' (p. 268) may have been their daughter.

Leonard and Nellie James lived at Wayside, Station Road. He was an insurance agent and joined the Home Guard. Their daughter, Betty, joined the W.A.A.F. She later married one of the Bunting family and was sister-in-law to Meg Bunting (née

Moore).

Miss Smith from the Wyck who also joined the W.A.A.F. later married Joe Pudney (above).

Mr Sayer was the local saddler and lived in Sycamore Cottages, Kelvedon Road.

Sydney and Clara Parker owned two general stores in Tollesbury and lived at The Stores, West Street. Their grand-daughter, Susie, remembers the shops as selling 'absolutely everything' and also remembers her grandfather as something of a romancer. Even in his last days in hospital he was telling the man in the next bed that he'd played football for Accrington Stanley. It was true that he had been gassed in WW1 but not true that he had been made a King's Corporal. When Margery gave him a copy of the book and he discovered that she had included this story (p. 188) he tore the page out and his family had to buy another copy to discover what had been said.

Ernie Chaplin is identified as assistant to Mr Doe the butcher. He may be connected to Irene Chaplin who lived at D'Arcy Cottage or to Frederick George Chaplin of White House Cottages, The Wyck, recorded as permanently absent on military/naval duties. Margery records a 'Mrs Chaplin's daughter's husband' as having joined up. His surname may be Rice.

Mr Dice, who lost the roof off his bungalow, lived in Tudwick but could have been at one of three separate addresses.

Members of the Osborne family, who ran the bus service, are recorded at five addresses in Tollesbury in 1939. Many people remember Ken Osborne chatting to his passengers as he drove.

Left: Harold Lufkin, Dick Rice, Joe Pudney and J Brady. (*Alan Smith*)

Below Left: Robert and Pauline Graves. (*Meg Bunting*)

Below Right: John and Dorothy Houlding's wedding. (*Dorothy Houlding*)

Bottom: P.Y.C., Jack Emeny, Norry Emeny and P.C. Dawes.

Right: Basil Golding and Arthur Moore. *(Meg Bunting)*

Below Left: Three of the Emeny siblings. *(Jack Birkin)*

Below Right: Three young wives: Violet Burmby, Nora Curtis and Dorris from Witham. *(Nora Curtis)*

Bottom: The Seabrook brothers circa 1933. *(Julia Seabrook)*

Appendix II

Diaries 1940 - 1942

1940

2nd March. Salter Relief Fund day. Em and Marcus over. Luard to lunch.

4th March. Getting on slowly – not working as fast I could wish.

5th March. Letters from Flo (remarkable effect of mine on her – minor personal triumph!) Bullough about Mrs Sydes, Postgate. Went to see Bea, found she has gone into King's poor girl. Phoned and wrote Bullough. Wrote Postgate. Bad afternoon's work but got going mid-evening. Norry still not sure about Maud's Venture's condition (foal). Sam to have 2/6d raise because of increased cost of living. He is at work on rockery. War news still confined to ships and German air attacks on them. Fall of Vipari seems imminent – general depression about it here. American press getting angry with Germany. Dorothy Thompson doing good work. Saw Ford in the street. Says he has complete scheme to set economic difficulties of country to rights. Wants to put it over on the radio with new comedian as medium! (Very <u>nice</u>, very tasty.)

6th March. Pip's appointment to R.A.S.C. arrived, a great wadge of papers. He is to report to Hounslow on March 18th. Do not like him going. Feel we're a three-legged stool with one leg going! Still what must be – am rather sad. Wrote Joslin's about the Adco. Did hardly any work. Later Pip came back from seeing Col. Campbell with good news. He's to go to Colchester for first three months and if we can get enough petrol can live here – am wildly relieved. Read two books for review.

7th March. Woodiwiss phoned to say that Maud's date was April 2nd for covering which means she ought to have foaled March 2nd - no sign of it yet. Wrote Cooee a card to tell her so. Did a little work, not enough but a bit. Got another book read. Fyfe (lieutenant in the Lights) came to dinner and gave Cocky enough information about uniform etc. Wrote Hiscot returning Bob's rates: phoned his desk and explained. The cottage was taken by friends of evacuees, not evacuees at all. The safe arrival of the *Queen Elizabeth* in N.Y. gave great satisfaction here and hysterical enthusiasm in the U.S.

8th March. Did a little but not enough. Pip to town buying his uniform (awful!) Maud definitely not to have a foal – Norry. Gassed myself sitting over hat cupboard when Mrs Fenner had over-disinfected the Baby House blankets. Read two books.

9th March. Wrote my reviews. Albert spent much of his day here talking about the car Pip needs. Cable from Reynolds asking for date. Said I'd get it in by early May. God I must work.

10th March. Sent off letters and reviews to Twine. Wrote Joslin's about fetching Adco. Got Pip to design rockery. Wrote Flo. Got Pip to instruct me in his job of D.F.A. which I'm taking over. Sad.

11th March. Pip to town. Put in morning on car business and A.R.P. and evacuation business. Worked hard all afternoon and evening on story. I like it. Hope to Almighty God it's all right.

12th March. Line from Reevo asking for a story. Wrote him. Pottered about with Pip until tea. Worked very hard afterward and finished chapter. Read it to him and we were both satisfied with it. News from Finland very dramatic and disturbing. It sounds as if Sweden has flunked the issue badly, a diplomatic victory for Germany I'm afraid.

13th March. Bad day for work. Worked out story but wrote little. Talk of Finland very depressing. News of O'Dwyer's assassination shocked everyone. Rockery coming on well. Beautiful warm day. Sent for plants.

14th March. Snow. Carter's uniform arrived. Dwye demanding permission to publish. Long letter from Meiggs. Did quite a good bit of work. To Graves to dinner. Saw James and Tita there.

15th March. Did a little more work but not a lot. Dr Macdonald called and stayed hours. Then McLaren came. Congratulations to P.Y.C. pouring in.

16th March. Spent whole day fooling with Pip in the sun. War news disturbing. New peace offer dangerous.

17th March. Wet day. Pip and I played patience and talked and packed and went to bed early.

18th March. Hitler meets Musso Brennan Pass. Pip joins up. Looks very fine in his lovely uniform. Mark and Jane come in. Grog out in A.R.P. Went to school to sign the register. Sent Meiggs a card and the American letter Mac sent me. Carter came in late having been drafted to Colchester thank God. He had gone up to town with Minney and they had agreed things look very black. He had also seen *Pinocchio* which he says is a classic. Did a bit of work myself but Ford came in with silly complaints about A.R.P. and wasted time.

19th March. Hitler's new peace terms announced early bulletin, devilishly clever but useless after Munich I should say. Pip to Colchester early. Masseuse came, also McLaren and Murrey in battledress, looks very young. Note from Watt to say he's sending me the Italian edition of *Shrouds.* It seems nuts we should be fighting. Did some work. Pip came in rather tired and hungry about 5.30. Afraid he may find it very depressing at first. Went to see Mark and Jane.

20th March. Woke to hear news of the bombing of the Sylt last night. Sounds to have been sensational show, only one of our planes down, thank God. Note from Dwye to say £250 coming April 1st but must be regarded as advance on first book of mine to come out. Wrote him accepting. Rockery going very nicely. Sam's only alarm that Hitler may bomb it. Did some more work. Pip came in much more cheerful and like himself. To bed early. Mrs Pearson (evacuee child's mother) came to get her form renewed. Only child so far to fill whole page – out of 225 forms!

21st March. Up at 7.30 as usual now. Did some gardening as soon as Pip had gone. Sam and I (and Roy, Sam's lad) put in sixty rock plants and looked them all up to see what they were. A.R.P. work for two hours and then Jane Degras came in with Mrs Clutton Brock about billeting. Wasted time with them until lunch. Review books from *Time & Tide*. Did a little work but not enough. Getting alarmed. Went to Tolleshunt Major First Aid demonstration mobile unit. Miss How and Dr Philip. Alarming if there is real danger. Brought Philip back for a drink and made friends with him.

22nd March. Pip had afternoon and evening off so did no work. Went to see Graves in evening.

23rd March. Wrote Mater and Miss How. Easter card from Flo! Worked very hard all day and finished chapter. It must be revised but there's a lot of it.

24th March. Pip had the day off so I did not work. It was a beautiful day just like spring. No war offensive although much expected.

25th March. Another glorious day. The Minneys and Thomas Moult came to lunch and stayed tea – very enjoyable. Gave Minney my idea for a pamphlet.

26th March. Worked on revision of the last chapter. Good letters from Reynolds. He is a magnificent agent. Says he's bullying Colliers to publish *Plumes*. I think he'll do it.

27th March. Up very early. Did A.R.P. and billeting in the morning. Finished revision of chapter in afternoon. Sent Cressy a p.c. Wrote Reynolds. Butcher offered me leg of Canterbury unrationed. Wrestled with conscience but refused. He then tells me that he's allowed to do it so succumbed. Apparently he had it 'over' and would not 'waste' it. Pip brought Wheatcroft 2/L to stay.

28th March. Read four books for review. Long day. Pip away all night on orderly duty.

29th March. Tried to get on with my reviews for *Time & Tide*. Did most of them. Pip back.

30th March. Pip had a half-day. A.R.P. Interference with work. Got reviews done. Trying to plan out story. Went round Tollesbury clearing up the mess.

31st March. Got reviews off. Planned out story to a certain extent.

1st April. Enjoyable but criminally wasteful day. Benneys came in the morning. Had to clear up some more A.R.P. muddle. Tried to map out chapter fairly completely. Went to T. Major gave 'em a pijaw and a pep talk. Bright and Motts came in.

2nd April. A.R.P. morning (this is taking too much time). Worked hard afternoon. Col. Cockburn and Drewett came to tea. Tried to get a bit done. Pip brought Lieut. Chamberlain in for evening and to stay.

3rd April. Worked fairly well all day but not doing enough. To Tollesbury for County Exercise with P.Y.C. Wildly funny. Met little Peter Gager, a child who will get on! Tollesbury F.A. Services very good indeed.

4th April. Wasted day – we shall starve. A.R.P. morning. Em to lunch. Man called Owen from Knights to tea (rather an ordeal). Saw Pauline, also Mark and Jane. No work.

5th April. Up early. A.R.P. Billeting. Mark all morning. Also awkward mission Mrs Christie on behalf of Salter Relief – successful. Got down to work in afternoon. Had to see Jessie after tea. Got down to work all evening, very satisfactory. Bed very tired just after eleven. Pip phoned, seems very happy. Miss him and am going to find it rather a strain when he's ordered off somewhere.

6th April. Watt sent cash. [...] Wrote him – also Dwye, Twino, Nerney. Billeting officer and Motts re Knights. Mrs Gilbertson and husband appeared – memo their cash Wednesday or Thursday. Did some work but nowhere near enough (going nuts). Mrs Christie to tea. Motts came in. Saw Jessie again re Salter Relief Fund.

7th April. Carter had the day off – up late. Wrote A.R.P. letters. Ronnie came in, also later Pip's Major, two Sergeants and a Corp. Rather heavy going – one Sergeant asked me if I used to hunt when I was young! That'll learn me.

8th April. Britain mined Norwegian ports. A maddening day – could not get to work for more than ten minutes. <u>Everybody</u> came in or rang up about everything. Mark, Mrs Gilbertson and husband (three times) Albert. Mrs Hush rang up for hours. Norry and Mrs Moore. Pip came in about 6.30. Went to bed early. Slept badly.

9th April. Woke to hear first rumour that Norway was at war with Germany and Denmark invaded. Tried hard all day to work. Still trouble from evacuees. Story not going. News ominous. Later in the day news still bad. Norway ratting. Acquired a short wave set.

10th April. War news cheering up. Norway standing firm. Billeting officer (Sennett) over, stayed to lunch. Did a bit but my god it's difficult. Mrs Brock to tea and stayed. Went to pm meeting on the Incident. Lasted from 6.30 to 10 pm. Very stormy. Fantastic performance. Old Cockburn put a remarkable display of muddled thinking, aided and abetted by a fellow called Wedd who took the biscuit for chumply inefficiency. Bright livid, Carter furious. All really funny – Enjoyed it like fun.

11th April. Trying to get down to work. More interruptions than ever. Phoned Cockburn and made my peace, also Drewett. Mrs Brock in, Mrs Gilbertson in. Carter returned unexpectedly at lunch. Spent afternoon working out story with him. Going slowly nuts but story okay. Churchill's pronouncement in House – not so good as rumours but still pretty good. Saw Jane and Mark and Mrs B. about Limesbrook. McLaren, Motts and Bright over in evening. [...] All barmy.

12th April. Massage girl came. More A.R.P. Got Mrs Gilbertson off. Got down to some work and was going quite nicely but had to lay off when Mrs Brock came in and then P.Y.C. News very exciting still. To Tolleshunt Knights to a Mobile Unit exercise. Not all bad. Met the celebrated Craig-Simpson act.

13th April. Got some more work done. Fairly satisfied but would like to polish it. Read a book for review. Albert came in and gossiped all the evening. Dreadful waste of time. Carter orderly officer, not back.

14th April. Pip back early with four of his sergeants and corporals. They stayed till after tea. News terrific. Read him my story but his mind not really on it naturally. Bed early.

15th April. In morning did all A.R.P. stuff. Rewrote whole of chapter and got it good. McLaren came to discuss exercise. Pip on orderly duty again so read book for review.

16th April. More A.R.P. News came that Mrs Todd's husband has gone down in the *Thistle*, poor soul. Tried to work out new chapter. Got it properly planned at least. Pip came in early – no real work on paper. That boy sent me his play, haven't looked at it at all.

17th April. A mad day. Constant interruptions. Just finished letters and getting down to work when hairdresser came. Hair all wet when Mrs Tuohy came – very worried poor soul about her boy with the B.E.F. in Norway. Hardly time to collect thoughts before lunch. Just back at desk when Margaret Wilson came (all A.R.P) Stayed tea, Went back to work and Mrs Seabrook came (school). Just back to work when P.Y.C. came home. Read a review book. Tired – but managed to get a chapter clearer. Feel all this outside activity is stimulating although worrying.

18th April. Got a little bit of work done but quite good. Read a review book.

19th April. A.R.P. and reviews ready. Mrs Robertson and daughter also vicar to tea. To dinner with Cocky to the Youngs in Tiptree – not much bottle.

20th April. Wrote reviews at speed. Carter brought his corporal Barrington and an A.T. to tea. Malcolm Easton came down. Heard explosion as North London factory went up. Guns going all night. Degras came in, Jane truculent.

21st April. Got reviews typed and cleaned and dispatched. Also Tollesbury exercise for Friday. Malcolm and Carter and Grog talking all day. Saw Degras new room. First real bright day of spring.

22nd April. Carter and his corporal [...] off reconnoitring. Long note from Meiggs who has joined Ministry of Supply. Malcolm went back. Line from Cooee. Going to send mares to stud this week. James came in. Wrote Meiggs a brief note. Did a little work. Carter back early but he went off again after tea. Did a little more work. Carter home with young Young. Raid on in evening but no warnings. Got Carter to bed with difficulty.

23rd April. Did a little bit of work but not enough. Nurse came in. P.Y.C. back early-ish. A glorious warm sunny day. Horses went off to Corbett. Valentine took Fox and Luke away.

24th April. Not nearly enough work done. James came and did some tables (casualty) for me. Had to go (forced by a telephone call from Mrs Golding) to the Annual Conservative meeting at the village hall. Good copy. Hairdresser. Cocky home full of the new mess room they are fixing up. Felt very much off the chain and rather lost.

25th April. Wrote practically all day. Glorious weather. News from Norway not quite so good – alarming. Bright and McLaren came in the evening. Pip back full of beans. Must be off very early tomorrow. Bed early.

26th April. Pip up very early also me. Did a bit of work. To Tollesbury in the evening to a Mobile Unit practise.

27th April. Did a bit of work. Robin came down. Pip home early. News a little bit better. Everyone expects air raids.

28th April. Pip home all day so got up late. Worked in afternoon and after tea. To James and Tita for dinner. Back round about eleven. Not much in the way of news. Anxious times. Getting the wind up about the story. Wish to God I wasn't so slow.

29th April. Did a bit of work and a useful piece of working out. Robin went back. Beau out in field alone for first time settled down well. Went to Mark's and Jane's with P.Y.C. Met Clutton Brocks. Very second rate.

30th April. Did a bit of work with great difficulty. Read two more review books. To Graves in evening. Heard terrific explosion about 11.15 (German plane coming down over Clacton) with bombs.

1st May. Sent *The World Aflame* to Cotterill & Cromb for Mother.

2nd May. Did some work – slowly getting on. Certain amount of A.R.P-ing.

3rd May. Worked hard all day. To Totham exercise, not too awful. Home early. Pretty bad.

4th May. Did my review. Pip back middle of afternoon with Cpt. Chamberlain and 2nd Lieut. Robinson – very pleasant interlude but not getting on.

5th May. Dictated reviews. News disconcerting. I must work, getting hysterical. Told Miss Moore no more reviews till June.

6th May. Put in a good day's work. Wrote young man (Howard Clarke) about his play on *Police at the Funeral.* Mrs Todd and Miss Bright to tea. Pip came in for a few minutes with 2nd Lt Vials. Pip back very late. News disquieting, looks as if Chamberlain will have to go.

7th May. Struggled all day with story. Occasional and irritating A.R.P. interruptions. Debate in House seems to have been very stormy. Was not impressed by Chamberlain's explanations.

8th May. Put in a steady day after some irritating A.R.P. stuff. Pip home to dinner. Went to Goldings in the evening, nice people. Political debate very exciting and alarming. Chamberlain shows up very badly. Churchill saves the government. Small majority.

9th May. Worked hard all day. Pip home late. Em and Marcus turned up briefly.

10th May. Woke to hear the 7am news. Belgium and Holland invaded, also Luxembourg. News right down. Grog making solemn preparations for air raids. Took the precaution of putting my precious story in biscuit tin. Terrific excitement. Pip confined to barracks on duty. Joyce and a Wren down.

11th May. Joyce here. Lot of coming and going. No P.Y.C. News sensational. Parachute troops used extensively in Holland. No work.

12th May. Pip home for the night. News still alarming.

13th May. Read late to Joyce who was impressed for the first time I remember. Children back to barracks. Saw Seabrooks about First Aid, not at all helpful. Order through to keep post manned and look out for parachute troops.

14th May. Reynolds called about *Plumes* 'Can they put in war atmosphere?' Replied 'yes', only thing to do. Trying to work. Orders to Wardens to patrol from dawn to dusk. Called up to explain my cable. '*Colliers* ruining construction' suggested coal miners sabotaging. Carter home for two hours, very tired. Tried to work late. Wrote Malcolm, finished chapter, bed at 10.50.

15th May. Grog called me at 4 to take my watch. Heard news of Holland's capitulation on 7 o'clock news. Miss Harvey – hair girl. Mrs Wilson et fam. all came. Nearly hysterical with temper at delay – very, very silly.

Pip phoned to say he would not be back. [...] about Tollesbury ambulance. Did a bit of work at last. Heard Old Queen of Holland – sounded like Boadicea.

16th May. Letter from S Paws asking for a story (!) Wrote him. Also wrote Watt to stir up Lane for cash. Trying to work. James came. Drewitt phoned. Bennet came! Yellow warning. Got down to work at last and did a bit (it's good). Pip home – very depressed, talking invasion. Very vivid memories of '15.

17th May. Getting my First Aid gang together in morning. Working afternoon and evening. First Aid class. Drewitt very good indeed – Pip late. James and Tita came in. News a little better, not good.

18th May. Held up, wasted time. Writing M. and C. News so disconcerting <u>had</u> to talk to someone even if only on paper. Jane and Mark incredibly depressing. Pip came home unexpectedly, seems a little happier. Agreed we must take whatever comes and meet in the Elysian Fields.

19th May. Wrote letters Granny and Em and First Aid. Went to Tollesbury checking stores with Drewitt. Saw Parker and Palmer. Odd people but nice. Worked like a slave from lunch until 11.30pm. Churchill made a fine 'backs to the wall' speech at 9 o'clock. A strange and terrifying time to be living in but ennobling times if the <u>mind</u> can take the pace.

20th May. My 36th birthday. Had a peach of an idea for the final twist in the book in the middle of the night. There was a lot of ominous 'banging off' too. Wireless down for a long time. Got down to work in the morning. Pip came in the afternoon. War news fishy. Weygand very popular, everyone expects a counter offensive and then hell's delight over here. Spent a peaceful evening walking in the garden but went up to Sayers with Pip to see the new pistol holster he is making for him. A very sad, worrying world. Don't feel very brave but astonishingly fatalistic. It must be age. Handkerchief from Mater, very small pair of stockings from Pauline, bless her.

21st May. Sent corrected proofs to Watt. Wrote Phil (who tells me poor old Tub is dead). Mater, Pauline, Drewitt, Mrs Hirsh. News terrifying. Germans in Amiens and Arras! Worked very, very hard as well. Did quite a lot. Pip home with an awful cold. Looked after him. Had two yellow warnings.

22nd May. A.R.P. phone calls and letters. James came, also McLaren, took until teatime. Tried to work but have caught P.Y.C's cold and feel frightful. Went to bed early. Heard the new bill on the radio. Its powers are terrific. I wonder if it's to be the beginning of new slavery. Germans on the coast of France.

23rd May. Such a dreadful cold couldn't work. A lot of soldiers (the 9th Cameronians) turned up on the doorstep. We're to have 120 on the meadow and a captain and 3 subs in the house. A nice major, others just army (polo and blood and can they see some action?). Cold so bad had to go to bed.

24th May. Cold still bloody. All the soldiers came. Did a little work. Pip came home, says he's being moved somewhere secret – God knows when I'll see him again. War news horrific. Nerney rang up. First Aid class. Heard the King's very fine speech, the 'smile on your lips, heads held high and we'll not fail' stuff.

25th May. Trying to work. Pip went off, rather sad. Nothing much to report until now, midnight. Went to bed at 12 and had been asleep for about two hours when heard a great rumpus and came down to hear that the Germans were attempting to land in Kent. Made some tea for the soldiers and only now while I'm waiting to hear about messages etc. have time to record that my reaction is pure astonishment and anger. Cheek. Absolute cheek. Gave soldiers permission to use the washhouse for baths.

26th May. Information seems to have been faulty last night or else they were driven off. News a little better. Carter home for an hour. Very tired indeed. Phoned Phil who sounded crackers. Had to go to bed I was so tired. Up at teatime.

27th May. Trying to work. Maddening cold. News appalling. Fixing First Aid at Little Totham. Pip home.

28th May. Terrible news about Belgian King ratting. Feeling bloody ill but trying to work. Sat up with Grog talking to soldiers.

29th May. Still trying to work and going very slowly.

30th May. Letter from Meiggs and young Phil. Certain amount of spy excitement everywhere. Did a bit of work. Cold has turned to a sinus – very painful.

31st May. Did a little bit of work. [...] First Aid class. News tremendous. How dreadful that they should have been under-equipped.

1st June. Pc from Twino put wind up me. Did terrific day's work. Good stuff. Frightened but only under the surface. Surface almost placid. The captain asked if his wife could come down. Said yes.

2nd June. Pip turned up for seven or eight hours leave. So no work. Discussed story which he liked. Seemed less worried than I am which is good.

3rd June. Worked hard all day. Gradually getting on. Only one (billeting) interruption.

4th June. Worked all day steadily. Very tired. News remarkable – 350,000 men saved from Flanders.

5th June. Sitting all day at work not getting any done. The gallant captain's wife turned up. A sort of army Betty Underwood. Ronnie came in. Quite a good evening.

6th June. Got rid of the Army lady after lunch. New soldiers came – King's Own Scottish Borderers to replace the Cameronians. Emmie and Marcus came in. Granny has been spy-hunting on Foulness Island. Finally McLaren came in. Cox of Box and Cox rang up to ask if I'd broadcast tomorrow and I said no. Girling ring up.

7th June. Worked very hard. Nearly done. Joyce came very fit and well. She's a Chief Petty Officer (!) Air raids all night.

8th June. Read late to Joyce. She's very enthusiastic. Pip came home at teatime. Very glad to see him. New officer (a ranker) very offensive about A.R.P. Put him wise firmly but gently.

9th June. Pip went off early. Very hot. News not good at all. Worked a bit. Joyce back to Town. Worked late.

10th June. Worked a very little. Worried. Getting house ready for dinner party. Italy came in. Bad news from France. Pip and Capt. Chamberlain and Mrs came. Not too nice a woman. They had to go at 9. Rather alone.

11th June. Worked like a nig all day and practically finished the whole thing except for polishing. Worked till midnight – news a worry. Mark and Jane to say goodbye. He's going into a factory training school.

- - -

18th June. France gives in.

- - -

21st June. Cressy came down. Air raid. Bombs at Wigboro'. I was rather frightened.

- - -

27th June. James came in to say that a friend had seen the *Dunkirk* in the Solent. I hope so. Bread and butter note from Cressy.

- - -

2nd July. Pip sent word in the early hours that the Ides of March fall on the 3rd this year. Soldiers filling sandbags. Wrote letters and made bandages – and waited. Feeling like a fight in a way. Think we'll win. Very hot and ominous.

- - -

6th July. Still waiting. Nothing happening.

7th July. A wasted day. Wrote a few letters. Listened to the news bulletins which seemed a little better. Phil sent all his furniture down here by three terrible toughs. Pip phoned. Feel rather lonely.

- - -

10th July. Gardened. Read book for review. Major Tritton came bringing two floosies. Philip's daughter and Oh Findlay

- - -

7th August. Gave Reynolds American book rights and powers of attorney.

8th August. Cable from Reynolds. *Colliers* publishing *Purse* ten instalments Sept 17th ending Nov 9th

- - -

17th August. Sam's wages went up

- - -

11th October. Small Pig Keepers Council, Turville Heath, Henley on Thames. Mr Ford. Leaflets. At least ten members.

- - -

20th October. Pip came over in beautiful new boots. Very full of a mine which just missed him on Thursday (night I was worried about him) and a Hun plane which disintegrated over HQ apparently without a shell being fired at it. ('They've found five feet so far.') I was so very glad to see him and very proud of him. Found him anxious for leave and glad to be home. Went to see Bobbie and Pauline. Pauline making socks and pullovers for the Home Guard and wardens. They were wondering if they ought to move because they were so near the church. Afraid it might be objective. Pip got a phone call from H.Q. which frightened us as he's not supposed to be over here, but it was okay and he went off about 10. I went to bed and decided if they were going to kill me it was no good thinking about it.

21st October. Woke up with bombs falling all over the place and an awful whistling sound which I took to be incendiaries. Fell out of bed and lay quiet. Got up and went downstairs. Great excitement. Wires down. Grog's hand cut. Bill and Basil C. came in, also Herbert, Cliff, Hammond, the Tollesbury wardens and 'Me' of course – did the telephoning and tied Joe up – Granny ok. One very near the church and Johnnie Reynolds's windows broken. Eatons bombed one each side but no harm done. All this at ten to one. Was in bed by 3.30, slept like a log. Memo – see to First Aid post. Got down to the book again. Am on a better track I think. Fell asleep after tea, went to bed early. Two bombs just before I went to sleep but decided they were miles away.

22nd October. Slept like a log. Heard this morning that 5 bombs dropped on Old Hall at 5am. No one here heard a sound which seems barmy. Saw the Rev. M. Hitchcock wild and fierce as a coot. Had to tick Sam off for making a fuss.

- - -

6th November. Nothing left but the S. individual because the situation was <u>new</u> – to civilisation. Barbary has never yet had as good or better weapons than civ. Situation quite <u>new</u>. Therefore individual counts – elementary.

- - -

20th November. Sent *The Oaken Heart* to Paul R.

21st November. Called Malcolm. Bombs last night at Tudwick. Don't feel very well.

22nd November. Woke up in a flap about Pip in the night. Very unusual indeed for me. Hope to God he's all right. Went down to see Suzy Emeny. Poor old dear is dying fast. Vic is very cut up but extraordinarily practical. She really is broken-hearted but she is arranging to move the wine and jams etc from the front room where the old thing must lie. (They can't get a coffin downstairs and it means taking out the windows). Couldn't think of anything to buy so I gave Vic £1. Very sad. Ought to be hundreds of kids – so there are in other branches of the family, but D'Arcy is a sterile spot.

1941

1st January. Had cable from Reynolds. 'Received *Oaken Heart* M.S. intensely interesting will cable after Doubleday reading.' Also letter from Malcolm. *Plumes* sold 7,000 so far and a sweet press. Disappointed but banking on *Purse*. Think he's wise. Granny has bad cold after shock. Poor Twino phoned. His mother (84) has developed neuritis after the shock of the bombing (which killed six of the family and wounded two – two including mother escaped). I said I'd take John if ever T. wanted to race off down to Cheltenham to see her. Made a very fine cheese. See Smuts predicts Armageddon over England. Bandia can't hold out long. Fump came in very anxious to make friends – did so.

2nd January. Rather a depressing day. Em arrived with Marcus bringing geese I'm to buy. Bitterly cold. Granny's bronchitis bad. I'm wondering if I'm nursing her properly! Em wants all the furniture she left here 5 years ago, also the stuff Joyce and Phil sent down. Had made up her mind I was going to be difficult – had the row anyway even though I was compliant. I gave her £3 and she began to pipe down a little. Bang about 9 – great excitement over the telephone, someone seemed to think it might be a plane down. Em and Marcus to bed very early indeed. Em sleeping in Granny's room. Heard a wallop or two in the night. Paid Em's interest and Marcus's 30/- for the two geese.

3rd January. Em and M. off very early. Em taking Granny's wireless although they do not know if they've got the current over there or not and they're not moving in yet. In their excitement they left a case containing Marcus's cassocks! Howling excitement over two mines and the wallop last night. One had burst in mid air and the other just broke up at Tudwick. Grog and McLaren had an awful time watching Sergeant A and two mad policemen pulling the thing about, setting light to it, stamping about in the hole and generally rubbing themselves with this stuff which is thought to cause incurable skin trouble. The bomb squad came and were as terrified by this as we were. Made friends with them (Lieut. and Sergt.) and sat and quaked while they brought a lovely dubious bit in with them.

4th January. So cold and snowy. Christine put off her trip until tomorrow. Terrific explosion at mid-day. Miss Withers's house damaged and many windows bust – naval squad letting off our mine! James came. Granny a bit better. Rather tired and a bit depressed in spite of myself.

5th January. Christine went home. Cooked and looked after Granny. Bitterly cold. Bandia fell. Heard at midnight. Grog came up to tell me. I was reading Compton McKenzie's *Red Tapeworm* in bed. Very funny.

6th January. Abbots Hall bombed yesterday. People having christening and carried on. Hope they don't call the kid Bombazine. More cooking and nursing. Very cold. Snow getting thicker. Geese absurd during air raid warnings. Hear Crittalls was bombed again and people machine-gunned in the streets (Witham). Too cold to bother about the various bangs. News from Libya very warming anyway. Albert came in with a dreadful tale of fungus which has attacked the Wheatsheaf and is eating it all up. Mrs McGrath had the same trouble in the other house. It seems to fasten on to everything and grow like mad. A sort of house-cancer. Frightened me more than anything else for months. Mines in the reservoir going off in the frost. Finished book – end not so good.

7th January. Awful headache, fear I've got a cold. Granny a little better but very sorry for herself poor dear. More cooking. Christine came back. Read *Kings' Masque* by Evan John – very able.

8th January. Cooking and cleaning all day. Tired.

9th January. Enthusiastic wire from Reynolds. Has sold M. J. the yarn for £250 advance and good royalties. Wrote Pip and prepared warm corner in the breakfast room in which to work. Air activity round about at night – probably Mersea got it.

10th January. Nice cable from Malcolm. Still working about. Did one review.

11th January. Letter from Pip. He seems all right. Miss him considerably. Also last minute book from *Time & Tide.* Had to read it quick, do the reviews and get them in the post. Attended to Granny who is better. Sewed, went to bed and read opening of D'Arcy book. Queer stuff but very honest.

12th January. Trying to start book again.

13th January. Joyce phoned midday that she was arriving in evening on embarkation leave. Joyce arrived very excited and fit, bringing me a magnificent Duffel coat. She's off to Singapore for 2 years or for the duration. Excited [...] all evening.

14th January. To London on early bus. Terrific day's shopping. No cotton to be had save at exorbitant prices and then scarce. Bought one good dress to be copied by Chinese out there. Treated her (7 guineas) at Marshall's. Very good style. Shirt, shorts and clip on scarf in yellow porous weave. Went everywhere. Harrods [...] (evening dress cotton (salvage!) for 10/- a beauty.) Saw Nerney who says Heinemann are very keen on the *Purse.* London very knocked about but wonderfully normal. Shops by no means crowded but very understaffed. Came home tired but satisfied with adventure.

15th January. Letter from Pip posted Monday. Thinks he may go 'on the 15th'. Don't like to think about it. Wrote him just in case I can catch him. Em writes she wants her furniture on Thursday. Spent long good day washing, ironing and marking.

16th January. Em and Marcus came. Collected her furniture. Sorted Joyce's clothes. Great upheaval but there you are so to speak. Granny cheerful.

17th January. Went to Colchester with Joyce and Christine. Shopped all morning and Joyce and I to pictures. (*Gaslight* – not good but newsreel of Eygpt impressive.) Chrissie wouldn't come.

18th January. Packed and washed and ironed. Man called Captain Nelson came from S. lights.

19th January. Got Joyce ready. Shall miss her very much but she ought to have a great time. Cooee wired to say could she come?

20th January. Joyce went early. Am rather ill. Afraid it's flu. Feel so awfully giddy. Stayed in bed until lunch but am not much use. Cooee came down on late bus. Seems very fit.

21st January. Long bad day. Cooee just the same. Felt ill. School managers' meeting in the evening. Bed after.

22nd January. A bit better but swollen glands and an awful cold. Had to put everyone off. The photographer and hairdresser and massage girl. Cooee assing about. Had to put things to her fairly clearly.

23rd January. Tobrook good news. Wire from Pip. Very mysterious and means he's away I'm afraid. Feel very shaky about it and depressed. My poor [...]. Edward and his wife came in. She's much better.

24th January. Cooee still fooling about and making trouble. Whispers everywhere. Feeling ill.

25th January. Getting better. Cooee up to mischief.

26th January. Cooee away.

27th January. Letter from Cocky. Never more delighted in my life – still in England. Margaret whispering to Christine – full details of Cooee's underhandedness (apparently senseless) carry out. Bored with her.

28th January. Getting better. Reading review books.

29th January. To Colchester with Christine to see *Great Dictator* (wrapped up very cautiously). Rather disappointed but funny in parts.

30th January. ARP-ing, school-ing, cooking, letter writing, reading

31st January. Trying to get down to work – very difficult.

1st February. Letter from Jane Degras. They've moved to London – why's that?

(diary then blank from February 2nd to April 27th)

April 28th. Cressy went back looking much better. Mrs Wilson and Margaret came in about the jam (borrow baby house table) Trying to work. Nerney rang up about book. Likes it. 'Me' came in – says military have scotched Sennet's scheme at Tollesbury thank God. No visitors save blood relations. Interesting. He thought Churchill had lost vigour and had something serious on his mind. Chamberlain no good but what did you expect – look at his Dad. War to last four years. Endurance – well no question who can last longest. French ought to be shot. 6,000,000 under arms and gave in! Pro-Germans in the government (French). What a night for the armistice! Cut his telephone wire. Christine on aims 'well we can trust each other.'

- - -

18th May. Roby de Cup buried. Norry very excited as they had the grand undertaker (who married a sister of Dick Rice's wife) in to see them. Spent all day getting the *Heart* off to the US. I feel it's very good and sincere but you can never tell how it's going to take people. Am so tired and dizzy I can't bear myself. I've written myself silly.

19th May. Spent the whole day tidying up my papers. Am stiff in every joint. Got the stuff in the post. Wrote M. and T. and decided to send the yarn to Bobby and Pauline to see if they think anyone will mind being mentioned.

20th May. My birthday. Spent it clearing out the drawing room. Pauline phoned to say she was reading the book to Bobby and they liked it.

21st May. Christine went to Eight Ash Green. They had bombs over there at Lexden. Farmhouse got hit but the woman put the kids to bed among the dust the next night just as usual. Mucked about. Feel very tired. Wrote Phil, Pip, Joyce. Got the chair covers back. Battle of Crete going on. Sounds terrific. Vet came to see Valentine's foal 'joint evil' (some sort of septicaemia) does not hold out holds. A pity. Very pretty little thing. No air activity at all. Wrote Watt and C.S.E. about *The Oaken Heart.* Coldish day. Everything still very late. Lilac not out and the bird cherry still in full flower. Narcissi everywhere. No flowers at all on the china peony this year. Bed fairly early – very tired but healthily so at last.

22nd May. Up at seven. Letter from P.R.R. (wrote him) and from A.R.P. as usual. Ashcroft says foal should be out. Vet told Norry foal should be in. Write letters and attended to billeting etc all the morning. Grog still deciding when he shall go into Colchester and give himself up as a soldier. Shall miss the old basket. Nerney rang up ecstatic about the book. That's good.

23rd May. Up early. Spring-cleaned the angel room. Pauline sent word she and Bobby like the book and they don't think anyone could mind being in it. They'd like to be in it more. Went down there after dinner. Saw Simon who looks an old man. Bobby is old and shaky but very alert in mind. Find we've got under the skin there with the book – there was a new intimacy and a great friendliness. Came in and saw Cliff and Johnnie and Grog. Late to bed. Bobby told me about young Bobby Jackson going up to see his parents (on leave). When he reached Curzon Street he found the house a heap of bricks and both old people dead. Sam thinking of making us a dugout. He and Christine, after seeing the week's *Picture Post* and hearing the news of Crete (is P.Y.C. there?) were discussing how one could get worked up enough to kill a parachutist or a German soldier. Chrissie thought she could do it if she had to! Grog went to Colchester to 'give himself up'.

Recruiting sergeant told him he must write to the labour exchange
– does so.

24th May. Wrote long letter to Malcolm. Slept (found it cheered
me up). Motts came in. Pauline sent book back – I think they
liked it. Motts said that in the last few days public opinion had
changed. Said that the tales of the Germans screaming for help in
the seas around Crete made people grin whereas a few months
ago they'd have been saying isn't it terrible. He says he'd been
lecturing on invasion etc and found people more prepared to
defend themselves with anything. Sam and Christine and Grog
talking nostalgically about flower shows – we intend to start the
D'Arcy one again after the war if we can. The foal is not better.
First mushroom sun today – a good rain. Bad news of *Hood*'s
sinking – we can ill spare her (9 o'clock news). Good news later.

25th May. A depressing wet day. News grim. *Hood* gone. Greek
king leaving Crete. Still we're fighting it out. Christine made me
send S.O.S. to Albert to clean chimney in the breakfast room.
Wrote Pip. Decided to go to London tomorrow and take Christine with me. Grog against it but feel it's ridiculous to funk it as I
need to go and if I don't show up and see Watt and Co there'll
be trouble I'm certain. I feel for goodness sake don't lets throw
away another ideal with the bathwater of snobbery this time. It's
not snobbish to want to be better than you are – the snobbery
surely lies in making a mistake about what is better. There has
been a great lowering of ideals in the last forty years – there's nothing new about that. One generation of 'nobs' lets the standard
down and so leads a whole crop astray. That seems to happen
regularly. It's the surge of genuine idealists coming up that puts the
aristocracy back on the rails again as a rule and I see no reason
why that should not happen this time. This time we are doing the
thing thoroughly and discovering the way to live pretty well from
scratch and it seems to me that we're [...]. God is returning like
courage without fancy dress. If it can but survive its birth pangs this
should be a very grand new world.

26th May. Christine and I arrived in London appalled by ride through city. Ceased to recognise the place and suddenly came on the Holborn Viaduct! Christine put flat in order (looks charming) and I saw Watt who was friendly - let Lusty have a copy of the *Heart*. Saw Tegan (gone ecclesiastical county) who admitted that the raid seen from Highgate was horrific. Said that the 'best people' in Highgate thought that going to a shelter was 'low' (!) so sat solemnly in their houses through it all! Took Nerney to Frascati's. Much more normal than earlier in the year. London very friendly but unchanged [...] save for the awful destruction. No strain as I remember it in 1917-18. Took Christine to see Maud and Ted at the Regent's Palace. Had some nice food with them. Refugee waitresses, gentlewomen, Czech and Polish. Polish army staying there. New poor. R.N. officer and his thundering English rose. Was very glad there were no sirens, I found.

27th May. Had my hair waved. Air raid casualty in next cubicle having her hair done to hide her scalp scar. To Ivy - unchanged. Even the food. [...] Leslie Banks, all the gang. News went round *Bismarck* sunk. Woman on door selling flags for animal casualties of raids. Went into shop in Soho and bought a pound of ginger (unheard of). Coffee shop just escaped an awful crater. Decided to have a party - rang Jane, Mark, Bocco and Cressy. Lusty came in delirious with joy about the book. Said he could have it. Party a riot. Boccarina couldn't come but Bocco the 'old poet' and musician. New wizard idea: 'Sun used to shine through the old church window, now old church window no longer there but sun still shines through it - see it?' Rough yet but see it? Cressy sad at first but cheered up enormously. Found he was on the roof all through the last blitz. Doesn't like it - it's awful to think about. Was again glad that there were no sirens. Jackdaw near the museum scratched and frightened me.

28th May. Decided to come home as spending too much. Christine and I had one rush round the shops. Saw Selfridges, Whiteleys and Harrods. Harrods worse than anywhere. Got some lemon juice (genuine) for Pauline and one for us. Also a tin each of Bath Olivers. Brought Nerney home with us for a quiet night and bombs fell all evening (far away). Found censor had cut out everything about unexploded bombs and mines. Five pages in all. Nice letter from censor.

29th May. Spent day getting censored bit back in shape again. Got it right and sent it off. Very tired. Christine spring-cleaning breakfast room. Nerney here.

30th May. Lusty very excited about the book. Wants it to go through at once. Sent it to printers etc. Very busy day. Edward and his wife came in.

31st May. Betty came down with family papers. Looks much older. Edward and his wife to dinner. He spilt ink all over the green Chinese carpet in the drawing room and left us to try and get it up.

1st June. Up early mucking about with oxalic acid on the carpet. Got ink out at last. Talked to Betty, made her a dress, gave her some shoes of Joyce's and set her up by washing her skirt. A helpless kid. So frightened of missing something that she misses everything. She's going into Women's American Ambulance – one of the snoopist shows. Feel it may suit her all right really. Good heart. Wrote Meiggs. Betty produced the opal ring mater left me and also the lucky [...] ring and some brooches. Told her to take whatever she wanted and leave the rest. Clothes rationing came in. Great surprise. Lucky I bought so much stuff. Secretly elated and stimulated by it all. Half gods are going fast.

2nd June. Got up early. Pressed Betty's skirt. Got her off safely with flowers for aunts etc. Finished letter M. Wrote Cressy suggesting next weekend or 20th not 14th. Wrote Maud. Cut out a new nightdress. Edward and wife came in. Stayed late.

- - -

24th June. Depressed walked about. Bat got in my room.

25th June. Airmail letter from Phil. Bless him. Wrote letters. Housework. Inez and Aunt Jane and Terry came over. Note from Reevo. *Strand* apparently dead. Russia doing fairly well.

26th June. Albert sweeping chimneys. Complains food short. Encouraging note Nerney - Tillie very keen on book. Wrote letters A.R.P., Reynolds etc, Jane. Russians keeping it up. Colossal. Our turn next - once more.

- - -

26th September Pip's birthday. Ten days since I heard of him. Seems a lifetime. Good news book U.S.

- - -

4th October. Norry came in bursting with gossip (silly Mrs B and Major P discovered dining in a hotel together - why not?) but went on to tell me about his mother finding the suicide in the old coastguard's house. All were frightened but she put his gun in his coffin. Why? said I. She said because it was his weapon and he should have it. Also as he was a Roman Catholic she put a penny and a piece of new bread in his hand. Sounds odd - must ask James.

- - -

7th December. Heard the news in the 6 o'clock bulletin. Japan attacks. Listened to the 12. Seems true.

- - -

10th December. Went into Colchester with Christine by bus. Had lunch with Twino by appointment. Saw news of *Prince of Wales* and *Repulse* in the window of the *Essex County Standard*. Could not assimilate it. Twino drunk. Rather shocked and alarmed me. Saw Sir Fred and Duffy. Twino says no married couple intact in the area. All seemed a bit tawdry and dull. Not amusing anymore. Town full and fairly cheerful. Air raid warning mid-day. Young John has to register. Judy in town, wants to go abroad. Came home by 4. Found Sam startled by news and Mrs Unwin frankly excited. Read Scott's *Journal.*

11th December. Cable from Reynolds. 'Malcolm delighted to publish thrillers permitting serious novel another house. You are a genius.' So that's okay. Now I've burned my boats. What a life. P.R.R. just isn't noticing the war I see. News came through 2300 survivors, thank god. Japs pulled very smart one. Nasty people. Feel war may last twenty years now. Went out and looked at holes for apple trees. It's a bit of a gesture but my new motto is 'I Stay'. Wrote about twenty letters. Interesting news about Cunningham's arrival in [...]. (Auchinleck seems to have the idea anyway.) News Russia good. Mrs Todd came in and wasted an hour. Hear Mrs Eve is very ill again. The Seabrooks have their share of troubles. Williams (A.R.P.) came in too. Mrs Husk making trouble again. Read some more of Scott. Just like any other hack writer's story but on a deluxe scale. Ours is not an art to abuse. Pegasus is a bad screw as all bloods are. Pompous observation result of reading Lockhart.

- - -

16th December. Collection of letters from Pip. Poems and drawings. All very good. Miss him very much. Finding life a bit of a sweat. Only thing to do is to shut mind and look ahead. Cabled Joyce, wrote Pip again. Went down to school and gave out my annual 6d prize – one to everyone and an extra for good marks. First Aid lecture at village school again. Did a little work. Apple trees being planted.

17th December. Letter from Meiggs who got married last Saturday. I wish him very well. There's a lot of good in him. Also note from Income Tax. Vast sums demanded. Must make it somehow. News from Singapore alarming. Better from Libya. Am only wretched <u>under</u> the skin. Actual life very quiet and peaceful.

1942

1st January. CABLE from Pip. Thank God <u>All right</u>. Finished my letter Dr. Lindsay. Wrote Reynolds. Pip. Aunt [...]. Wired Pip. News bad Singapore.

2nd January. Wasted day. Wrote necessary letters, fooled about – amazing how I can waste time. At desk all day.

3rd January. Another day in which I did not enough. News from Singapore bad. Lovely letter from Pip written in November. Made me realise again how much I miss him. Unsettled. Sam's wages went up to £3. All apple trees in.

4th January. More bad news Singapore.

5th January. Nice note Lindsay. Wrote him neat little acknowledgement. He thinks I'm daft. Wrote Maud.

6th January. Did a bit of work. Went to First Aid lecture. Nerney sent me Macready in two vols 10/-

7th January. Cooee wrote. She's getting married, sent her £5. Did a bit of work.

8th January. Worked. Nice letter Nerney. Funny argument with Fump. Wrote Pip a long letter.

9th January. Wrote Lindsay in return to one of his.

10th January. More letters. Wasting time. But want to write Pip.

11th January. Wrote Phil, Joyce. Parker came. Snow. Bed early. Told [...] about Cooee. She rather cross!

- - -

6th July. Nervy day. Worked a little. Fidgeted. Saw M. Seabrook. Borrowed Piano Doe. Couldn't get a tuner. Worked some more. Long Pig Club committee meeting all evening.

- - -

8th July. Cable from Pip. Thank God.

- - -

26th September. Pip's birthday. Cable from him dated 22nd.

- - -

Right: 'The Unhappy Warrior'
by Youngman Carter.

Left: Margery in the
conservatory.

Appendix III

Censored

On May 28th 1941 Margery returned from London to discover that the censor had cut out much of her material about mines and unexploded bombs. She made no complaint and settled to reorganising the pages around the deleted section. The censored passages begin on page 237.

There is a great deal more to it than that, though, as the tales of the casualties tell, Auburn has better chances than most.

Several of the villages round about lost their churches and this was thought to be deliberate by many until it occurred to somebody that most of the damage was caused by the parachute mines which float gently down in couples, like giant pillar boxes and are apt to hit a high building before a low one. These are horrible things, senseless, aimless bundles of idiot destruction. Sometimes they do not go off for a long time and then they are a nuisance and a great worry and very brave young men come out and take them to pieces and haul them away without making any fuss about it. They make so little fuss that one might almost be excused for thinking them unimaginative, but every now and then something happens to open one's eyes.

A boy came to see me one day, looking for an unexploded bomb. He was a lieutenant and he had a sergeant in a lorry outside. He was very young and was the sort of lad one would normally expect to find lying on his back underneath an old sports car. I told him where it was up on the hill and that it was thought to be an unusually large one since the clear circular hole it made was unusually wide. He thanked me kindly and I offered him a drink. He said he did not think he would until afterwards, if I did

321

not mind because – well, naturally he'd need to be absolutely clear-headed. I suddenly realised exactly what it was he was going to do and said, involuntarily and idiotically, 'Oh be careful.'

He laughed like a child at me and went off, chuckling.

The passage about Courage on pp. 238 – 239 follows here.

Of course there were people who approached unexploded bombs, and even mines, in other ways than did my visitor, whose attitude towards them was so unassuming and intelligently brave. There was the old man in the orchard in Goldenhind who went on picking his apples while one of the wickedest looking holes in creation lay at his feet, for, as he said, he wanted the apples and if death came he didn't know but that he hadn't been knocking around long enough.

The there was the other old gentleman nearby who found a great mine on his farm and crawled over to it and laid his head on it to see 'if it were a-ticking'. When he found it was not he decided it was all right for a bit and rung up the authorities in the dinner hour. There was also the retired colonel who had a passion for the things and smelt them out like a blood hound. He came in with a tale of one glorious day when he was in on a party for moving two of the largest mines from a ploughed field which had become a morass. On getting the first onto a lorry they discovered that the vehicle had sunk up to the axles, had to lower the thing again, and then, at the Colonel's instigation, set about rolling both mines ('very cautiously y'know') some eight hundred yards to the hard road.

There was the completely barmy and purely country story of 'whoosh-flap-flap' which had better be told as I heard it, always remembering that the local voice conveys intense excitement and rise to a shout on unexpected words, which I will italicise.

'Pimpey was a-ridin down the road on a *bicycle*. Top o' *Moss Hill* that were. Very *lonely*. Very *quiet*. Heard a *plane* overhead. *Circling*, that were. Twisting and turning. Suddenly he heard that very *close*. Whoosh-flap-flap, that went, whoosh-flap-flap. Pimpey was *frightened*. Went on pedalling. Very lonely, Very quiet. Plane went away. Heard that *again*. Whoosh-flap-flap, whoosh-flap-flap. Pimpey was right *terrified*. Thought of ghosts. Whoosh-flap-flap, that went. Whoosh-flap-flap. In's ear. Throwed hisself off his bicycle. Got in a ditch under a *wall*. Lay there a *long time*. Put his head out. Whoosh-flap-flap. Whoosh-flap-flap. Whoosh-flap-flap. Just by his *head*. Looked *behind* of him. See a great *parachute*. Coming a-down on 'im, that was. Sprang away from that. Looked over the *wall*. See a great *moine*. As big as a *piano*. He leapt for that bicycle. Still out of *breath*.'

There was the other story too, almost too horrible to tell, which a friend of P.Y.C.'s told me when they came over on day on short leave. He was present at a disposal. The protecting sandbags were put in place at the required distance and everyone lay flat behind them, as usual, except the man whose job it was to do the dangerous work. He went quietly towards the missile, green with terror, beads of sweat standing out all over his face, and had come perhaps within a foot of it when it exploded. There was no trace of him.

Grog and the Head Warden themselves had one of the more dreadfully serio-comic adventures with an unexploded mine. Auburn had been very lucky about mines for a long time and, when its turn did come at last, the luck still held. The usual two mines fell together just over the village but one exploded in mid-air and did no damage at all but blew its fellow off its parachute, so that it fell some considerable distance away in the wilds instead of floating gently and dangerously to earth in the middle of a more populated district.

A parachute mine, by the way, is one of the enemy's more complicated products containing, as a rule, besides a lot of explosive, quantities of extra gadgets in the way of booby traps, poisonous paints and other frightful fancy work. It is as complicated a bag of trouble as any of the industrious destructionists have yet produced. This particular specimen did not explode but broke to pieces on impact, which transformed it into a very unpleasant kettle of fish altogether.

At first there was no clear idea in Auburn what had happened at all. Something had certainly gone off in the sky and all Grog could gather was that it had been 'wonderfully pretty', but when the sun came up, quantities of fragments, by now familiar, began to turn up all over the place. P.C. Me collected all manner of stuff and persuaded young Miss Margaret from The Tye to bring him and his haul back to the village in her car. They paused outside our house to let Grog in on the discovery. I was allowed to look too and we put our heads in the run-about to inspect what looked like the assembled wreckage of a small railway engine struck by lightening. Norry came across from the Forge in his goatskin and I think Tiff was there and one or two others.

Amid a lot of general admiration for the workmanship, (for Auburn has a blessed grasp on the satisfactory things of life), and a lot of fascinated speculation, it gradually began to occur to everyone that there was more than enough harness for one mine and the speedy discovery of the other became a vital interest to all concerned.

Finally, after a great deal of detective work by telephone, Grog located something, and, with the Head Warden, went up to the far end of the parish, where the world is quiet and undisturbed in the normal way, and, after crossing a bog, a section of close-planted thorn, a wood and a small marsh, burst suddenly on what I can well believe was one of the most alarming sights of their career.

In a quiet dell lay a broken mine of the largest kind, whose very weight had made a small nest for itself in the soft earth, and upon it, working with the joyful enthusiasm of the genuine collector were no less than five hearties struggling with pick, shovel and blacksmith's hammer to detach the nose which they fancied as a door stopper. Sinister wires, gobs of grey explosive, knobs, ominous buttons, detonators, bits of steel and mysterious clock entrails covered the moss around them and there was a small patch of burnt earth nearby where they had been making a little fire to see whether the grey stuff would ignite. Nor would they be convinced.

'Har, that's all right, that's sort of half gone off,' they said. 'That's not dangerous, that's broken.'

There ought to be some sort of frightful cautionary ending to this monstrous story, but on that day the angels, rendered compassionate no doubt by the very enormity of the rush in, were being kind to utter fools. However the coruscating remarks of the professional Bomb Squad, when at last it could bring itself to speak, together with the size of the explosion when the horror was finally 'rendered harmless', were salutary and once again, by the grace of God, nobody died.

My own personal experience of the unexploded menace was probably not at all dangerous but it gave me a bad half hour. One day I came into the breakfast room to find Grog entertaining a Bomb Squad officer and his great gaunt Welsh sergeant, who had been collecting some gadget or other which interested them from out of the fields. They were all very keen on the subject and as it was dark it occurred to them to bring their find in and take a look at it in comfort. They were chatting away about various aspects of the work and the war, and one subject and another, and the sergeant, wishing to be polite and bring me into the conversation, indicated an enormous hot-water-bottle-stopper of an object which lay on the hearth rug, and remarked pleasantly that they usually came smaller and you had to be careful of them, because his pal, who had given one only a quarter of the size a slight 'bit of a twist', had lost his hand for his trouble.

I said 'Oh dear' rather faintly, and, thinking I was mainly concerned about his friend, he went on to dilate upon the story.

Meanwhile the thing lay on the mat in front of the nice bright fire. The sergeant nearly kicked it with his half-hundred-weight boot when reaching for a cigarette, but avoided it in time and the party went on. I was very frightened and pretended I wanted to telephone and went out, but felt a fool at once and came back and tried to listen intelligently. Finally I said to the sergeant that I hoped it would not go off in the house, which was putting it mildly, but he said nonsense, bombs and booby traps were 'like warsps'. They would not hurt you if you did not give them a bit of a twist.

He then went on to tell us a story about a crowd of Welsh men going over to Belfast for a football match and how they never got out of the pub next the quay and missed the match, and how, by judicious fictions they disguised this fact from their football-enthusiast wives when they got home, until some weak fellow gave the show away. However, that was days later, he said, and by that time 'the wrath had gone out of the women'.

At last they went and took their prize with them, and, although they were delightful people, I was very glad.

DEMOLITION OF AN ESSEX CHURCH—SEPTEMBER, 1940

J. E. Studer, Colchester, photo.
Our readers will be aware of the identity of this Church, utterly demolished by enemy action.

Above: Church demolished by bomb.
(Essex County Standard)

Appendix IV

Letters to Joyce

Left: Margery Allingham
— and the duffle coat. see
13th January 1941

D'Arcy House,
Tolleshunt D'Arcy,
Nr Maldon, Essex.
October 18th 1941

My dear old Joyce,

Your June letter has been passed round the family and tremendously enjoyed. You give a very vivid picture of the place. It's impossible to answer it in any ordinary sense because of the delay in the mails. Dick Pepper arrived without letters but very pleased with himself. I think we almost convinced him that communism in his sense was *vieux jeu* and that England was pleasantly not to say rosily red just like him. The little ships were a delight. Some of my letters may have gone astray but I hope you get this one. News of the troops is good. Pip is a captain and has met Phil in the desert. They had a great meeting apparently and all was well. Grog is a Pilot Officer training in the west. I don't think this means that he flies. Granny and Christine and I hold the fort alone.

The *Heart* (I hope you've got your copy. I told New York to send you an early one months ago) has been a great success over

here but as far as I can hear has made little impression in the U.S.
Still, it's early days yet. To my relief the local paper gave it a terrific
boost and the village decided to be very pleased – a mercy all
things considered! The press over here gave it a terrific show.
Whole columns in the Sundays, front page of *John O'London's*,
great wodges of it everywhere. So far, six weeks after publication,
sales at 10/6 are 13,000. Lusty has got me to do him a novel next.
The novel, the one we discussed. You know, the 'who are you?'
one. This is a real break for me if I can only pull it off. Pray for
it.

I'm very quiet and good-tempered down here practically on
my own. Granny remains in form. She came bundling in in great
excitement the other day having seen (apparently for the first
time), a map of Europe. 'Isn't it wonderful they're on our side,'
she said, bursting with delight. 'Who?' I said. 'They're right on top
of us,' she said. 'If they were against us we should be for it.'
'Who?' I repeated. 'Why,' she said, 'The Scotch!'

I had a letter from Meiggs the other day saying he's getting
married to an attractive historian sometime this month. He was
rather angry with me over *Traitor's Purse*. Took it very personally.
It may have done him good. I hope he'll be all right. An odd, difficult chap, but there was no one ever quite like him as far as I was
concerned. Which is just one of those things. It's an odd thing to
say but you'll probably understand when I say I really do feel (and
most unexpectedly) curiously relieved. The tale did have an end
anyway!

Nerney is in tremendous form. The worry of the war and the
fact that she's virtually boss-less has made her rather more so than
usual. She 'manages' so violently these days that I'm half afraid to
go near her. Still she's a good old girl and a great good sort.

I hear a little of the gang via Grog via Coop. Mrs Box has
startled everybody by running away from Bocco. Moll has definitely left Bobby who is a rear gunner or a bomb aimer. Jack is an
ack-ack gunner.

The village has been in great form. It's made jam (communally) and kept pigs and prepared for invasion all in remarkably good humour.

I had a note from Claud. He's at the desk in a very posh Woman's Club and seems quite happy. Granny writes to 'dear Inez', 'dear Amy', 'dear Poppy' and 'dear Toots' all of whom seem to have exactly the same news and just what you'd think.

Nerney took me round to see Clemence Dane who I found (secretly) rather over-poweringly charming and so like Miss Bagley that she quite frightened me. She was a bit of an 'awful warning' I felt in my heart and I was glad to get back to the bokels. I only saw her for a little while and may have misjudged her.

Em and Marcus are getting on very well in the House. I got Maud and Ted down for the weekend and we all went over. The <u>work</u> in the place and the size of it! Gave me a great respect for the old girl. She's got such a <u>nerve</u>. I liked the church and garden but was not altogether taken by the house. It was designed by a chap with a mania for what Grog calls 'ecclesiastical wood'. Still it's very good and impressive. They're very happy. It is a miracle.

Our place is odd, empty like this. I got all kinds of flu and bronchitis and what not working in the drawing room so, when Grog left, I turned the studio into a sort of Panda cage. I work in Pip's part (having had a tortoise installed), I sleep on the raised part and the long bit is my 'run'. It's very warm and comfortable and Christine keeps it very shiny.

To return to the *Heart* – I was so fed up at the lack of interest in the U.S. (Doubleday presented it very badly I thought), that I got all the people in it to sign it (except you folk in active service) and I sent the copy to Winant with a long intimate letter asking him, if he thought it a good idea, would he, as <u>ambassador</u>, send it to Mrs Roosevelt? I got one of the most kindly personal letters (really understanding) back and the book has gone on. There the matter rests. It's up to her. I'm keeping very quiet and praying. Nerney was startled by the idea but the bokels thought it very sensible and reasonable. It's one of those things you couldn't do if you weren't absolutely sincerely disinterested. I hope she does something. I think they <u>ought</u> to read it if they do want to know something about England.

The war news is not good – the Huns are just outside Moscow but do you remember our prophecy – 'when there is fighting hand to hand in the citadel then the war will be nearly over and the invading hoard will be crushed'? I hope St whoever-it-was is right I must say! I think of you out there. Things must be in a bit of a flap there now but it's a terrific time to be alive in.

No more news from here at the moment – I'll write you again soon – <u>Lots</u> of love from us all ducky

yrs ever

Marge

P.S. Things are very quiet here. It's just like the beginning of the war – the first year, but not so optimistic of course. Everyone feels we're all set for a struggle and then victory. I'm the only really optimistic person I know and I'm just illogically cheerful. I think things are going to be good.

* * *

D'Arcy House,
Tolleshunt D'Arcy,
Nr Maldon, Essex.
November 27th 1941

My dear old Joyce,

I've just discovered I am allowed to send you the enclosed two pounds, which may be useful. I have had a card from you and Granny got some sweets, which delighted her and she's written you. You may not get these for Christmas but it shouldn't be long after. Just at the moment it's a bit of a nervy time as the Libyan battle is in full swing and both the boys are on general transport. Still I'm completely confident they'll be all right.

There seems to be a lot of excitement at your end but I see the wogs are talking turkey again this morning, thank god. What a time it is – how we shall bore our children in fifty years or so.

I do hope you got your copy of the book and that you liked it. It's still going very well here. The trouble is to get it printed. The U.S. is reviewing it wonderfully but not buying it.

The new call up is published this morning – I shall look funny in the A.T.S.!?! Meanwhile I'm really getting on with the book very slowly. It's meant a lot of reading, especially 'lives', but it's astonishingly interesting. I don't think they'll take me away from here as I'm rather useful, and also Pip is a soldier, but I'm afraid Christina will have to go, which won't be fun.

Grog came down on leave looking very fine and astonishingly clean in his P/O uniform. The R.A.F. has bitten him and I think he's making good. Bob Gee is still missing but we're all still hoping. Molly is or was on the verge of a divorce. Mrs Box has run away from Box. Pippa on the other hand has settled down very happily in the country, the kids going to the local school. Bill and Bernstein apparently 'behaved very well' when the news came about Bob. They went down to the station said the right things in the right way. Meanwhile dear old Mrs Gee has remained steadily in Hampstead (now called the Gateway to the East) through shot and shell and nobody knows her reactions (which is life!).

I heard from Francesca yesterday, I think she's feeling this blasted battle.

Maud and Ted are remarkably better and fitter and happier. I saw them in Town.

I went to Town for a week and took Christina. Nerney looked after me like the Crown Jewels but I got out to the zoo with Cressie and to a theatre. The old man is remarkably unchanged – still grumbling, still rude and lazy. I shall be interested to hear his reactions to military conscription for all men under 50. The famous age question may have to be reviewed! (What an old cat I am.) Jeri, I hear, has got another three children – making about eleven, I fancy.

Birdie came over with two local 'ladies'. Fans of the *Heart*. She looks a bit older but is very sprightly. Rush has been doing new views of London's famous buildings – St Paul's seen from the north for the first time and so on.

I saw the old Miss Luards the other day. They asked most kindly after you. Poor old dears, they feel a bit helpless, I'm afraid, a new experience for them and not too good at that age. The *Heart* is having a most unexpected effect on the district. Everyone is getting so <u>matey</u>. I fancy we've started a fashion. There's a cricket-party friendliness about. It may not last but it's a good thing when it does.

I've got caught by a lot of 'Church' persons again. Anglo-catholic monks this time. Someone wrote and invited me to write a religious book and, not wishing to be discourteous, I said 'I wasn't <u>ready</u> yet' and that I ought to be more educated in the subject. This seemed final to me but the old boy got busy and put a most sincere and earnest monk onto me who recommended some 35 good books and did his best to convert me. I couldn't understand the interest until I pulled myself together and realized that it must be because they're all so cross with Sayers!

I did tell you, didn't I? that I'd been able to fix it with C.S.E. so that I could do the new book *Dance of the Years* ('Chaff of the Mountains' under a new title) for Lusty. I'm very glad about this. The *Heart* has done nearly 12,000 so far and is still selling well. It's got down into the second strata of readers, I think, and may go on for ages. I hope so. Income Tax is just silly – about £700 next year!

Oh dear me, yes, I forgot. I've undergone a remarkable and impressive change. I got bored of my looks and went to the barber's and had my hair cut off and the tufts curled tight on top. Curiously enough the change is a terrific success. I'm said to look more like you. It's not at all bad and very easy. You just brush it on end and shake it – falls into curls.

No more news of Meiggs and his marriage. I hope it's come off.

Any muck up would be thunderingly bad for him and would shove him right down the path to 'barmy-old-prof-hood'. It's an extraordinary thing but I can't get up any feeling for him except earnest maternal solicitude – I hope to God he's got a good 'un. I've met one or two Oxford men extraordinarily like him in mind. Maybe he wasn't so very extraordinary but he was a good chap.

Granny is in tremendous form. She's a little older but not much and still patches (in bright colours) anything she finds lying about in the bathroom. I've got one nightshirt with a crescent on the stomach and a sort of swastika on the seat.

No more news at the moment ducky – All my love – Hope to God you're all right and happy – Bless you –

Marge

* * *

D'Arcy House,
Tolleshunt D'Arcy,
Nr Maldon, Essex.
February 7th 1942

My dear old Joyce,

Granny and I are still rejoicing that you're out of Singapore. Granny came running along in a great state of excitement the other day but it transpired that she'd got Colombo mixed up with Borneo and I was able to set her mind at rest. I think I shall have to buy her a globe.

There's a great absence of news just now. I heard from Pip (and indirectly from him of Phil) Jan 11th but nowt since. It's no good worrying, I know, but if they wanted excitement, they've certainly got it, poor lads.

Cooee wrote that she's married the Executive Officer of the Hants War Agricultural Committee. In peace he's a farmer and I really think it's the most sensible thing I ever heard of as long as she doesn't play the goat.

Meiggs too, I think I told you, got married and wrote me a long letter on his four day honeymoon carefully describing everything except the girl. I sent them both a silver milk jug (antique and very 'decent') and he replied using an envelope with Mrs Meiggs on it, lightly crossed out. I believe I'm beginning to see through him at last. I'm afraid the girl's in for a bad time if he's got that kind of complex. How Gawd looks after me. 'Rough but kind' as we say.

I don't expect you got the cash I sent you but I hope you got your copy of the *Heart*. It's still selling and has produced a lot of interesting people, including the Master of Balliol, with whom I'm having a great correspondence. I like the old boy's attitude, not at all unlike Daddy's.

Nerney is going very strong. I think I worry her. A very funny thing happened. She really engineered me away from Heinemann to Lusty without exactly letting her left hand know what her right was doing. I fixed it up with C.S.E. very neatly and contracted with him to do the thrillers if Lusty had another novel. Having found out how to do this though, I taught P.R.R. how to do it in the U.S. and he's done the same thing with Doubleday. Malcolm is delighted. Little Brown gets the novel if they want it (and I think they will, it opens pretty decently) and Nerney is wondering how it all happened. However, she's an old duck and is helping me with the book. I think she's a bit wild with Malcolm who is just relieved because he doesn't think I can do a novel and was afraid he'd have to publish out of friendship. So that's that.

I am very well and working. Oddly enough, I don't get as lonely as you'd think. People still come in to see me and the village is very matey.

Grog writes cheerfully from the west. His work seems arduous and difficult but is also dead secret so he has less to say than ever: I can't think of a better chap to give a secret job to. He sounds as if he's got younger than ever, is reading Dumas Père and, when made to play hockey against the W.A.A.F's 'got a lot of fun by frightening them but not really hacking their shins'(!) Robin's wife sounds a strong-minded wench – Grog says she 'wasn't bad when she took off her spectacles'. They're a funny family.

I see Cressie occasionally. He's an odd chap when you get to know him. It may sound unlikely but he reminds me more of my early girlfriend Angela than anyone I ever met. We get on all right, we're not unlike each other temperamentally and it's very nice to have some one left out of the gang to talk to occasionally. He's my only link with the original crowd. When I go to London (about twice a year) he takes me to the Zoo!

The Novel is very exciting to do. I think you'll like it. It's the one we talked about and you thought would be just right for the end of the war. It's not easy by any means but it's 'coming' slowly. *Dance of the Years* is the title – pray for it.

There's a great deal of talk about us going labour and so on but I smell a sort of reaction from the working folk themselves – I can't describe this but they don't seem too keen on sweeping changes.

One interesting thing that is cropping up is a new Time theory. James Laver has written a book on Nostradamus, the 15th century prophet and astrologer. He's approached it from our (the reasonable materialistic) attitude and has done a good job. I exchanged a letter with him and I find he's working on our lines, as are some of the Russians. Great fun.

Roughly, the theory is that there is no general time – ie everything has its own time (which is the measure of growth and decay of the object). The people who are alive at the same time are the 'seeing' part of the whole. The whole thing is like a light slowly creeping [...] sideways – instead of a procession from past to future. So Nostradamus. By seeing sideways, or having a hole in his blinkers so to speak, he caught glimpses of something going on at his elbow. I've said this badly, but you'll see what I mean.

The astrological folk are bad or wrong as usual, but I think myself that that's because they won't stick to people and will go trying countries and states, which are not the same thing at all. There's a great deal of thinking going on anyway.

We're all right for food. In fact it's nothing like the last war yet.

Things are getting short (clothes, furniture, books etc) but if one's got simple tastes, one's more or less all right. I'm all right anyway. The Panda house seems much as ever. I just work and listen to the wireless and read and read.

My only venture has been to plant 100 apple trees down past the summerhouse - Coxes Orange and Pippins and Bramley seedlings.

I've got an ex-army widow pal in the village who knows Colombo well. The manager of the Nat. Provincial Bank is a pal of hers. She's a Mrs Tuohy (Ferdinand's sister-in-law) and I hear from her that it's a good place for which I am truly thankful. You seem a long way away, dancing round the world in this blessed circus. What a set out it all is!

The disaster to the two big ships must have hit you all pretty hard - it shook us up over here.

All my love ducky -

Granny sends hers. She's in tremendous form. Amy sent her a card for Christmas saying 'love from Amy' and Granny thought 'dear Gracie' would like it, so she wrote 'to all' after the 'Amy' in what she says was disguised writing (!) and sent it on. Grace is just confused of course. She also gets hold of any clothes I leave near her and puts big coloured patches on anywhere where 'it's thin' with the result my night shirts and pants are beginning to look festive. She likes bright colours you know.

Em is herself too - very full of beans. She now has a little puppy who is house trained but never corrected otherwise. She bought him at Christmas and Theobald had to submit to a mauling and wasn't even allowed to teach him Queensbury rules. He bore it for two hours solid and then asked meekly to go out. I let him and he went straight to the stables and killed all the rabbits. The perfect host dog.

Once more all my love

Yrs ever,

Marge

P.S. Lovely Christmas card from you – wonderfully attractive. I wrote you thanking you for the parcel but have just thought you may not have got it. Anything I can send <u>you</u>?

* * *

D'Arcy House,
Tolleshunt D'Arcy,
Nr Maldon, Essex.
March 5th 1942

My dear Joyce,

Many thanks for your letter which was good to get. How nice you running into uncle. I bet the old so-and-so is brown but not 'browned off' I trust. All my love. Well, well eh? Pip and Phil seem to be oke to date – Phil reports the capture of an Italian dear little-fing wagon right up in the forward area, but empty. (Extraordinary people.)

We're all right to date. No excitement at all. Granny is still staggered at the unexpected wickedness of 'Hilda' as she persists in calling Adolph – not unexpectedly 'naughty' so much as 'successful' I fancy! She's just the same – annoyed because she had a touch of lumbago. She says she's 'only ninety'.

At the moment I'm very much the Panda in wonderland. I've got into another highly complicated correspondence this time with the Master of Balliol (unbeknownst to Meiggs). He's looked me up, seen I was 'educated' in Cambridge and seems to think I'm a blue stocking. So far I've been undiscovered in spite of dozens of letters but I fear it won't last. He's begun to discuss Aristotle(!) I've also got Dot Sayers on my hands. She <u>likes</u> me like anything and came over by bus to lunch. A nice old duck really when you know her. Just determinedly belligerent. I'm trying to work and am getting on with the book but not fast enough. God knows what you'll think of it. I'm sending you another copy of the *Heart* as you haven't got yours. Malcolm was supposed to have sent it. Twerp.

I had an extraordinary visitation the other day. Cooee's <u>father</u>.

He'd been writing me very fishy letters for ages and I'd been ignoring them. (He'd seen the *Heart* and was cashing in) and then he <u>arrived</u>. Awful. A real little old <u>crook</u>. As smart as a hundredweight of monkeys. He's <u>old</u> now and has evidently got more obvious but his methods are alarming. He carries photographs for reference – old snaps of himself in uniform, snaps of his yacht circa 1909, snaps of Cooee at all ages and dusty legal documents. I couldn't decide what he was after – anything, I fancy. Anyway, with great presence of mind, I remained absolutely dumb and blank. I said 'Quite', 'Indeed' and 'Really?' and no more whatever, for two solid hours while he told me everything, from the point at which he joined 'dear old Winston's staff' to his 'important secret job' in this war. Finally he left. It rather explains Hippo. I'm all right but adventures seem to come and sit on the doorstep. I began to clap my bear's feet and say 'Oh my'.

I'm sorry you're missing all this particular sort of fun. You'd enjoy it. I'm the Panda just arrived at 'pets corner'. It'll die down but at the moment it's ridiculous and silly not to enjoy it. It may never come again. Sales <u>only</u> 15,000 but at 10/6d and still going quickly. (All my other books O.P of course and we can't reprint!) I don't see many people (except for the two old visitors recorded) but the post is exciting.

Nerney is going strong. She came down and we walked over to Layer Breton? Sad to see it like that. It's still dry you know but overgrown and black with neglect. She's getting older and is threatening to retire and come and mind me. I <u>couldn't</u>, Joyce. Such a nice old duck but I couldn't. I'm <u>out</u> – off the chain and I look coldly at the carrot in the box.

I see old Cressie occasionally – not often. It's a funny relationship. We meet two or three times a year and have very little interest in each other's activities in between times (or so we pretend very successfully – it must be <u>age</u>).

This whole letter sounds as if I was unaware of the war – that's not true of course. One can't miss it. The country thinks of nothing else and one's spirits rise and fall with the news, but I'm determined to go on living too, while I can.

The Russian show is terrific. It just goes on like a steady good thing amid the chaos. [...]

Lots and lots of love, will write again soon,

Marge (amid the intellectual honey pots)

* * *

> D'Arcy House,
> Tolleshunt D'Arcy,
> Nr Maldon, Essex.
> May 8th 1942

My dear old Joyce,

Many thanks for your grand letter and the airgraph – much to my annoyance I find I can't send one back yet. You should have had this before but the idiotic Marcus said they'd had a cable from you with a new address and I've been waiting for it – now it turns out to be *sans origine*! He saw it at once when I pointed it out of course – Chump!

Grog has gone off to join the boys and has not been heard of since so Granny and I hold the fort. I'm afraid she's getting a little bit older and won't be fit to be the General in the A.T.S. (a post I've been promising her) unless they hurry. Both Christine and I have registered and so far they've decided to let Chrissie remain. I have not had my case reviewed yet. I am thinking of a nice job on the railway tapping wheels which sounds about my mark.

Both Phil and Pip are oke so far – thank God. I'm afraid they had a near shave further back in the year when they seem to have been surprised in one of those recaptured towns but they got out. [...] Pip writes wonderfully cheerfully. I wish he was home though.

I'm glad you liked the *Heart* and very annoyed you didn't get your copy from Doubledays; they are unreliable blighters. It has done about 15,000 so far and is still selling quickly. The U.S. of course has no use for it. I am getting on very slowly with the new book. The will to work is there but as you can guess there are interruptions. We are now a totally restricted area and can't have visitors, which makes for quiet in one way but is a bit depressing. I go to Town when I can but must get on or I shall be in the soup as usual. However, I can't say I worry as much as perhaps I ought – I get entertainment from my correspondents in the church and universities and I work and read and ARP and prepare for invasion all the rest of the time.

Your adventures sound considerable. I've passed your famous letter round and it is much enjoyed and appreciated. I envy you, you know. See all you can ducky. Feel all you can too.

I think I told you in my last letter that Littley Wright got killed in Sumatra – Bunny was very cut up. The rest of the gang is well. Jolly Jack H has got a commission in the Tanks. Edward has got more gold lace and will probably become a brasshat if someone doesn't put him in a bucket first. Bill I think is doing well. Robin is still schoolmastering and has got his wife a job down there at Hurst teaching. Box sounded like 'a man with a grievance' last time I heard him on the 'phone. I see a bit of Cressie some times. [...] His famous and mysterious shellshock is pretty terrifying when you see evidence of it – fits of ungovernable and senseless fury. (I seem to have some odd pals). Meiggs is apparently very happy. He does his usual trick, fishes for an invitation assiduously until he gets it and then ignores it for a couple of months and writes a long effusive apology. He is rather hampered in this by the restriction order but still does it. I hope this sort of thing doesn't grow on him! At the moment I think I've rather startled him by inadvertently becoming a pen pal of his boss at Oxford. I want to see his wife I think by all accounts she's very young and a bit hard which is what he wants. He writes me long accounts of them going 'wooding' together. It really is disgusting and, if I were younger, would upset me as he intends but I ain't young any more and the old Panda is doing pretty well in a chuckleheaded fashion.

I've made quite a pal of Dot Sayers and went to see the famous husband. He's a <u>Ted</u>. In fact the whole do reminded me of Sunday afternoon at Maud's without Maud and in her place a headmistress. Sensationally hard work.

I also saw Miss G and Miss Rose the other day. They're old. They sent you all their love and were peculiarly pathetic and backwatery but wonderfully <u>gallant</u> you know. They've got guts. I'm hardening up towards breeding in spite of myself. You need it in a row like this. It stands out miles and is rocky in the sands.

By the way practically the whole of the first page of your grand long letter was censored – did I tell you? I mention it again anyway. I'll have to wait until after the war for that bit.

Conditions here are good. Food is still cheap in the main and, unless you are a natural hog, I can't think you can be much hit. The Baedecker raids have made little general impression. Our own stuff is so much more sensational. I don't think people quite realize how good they were in the real Blitz and this new little spurt seems chickenfeed beside them.

I hear the Americans are taking things very seriously which is good. Of course, they've ceased to be our audience and are now just one of the gang and are therefore not so important from our 'public' point of view. We just feel 'get on with it, boy' apparently now.

It's not possible to comment on the situation now of course because we're waiting for the fun to begin still [...] I loved your ad. from the local paper. I think I can beat it almost from Towzer though, 'Lady with own cow requires comfortable and congenial home.'

For the rest the house is just as it ever was to date – rather better kept because it keeps tidier. The new apple trees are in bud all 100 of them and they look pretty good. Even the lawn is cut and there are about 1500 tomato plants in the conservatory.

Nerney still phones from town to see if I'm still alive and intelligent. I still get books to review (rather thin and printed on a sort of disintegrating substance like an old ice cream wafer) and

I'm still months late with my copy. *Vogue* still comes out with rather idiotic suggestions for brightening the home with bits of old wallpaper etc.

I have just discovered that my clothes coupons run out of date by the end of this month so I'm going to town to buy some pants and a dress as I've got all my card and am in not too picturesque rags at the moment. Oh yes, you'll be amused to hear that the *Heart* has had a most salutary effect on Auburn. Christine says they're 'living up to it' and are being virtuous noble chaps about the place.

Here is the news just come on. The battle in the Pacific is in progress. It sounds terrific - it'll be called The Battle of the Coral Sea I suppose. Terrific times.

All my love ducky - I think of you all the time.

yrs ever

Marge

Right: Joyce Allingham in tropical uniform.

Notes

p.xxiii   'Auburn': Tolleshunt D'Arcy. Name from Goldsmith's *The Deserted Village*.

'an American': Malcolm Johnson, Margery's U.S. publisher.

p.xxiv   'I lived down the road': the Allingham family lived in Layer Breton 1909-1917.

p.xxv   T & M: Tina and Malcolm Johnson.

p.9   'Albert and his father': Albert Smith and his father Alfred Smith (see Appendix I).

'the Old Doctor and Mrs Graves': Dr J. H. Salter, former owner of D'Arcy House. It is not clear whether the Mrs Graves mentioned is Reverend Robert Graves's first or second wife (see Appendix I).

Norry and Jack Emeny: (see Appendix I). 'Mycroft' was the older brother of Sherlock Holmes.

p.10   *Snow White and the Seven Dwarves* was produced by Walt Disney in the U.S. in 1937.

Reg: Reg Hammond, storekeeper (see Appendix I).

p.11   Cis helped her parents Mr & Mrs Thomas run the Red Lion P.H. in Tolleshunt D'Arcy. Surname later Eaton?

W.A.A.F. Women's Auxiliary Air Force 1939-1948.

'railway': The 'Crab-and-Winkle Line' ran from Tollesbury to Kelvedon 1904-1951.

'Flinthammock-on-Estuary': Tollesbury.

'the school': St Nicholas C. of E. Primary School was threatened with closure in 1938. Margery Allingham's household were involved in the struggle to avert this. It is flourishing today with, currently, 117 pupils on roll.

'What Happened to France': *Tragedy in France* by André Maurois was published in the U.S. in 1940 and serialised under the title *What Happened to France*.

p.12   Vernon Bartlett (1894-1983) Journalist, broadcaster and politician. Presented 'The Way of the World' weekly talks on BBC radio from 1928. Opposed to appeasement. MP for Bridgwater 1938-1950. Co-founder of Common Wealth party 1942.

Germany and Japan withdrew from the League of Nations in 1933.

Charles Ulm (1898-1934) Pioneer Australian aviator.

p.13   Austria was annexed to the German Third Reich on 12th March, 1938.

p.14   'two schoolma'ams': Mrs Moore and Mrs Gager (see Appendix I).

'old 'Anry': Could be a reference to a character in Margery's novel *Mystery Mile*. More likely to be a generic term for any Suffolk rustic. 'Heath': Tiptree.

p.15   'bread and pull-it': a hard-times expression meaning bread and more bread (possibly the joke is on pullet, a tender young chicken, unaffordable for the poor).

p.17   'Earl Baldwin': Three times Prime Minister Stanley Baldwin (1867-1947) was given the title Earl Baldwin of Bewdley on his retirement from politics in 1937. His handling of the Abdication crisis in 1936 had made him generally popular. This was modified on the outbreak of WW2 when Churchill especially criticised him as having been slow to commit Britain to rearmament. Baldwin supported Chamberlain's Munich Agreement.

p. 18   'the Anschluss': annexation of Austria, 12th March, 1938.

p. 19   Sam: Sam Taylor (see Appendix I).
        P.Y.C.: Philip ('Pip') Youngman Carter, Margery's husband.
        Grog: Alan Joe Gregory, school friend of P.Y.C., living in D'Arcy House. Joined R.A.F. Did not return to D'Arcy after the war.
        Cooee: Mary Orr, college friend of Margery, living in D'Arcy House. Joined A.T.S. Did not return to D'Arcy after the war.
        The Newmarket Town Plate: 3 mile 6 furlong flat race open to amateur riders.

p. 20   'Sudeten trouble': Following the annexation of Austria in March 1938 Hitler turned his attention to the ethnic Germans living in Czechoslovakia. Tensions mounted. In August 1938 Lord Runciman visited to see whether agreement could be reached between the Sudeten Germans and the Czechoslovak government. In September 1938 Henlein, pro-Nazi leader of Sudeten Germans, demanded takeover by Hitler's Third Reich.

p. 21   'the boarding school': Margery was at Endsleigh House, a prep boarding school in Colchester from 1915.

p. 23   Foresters: a Friendly Society enabling members to save money and insure themselves or their families.
        Rose Show: important annual event in Colchester, Essex.

p. 25   Legion: the British Legion was formed in 1921 by the amalgamation of four WW1 servicemen's organisations.
        Margaret: Margaret Nicklin (see Appendix I).
        Chrissie: Christina Carter, housemaid. Came to work for Margery at Viaduct Farm, Chappel, in 1933 and stayed with her and then with Joyce Allingham until her death in 1994.

p. 27   Mr Doe: butcher (see Appendix I).

'Marshling': Virley.

p. 28 'Different men have different opinions: some like apples and some like onions' (English proverb).

p. 29 E. Phillips Oppenheim (1866-1946) was an early writer of spy fiction. *Limehouse Nights*: 1916 collection of melodramatic stories by Thomas Burke (1886-1945) centring on Limehouse district of East London.

Vic: Miss Victoria Emeny (see Appendix I).

'Pontisbright': Chappel. Name also used in *Sweet Danger* and other of Margery's novels.

p. 30 'that terrifying day': probably 24th March 1917.

the Lancers: a set piece dance, a quadrille.

the Harlequinade: a theatrical performance piece with set characters.

p. 31 'one of His Majesty's Recorders': Edward Terrell Q.C. (1902-1979). Weekend cottage in Tolleshunt D'Arcy (see Appendix I).

p. 32 Czechoslovakia and France: the Munich Agreement, ceding the Sudetenland to Germany, was signed on 29th September 1938 by Chamberlain, Daladier, Mussolini and Hitler.

p. 33 'a village not far away': on the night of 23rd September 1916 a German Zeppelin was brought down at Little Wigborough and the crew taken prisoner.

p. 34 'the county town': Chelmsford.

P.C. 'Me': Police Constable Dawes. Lived at 11 Spring Crescent, Tolleshunt D'Arcy.

p. 36 'Fishling': Maldon.

'Bastian': Colchester (elsewhere spelled 'Bastion').

p. 38 Charlie: Charles Flack (see Appendix I).

'the Prime Minister': Neville Chamberlain.

p. 40 Joan and Cynthia: Joan Barker and Cynthia Tatchell (see Appendix I). Mr and Mrs Carr Seabrook (see Appendix I).

Spanish Civil War 1936-1939. German intervention on the Nationalist side had included the terror bombing of towns, eg Guernica in April 1937.

p. 41 Ronnie and Mary Reid, long-standing friends of Margery and Pip.

Dr James Madden, another life-long friend lived in Tollesbury where he was the G.P. He is remembered by some patients as being blunt, 'if he thought you were skiving he told you so'.

Cliff: Cliff Otway (see Appendix I).

Sir Edmund Ironside (1880-1959) was a British Army officer who became Chief of the Imperial General Staff on the outbreak of WW2.

p. 43   'the Tye and Shadow Hill and Abbot's Dyke': Tudwick, Oxley Hill,
         The Wyck.
         'Clover or Cornell': Tolleshunt D'Arcy families (see Appendix I).
p. 44   Olive: Olive Nevill, daughter of Alfred Smith (see Appendix I).
p. 45   'the Premier's decision to fly to Germany': September 15th 1938,
         Chamberlain met Hitler at Berchtesgaden.
p. 46   'the second flight': Chamberlain met Hitler again at Bad Godesberg
         on September 22nd-23rd and flew for the third and final time on
         September 29th-30th for the Munich Conference and then for a
         private meeting with Hitler at which he obtained a signed paper
         expressing the desire of the two nations 'never to go to war again'.
p. 48   Clara: Clara Dickenson, daughter of Alfred Smith (see Appendix I).
p. 49   Ralph: Ralph Unwin, Tolleshunt D'Arcy youngster doing odd jobs
         for Margery's household (see Appendix I).
         Mrs Golding: Jessie Golding (see Appendix I).
p. 50   Miss Drudge lived at High View, Station Road, Tolleshunt D'Arcy.
p. 53   'the A.R.P. officer': Margery's diary mentions various men from out-
         side Tolleshunt D'Arcy who were prominent in the organisation of
         local defence. Messrs McLaren, Motts, Drewett and Bright are
         among them.
p. 54   'When Adam delved': part of a sermon by Lollard priest, John Ball,
         during the Peasant's revolt of 1381.
p. 56   Bill: Bill Cottis (see Appendix I).
         Charlotte: Charlotte Smith (see Appendix I).
p. 58   The term Civil Defence came into widespread use in the late 1930s
         though several of its constituent parts, (such as Air Raid Precautions)
         had been in existence since WW1.
p. 59   Granny: Emily Jane Hughes, born 1852. Her father was William
         Allingham, born c1800.
p. 61   P.B.I.: poor bloody infantry.
p. 62   Orkney Scottish ex-Army instructor cf. note on p.53.
p. 63   Illingworth: Leslie Illingworth (1902-1979), Fleet Street cartoonist
         then working regularly for *Punch*. Joined *Daily Mail* 1939.
         Oleograph: colour lithograph on canvas imitating an oil painting.
         Process first developed in Germany, late18th / early19th century.
         'The Light of the World' is by Holman Hunt: 'The Infant Samuel'
         is by Sir Joshua Reynolds.
p. 65   'the rape of the rest of Czechoslovakia': March 1939. On returning
         from Munich in Sept 1938 Chamberlain compared himself with
         Lord Beaconsfield returning from the Congress of Berlin in 1878.
p. 66   The Observer Corps: the Observer Corps had been mobilised

briefly at the time of the Munich Crisis. Organisational problems identified then were worked on at intervals throughout 1939. Observer posts were manned continuously from September 3rd 1939 to 12th May 1945.

Mr Eve: Mr Weston Eve (see Appendix I).

'The Specials': Special Constables. Margery Allingham's father had served in this way in WW1.

Recruiting sergeants were traditionally allowed to recruit 'by beat of drum', a means of attracting attention and exciting potential recruits before they were persuaded to take the king's shilling.

p. 67   *Old Moore's Almanack*: an astrological almanac published annually in Britain since 1697.

Miss Susie: Miss Susannah Emeny (see Appendix I).

Maginot Line: fortifications constructed between 1930 and 1940 along Franco-German border. Believed impregnable but actually outflanked by blitzkrieg tactics.

Albert Canal: dug 1930-39, connects Antwerp and Liège.

p. 68   Mr. Saye (see Appendix I).

p. 69   Alec: probably Alec Coker (see Appendix I).

Jack Hargreaves: 1911-1994, friend of Margery & Pip. Later well known as T.V. presenter of *Out of Town*, served in Royal Artillery during WW2.

p. 70   Cressie: Leslie Cresswell (1896-1979) friend of Margery & Pip. Highly regarded technical illustrator specialising in sectional drawings of cars, boats, engines. Suffered from shell-shock in WW1.

p. 77   German invasion of Poland, 1st September 1939.

'Uncle Beastly': BBC announcer Alvar Liddell (1908-1981). Later in the war 'this is the news and this is Alvar Liddell reading it' became a catch-phrase.

'Lady of Shallott weather': In Tennyson's poem 'The sun came dazzling through the leaves, / And flamed upon the brazen greaves / Of bold Sir Lancelot.'

Guildhall fire: 29th December 1940.

p. 78   'her brother': Christina Carter was one of nine children. The second eldest brother was Frederick. Margery's nickname for Christina was 'Fump'.

p. 79   'they all': Herbert Bullard (see Appendix I).

'Driffy': Driffield Smyth (see Appendix I).

Johnny Reynolds (see Appendix I).

Remount station: Army remount stations for the provision of horses and mules had been established in the 1890s and were especially important during WW1. Civilian grooms were needed in times of emergency. During WW2 the service was merged with the Army Veterinary Corps. The Essex depot was at Brentwood.

p. 80   'my brother Phil': Phil Allingham (1906-1968) author of *Cheapjack*.

p. 81   Medical Officer: Dr Bullough

p. 83   'the blood writers': writers of popular adventure fiction – such as Margery's father Herbert Allingham. *The Wizard* was one of the D.C. Thomson 'Big Five' comics. In 1930s the adventures of Sexton Blake, 'the poor man's Sherlock Holmes' were published in Fleetway Publications' *Detective Weekly* (previously *Union Jack*) and also the Sexton Blake Library.

p. 85   'my own work': Margery was in the early stages of her thriller *Traitor's Purse*.

p. 86   September 3rd 1939, declaration of war.

p. 88   Miss Christie: Miss Theresa Christie lived in Church Street, Tolleshunt D'Arcy.

p. 89   'ten-and-six': ten shillings and sixpence is fifty two and a half pence in today's money. A meaningless figure. Perhaps easiest to understand in comparison with Sam Taylor's weekly wages as a gardener, thirty five shillings and sixpence (one pound seventy seven and a half pence) for a married man with two young children (plus insurance). Or the rent of a cottage, between three shillings and seven-and-six per week.
'Better *is* a dinner of herbs where love is, than a stalled ox and hatred therewith' from Proverbs 15.17 (King James Bible translation).

p. 90   'ack-ack fire': anti-aircraft fire

p. 91   The *People's War* site includes an account of similar red double-decker buses arriving at Tollesbury. (www.bbc.co.uk/ww2peopleswar/stories/82/a8788882.shtml)

p. 93   'ballad': quote so far unidentified. The pregnant evacuated mothers, and those with very young babies, made a special appeal to Margery. She used the 'pink tickets' and general confusion as background for her later novel, *The China Governess*.

p. 95   Bret Harte (1836-1902): American author and poet, much influenced by Dickens.
Mark Benney (real name Henry Degras): b 1910, best known for autobiographical *Low Company*, the tale of a reformed burglar.
Jane Degras: left wing economist, specialising in Soviet and east European planned economies.

p. 97   Jessie Matthews (1907-1981) English actress, dancer, singer, born in London in a large, relatively impoverished family.

p. 98 Mr Spooner (see Appendix I).

p. 100 food committees: set up at the outbreak of war. Local traders and consumers charged with implementing ration and coping with unexpected surges of demand from arrivals of evacuees.

p. 101 Jessie Bacon: housekeeper to Dr Salter (see Appendix I).

p. 107 'Goldenhind': Goldhanger.

p. 109 Mr & Mrs Eaton (see Appendix I).

p. 110 Charles Haddon Spurgeon (1834-1892) born Kelvedon, Essex. George Price (1901-1995) contributed cartoons to the *New Yorker* for over fifty years.

p. 111 Phoebe 'had seen a bus and got on it' – clear influence on the plot of Margery's *The China Governess* (1958).

p. 113 The Unemployment Assistance Board was set up in 1934 to provide means-tested benefits.

p. 114 Reception Area: under the scheme drawn up during 1938 by the Ministry of Health the country was divided into three areas, evacuation, neutral and reception, each comprising roughly one-third of the population.

p. 115 Miss Gene and Miss Beattie Emeny (see Appendix I).

p. 118 'Now the bombs have really come': Margery was writing *The Oaken Heart* during early part of the Blitz period. This lasted from 7th September 1940 to 10th May 1941 when London was bombed for seventy-six consecutive nights. By the end of May 1941 43,000 people across the country had been killed by bombing.
'Didikye': usually spelled didicoy. A term for travellers who are not pure Roma. Can be used to refer to all Gypsies.
Swiss Family Robinson: shipwreck novel (1812) by Johann Wyss intended to instruct children about family values, self-reliance, uses of the natural world.

p. 119 'female Blimp': Colonel Blimp was a cartoon character drawn by David Low for the London *Evening Standard*, satirising the Army and reactionary values (rather in the same way that Margery's household had joked about the Regular Army as 'Featherstones'). The film *Life and Death of Colonel Blimp* came out in 1943.
'barnstormers': in 1920s this term referred to stunt pilots giving aerial displays as part of a flying circus. Also applied to U.S. political campaigns in rural areas.

p. 122 Mr Spitty: not identified.

p. 123 'Cynthia's mother': Cynthia Tatchell and Joan Barker were the daughters of Mr & Mrs Hortin who owned the Guisnes Court estate. The Mama's House is described by Margery as a coastguard cottage but is remembered by Alan Smith as the gamekeeper's cottage.

p. 124   Bea: Beatrice Smyth (see Appendix I).
          Mrs Foster (see Appendix I).

p. 125   'Never mole, hairlip nor scar': from *Midsummer Night's Dream*.

p. 126   'grass-widow': a woman separated from her husband.

p. 127   Joey: not identified.
          'balloon': the phrase 'the balloon's gone up' (meaning there's about
          to be action) comes from the use of barrage balloons in WW1.

p. 128   George's mother: could be mother of George Whipps or George
          Read, both Tolleshunt D'Arcy residents (see Appendix I).

p. 132   The Somme, etc: Historian Juliet Gardiner suggests that more than
          30% of all men aged between twenty to twenty four in 1914 were
          killed in the First World War, and 28% of those aged thirteen to
          nineteen.

p. 135   *Inferno*: reference to Dante's *Divine Comedy*.
          'Coop's cat': Robert St John Cooper, friend of Margery & Pip, was
          a cartoonist, animator and later script-writer.
          William Hickey: Tom Driberg (1905-1976) was 'William Hickey'
          from 1933.
          Beachcomber: pen name for J.B. Morton (1893-1979).

p. 136   *News Chronicle*: daily newspaper (1930-1960) owned by the Cad-
          bury family. Liberal in politics eg anti-Franco in Spanish Civil War.

p. 137   Sir Samuel Hoare (1880-1959): Conservative politician, Home Sec-
          retary 1937-39.
          Cosmo Gordon Lang (1864-1945) was Archbishop of Canterbury
          1928-1942.

p. 138   'George Playle and Long Un': people Margery remembered from
          WW1 in Layer Breton.
          Lord Haw-Haw: announcers (mainly William Joyce) on the propa-
          ganda programme *Germany Calling* which was broadcast from
          Hamburg 1939-1945.

p. 140   Russian invasion of Poland: 17th September 1939. Fall of Warsaw
          28th September.
          'Low's caricature "Idealism ...": see illustration.

p. 143   Martha Cracknell (see Appendix I).
          Invasion of Finland by Soviet Union: the 'Winter War' 30th
          November 1939 – 13th March 1940. British and French attempts to
          intervene were thwarted by Norway and Sweden refusing access
          through their territories.

p. 145   Tiff and Mrs Tiff: Mr & Mrs Lingley (see Appendix I).
          'Mrs Tiff became devoted to the child': interesting parallel with the

situation in *Doreen* (1946) an evacuation novel written by Margery's
later colleague Barbara Noble.

p. 146   William Hogarth, artist, 1697-1764.

p. 148   Woolworth's: founded in U.S.A. 1879 as a 'five-and-dime store',
came to U.K. 1909.

p. 151   Dick Houlding (see Appendix I).

Mr Maskall: Richard Maskell, undertaker, lived in North Road,
Tollesbury.

'won the shield: Local competitions involving challenges such as
hose-running drills were still held in the early years of the war.

'heroes in the Blitz': this could refer to assistance in Essex fires, for
instance at Thames Haven which was frequently bombed, or the
Tollesbury brigade could have exchanged with one of the London
services to give them respite (as Witham did with Walthamstow).

p. 152   'the Major': Gerald Tatchell. The others mentioned are Albert and
Sam Clover, George Bouttell, Joe Pudney, Fred Cockle (from Salcott), Alec Coker, Stan Goody, Geoffrey Townsend, Mr Ford and
his sons, Fred Braddy, 'Smiler' and 'Tiddles' Cornell, Alf Goody,
Frank Hart, Mr Spooner, Harold Curtis, 'Mrs's Chaplin's daughter's
husband', George (?Whipps), Johnny (Jimmy) Burmby, Mr Todd,
Tony, Francis and Brian Seabrook – (see Appendix I).

'submarine': This was the *Thistle* sunk on April 10th 1940 by the
U-boat U4.

p. 153   The *Rawalpindi* was the first of fifteen Armed Merchant Cruisers to
be lost in WW2. An exceptionally vivid account by one of the few
survivors can be found on the BBC *People's War* site
(www.bbc.co.uk/ww2peopleswar/stories/79/a1984179.shtml)
Betty James and Miss Smith (see Appendix I).

The R.A.S.C. (Royal Army Service Corps) is responsible for deliv-
ering all supplies up to the front line.

p. 154   'my father': Herbert Allingham (1867-1936) cf. *Fifty Years in the Fiction Factory*.

p. 157   'Joyce ... on leave from the Wrens': Joyce Allingham joined the
W.R.N.S. early in the war and served until the early 1950s.
searchlight unit: unidentified.

p.158   a buggy was a light two wheeled carriage common in the 19th and
early 20th centuries.

'Mudlarking': Salcott.

'roughing horses': usually roughing a horse off means turning it out
into a field or reducing its work. Here the meaning is more likely to
be taking off the shoes, heating them in the forge and turning down

the heels so as to form a sharp projection that will cut into ice or frozen snow.

'paraffin-lit winters': no electricity in the Layer Breton house.

p. 159 'Cobber' Kain (1918-1940). New Zealand-born R.A.F. flying 'Ace'. Awarded Distinguished Flying Cross in March 1940. Killed in June 1940 when performing low-level acrobatics in his Hurricane.

p. 160 'Fordie': Joseph Ford (see Appendix I).

p.161   'the splendid folk from Poynters': unidentified.

p.162   'The fall of Finland': March 13th 1940.

Loss of the *Thistle* April 10th 1940 (Margery heard news on April 16th). By an odd co-incidence a Tollesbury fishing smack, also called the *Thistle*, was sunk by a mine off Clacton beach in 1940.

p. 163 'the nation had found its soul': Comment made by Churchill around March 27th 1941 when Yugoslavia briefly defied Germany and over-threw the government who had signed the Tripartite Pact. Hitler invaded and conquered the country in April 1941.

p. 165 'the evacuation from Dunkirk': 26th May–4th June 1940. Cf. account of the Tollesbury smack the *Iris Mary*. (www.bbc.co.uk/ww2peo-pleswar/stories/51/a7915151.shtml) The *Iris Mary* was halted at Ramsgate as deemed too small to continue. The sailing barge *Tollesbury* was towed from Dover to Dunkirk with stores and towed back on June 1st with 200 rescued troops. (For details see www.adls.org.uk/t1/node/521).

p. 166 'Hitler had missed the bus': 4th April 1940 Chamberlain claimed that Hitler had failed to follow up his initial advantage. A workman's bus would have left much earlier.

p. 167 Denmark captured April 9th. Landings in Norway began that day. Final surrender June 10th 1940.

p. 168 'Naught shall make us rue' – from Shakespeare's *King John*.

B.E.F.: British Expeditionary force.

May 7th – 8th Parliamentary debate – no confidence in Chamber-lain. For a clear and compelling account of the debate cf. *The Age of Illusion* by Ronald Blythe.

p. 169 Winston Churchill became Prime Minister May 10th 1940.

'the unchanging bulldog': Churchill himself pointed out, in 1916, that a bulldog's jaw allows him to breathe whilst continuing to bite.

p. 171 Nerney: Winifred Nerney was U.S. publisher Doubleday's repre-sentative in London and a close friend of Margery.

p. 175 Herbert Allingham's story *The World Aflame* had been written in the early months of WW1.

p. 176 William McFee (Mac) (1881-1966): author, ship's engineer,

Allingham family friend.

Thermopylae: famous last stand of the Greek city-states defending themselves against Persian invasion.

p. 177   Paul Reynolds: Margery's U.S. agent. Cf. Margery's diary entry 14th May 1940.

p. 178   Queen of Holland: Queen Wilhelmina (1880-1962) ruled the Netherlands from 1890-1948 and proved an inspiration to the Dutch Resistance.

p. 179   Mr Sayer: saddler (see Appendix I).

p. 183   Mrs Molesworth (1821-1921). One of her best-known books was the *Cuckoo Clock*, which emphasised charming and wonderful German workmanship.

'The Nuremberg Stove' was a story by Ouida, published in 1882.

Arthur Fletcher worked for the Allingham family at Layer Breton.

Lord Northcliffe, founder of the *Daily Mail*, was in charge of propaganda to enemy countries in the last years of WW1. Within Britain his papers have been held responsible for inflaming anti-German feeling.

'the Glebe garden': The Glebe was a separate building attached to Layer Breton Rectory where the Allingham children lived.

p. 184   Cissie: nursemaid at Layer Breton.

p. 187   'On Sunday morning': May 19th 1940. General Gamelin (1872-1958) Commander of French General Staff. Assured Prime Minister Daladier that France had the greatest army in the world. Sacked 17th May 1940.

Mr & Mrs Parker (see Appendix I).

p. 188   Robert Graves *Goodbye to All That* was published in 1929. Edmund Blunden's *Undertones of War* 1928.

p. 189   L.D.Vs: Local Defence Volunteers, better known by Churchill's name 'the Home Guard'. Call for volunteers 14th May 1940. 250,000 men came forward within 24 hours. A glimpse of the Tollesbury Home Guard can be found on The *People's War* site (www.bbc.co.uk/ww2peopleswar/stories/41/a7920641.shtml)

Churchill's first broadcast to the nation as Prime Minister (May 19th 1940) took as its text 'Be ye men of valour'. His 'fight them on the beaches' speech was made on June 4th 1940 after the retreat from Dunkirk.

Queen Elizabeth's famous speech made at Tilbury, Essex, on the eve of the Armada 1588. 'I have the heart and stomach of a king and a King of England too.'

p. 190   When Churchill visited Paris he discovered that the French were defeated and Britain alone in Europe.

General Weygand was recalled from Syria to replace General Gamelin.

Margery's 36th birthday: 20th May 1940.

p. 191   Samuel Pepys (1633-1703) Great Fire of London 1666.

'my thriller': *Traitor's Purse*, published 1941.

'Great-grandfather': William James Allingham (1803-1874).

p. 192   'Grandfather': James Allingham (1841-1920).

'On the Wednesday night': May 22nd 1940.

The Emergency Powers (Defence) Act 1940 required persons 'to place themselves, their services and their property at the disposal of His Majesty'.

p. 193   'a great foreigner': Joseph P. Kennedy senior (1888-1961), U.S. ambassador to Britain 1938-1940. Term of office ended abruptly in November 1940 when he said that there was 'no democracy left in Britain'. Previously he had asserted that 'the British are a lost cause'.

p. 194   Soldiers from the Ninth Cameronians arrived at D'Arcy House 23rd May 1940. The battalion had been raised in 1939 and formed part of the UK defence force. In December 1942 they began training for D-Day and finally sailed for France in June 1944.

p. 195   Kiel was a major naval base and ship-building centre for the German Reich.

p. 198   King's speech: 24th May 1940.

'the address before Agincourt': from Shakespeare's *Henry V.*

p. 199   'I had been asleep about two hours': cf diary May 25th 1940.

p. 202   'capitulation of the Belgian Army': cf diary May 28th 1940.

King Albert of the Belgians (1875-1934). Succeeded by his son Leopold III. Belgium was invaded 10th May, co-ordination with the British Expeditionary Force was unsuccessful but the Belgians continued to fight long enough for the B.E.F. to retreat to Dunkirk. Leopold remained in Brussels after his surrender.

p. 203   Dunkirk: Battle of Dunkirk lasted from May 25th to June 3rd. On 4th June 1940 Margery stuck a 4 leaved clover in her diary. The first request was for shallow draught vessels 30' – 100'. Later requirements changed and some of the vessels that set off from Tollesbury (such as the *Iris Mary*) were stopped at Ramsgate as being too small. 338,226 people finally recovered.

p. 206   'Fifth Column activity': Margery's diary for May 30th notes 'a certain amount of spy excitement everywhere'.

'elephant's child': reference to Rudyard Kipling's *Just-So* stories.

'the period of probation': Gloria Greci, later Margery's secretary, used to visit her parents in Tolleshunt D'Arcy during the war and was surprised by the village unfriendliness to strangers.

p. 209   Paris was occupied by the Germans on June 14th and signed armistice June 22nd.

p. 210   Roosevelt introduced the Lend-Lease Bill to the House of Representatives 10th January 1941. He compared his proposal to lending a neighbour a garden hose to put out a fire.

p. 212   'Aunt': Maud Hughes, editor of *The Picture Show*.

p. 213   Mr Swing: Raymond Gram Swing (1887-1968) broadcaster. Chairman of the Council for Democracy which was formed in 1940 to combat American isolationism.
Mr Willkie: Wendell Wilkie (1892-1944). Opposed Franklin Roosevelt in 1940 Presidential Election but shared his ideals re Europe and travelled as an informal ambassador-at-large.
Mr Winant: John G Winant (1889-1947). U.S. Ambassador 1941-1946. Declared on arrival in March 1941 that 'There is no place I would rather be at this time than in England'.

p. 214   Capitulation of France: cf. Margery's diary 17th June 1940.

p. 216   soldiers: King's Own Scottish Borderers.
The M.M. is the Military Medal and is awarded for bravery. The Mons Star is a WW1 campaign medal.
'our first genuine air raid': 7th June 1940.

p. 217   'all the Wardens': Joe Gregory, Cliff Otway, Reg Hammond, Sam Taylor, Johnny Reynolds, Herbert Bullard (see Appendix I).

p. 218   'where a Zepp came down': Margery's diary notes bombs at Wigborough 21st June 1940.

p. 222   Battle of Britain: June-September 1940.

p. 224   Ernie Chaplin (see Appendix I).

p. 227   Mr Withers's bungalow was in the neighbouring village of Tolleshunt Knights.

p. 228   'how very small': As Churchill said on 20th August 1940, 'Never in the field of human conflict was so much owed by so many to so few.'

p. 229   'just before the beginning': the London Blitz began 6th September 1940.

p. 231   'the Mayor of the county town': Mr John Ockleford Thompson, Mayor of Chelmsford and Editor of the *Essex Chronicle*. Thompson had edited a single volume of Dr Salter's dairies. All the rest of Salter's papers were destroyed in this catastrophe.
'Mr Eaton had his own farm straddled twice': 21st October 1940.

p. 233   'after the first big night raid': On the afternoon of 7th September 1940 London was attacked by 364 bombers, escorted by 515 fighters.

Another 133 bombers attacked during the night. The bombs were mainly aimed at the docks but many also fell on neighbouring residential areas killing 464 Londoners and injuring 1665.

p. 234   'oil bombs': incendiary devices which ignited oil on impact.

'time bombs': bombs fitted with delayed fuses or timing devices to increase fear and uncertainty in the civilian population. Unexploded bombs also presented problems. During 1940 the Royal Engineers began to encounter fuses incorporating anti-handling devices, specifically designed to kill bomb disposal personnel.

'home on a mud island': Foulness Island.

p. 239   'as the Greeks have shown us': Greece and Yugoslavia resisted the Axis invasion for three and a half weeks from April 6th 1941.

p. 241   'exact location of each crater': incident books recording bombs dropped in the Tolleshunt D'Arcy area are stored in the Essex Record Office.

p. 243   Mr Read (see Appendix I).

Mr Dice who lost the roof of his bungalow lived in Tudwick but could have been at one of three different addresses. 'Mexico' has not been precisely identified.

'full-dress fight': rural fire brigades were frequently required to help in the more severely bombed areas.

p. 244   Ken: Ken Osborne whose family owned and ran the local bus service.

p. 247   'top floor of a big block of offices not far from St Paul's': assume this was the Amalgamated Press offices at Fleetway House.

Roof-spotters were posted on the tops of buildings to sound alarm in case of imminent danger.

p. 248   'the little flat': Middle Row Place, High Holborn.

p. 249   German films: produced in Weimar Republic 1919-1933 in expressionist style. *Alraune und der Golem* (1919), *Die Nibelungen* (1924), *Faust* (1926).

'the very old church': St Giles in the Fields, just off Charing Cross Road in London's West End. Lost all its glass in the war but otherwise escaped serious damage.

'the restaurant': Frascati's, 32, Oxford Street.

p. 252   The King: George VI drove through Tolleshunt D'Arcy to inspect defences at Tollesbury on 31st October 1940.

p. 253   'When his best house was bombed': Buckingham Palace was damaged on 10th September 1940. Queen Elizabeth said 'I am glad we have been bombed. It makes me feel I can look the East End in the face.'

p. 255   'our new neighbour': Mr Ford.

p. 256   'hokey-pokey': slang term for ice-cream sold by street vendors, mainly of Italian origin.

're-election of President Roosevelt': 5th November 1940.

p. 257   'relations at Coventry': Coventry, an industrial city with munitions factories, was bombed many times in the autumn of 1940, notably on the night of 14th November when approximately 600 people were killed and 1000 injured in the one night. Portsmouth, as an important naval base, was also heavily bombed. 930 people were killed and 1,216 people were injured.

'other friends were not so lucky': cf. Margery's diary 1st January 1941.

p. 259   Aunt: Maud Hughes continued working as editor of *The Picture Show* and moved into the Regent's Palace Hotel.

p. 260   Marie Lloyd (1870-1922), music hall singer. Song may be 'One of the ruins that Cromwell knocked about a bit'.

p. 262   Noel Coward (1899-1973). *Cavalcade* (1931) included WW1 scenes. General Strike, May 1926. Margery's parents had moved out to Suffolk leaving her in a studio flat.

p. 263   Aunt Halifax : unidentified.

p. 266   Emily Hughes was at a finishing school in Germany.

'when Julia used to read the Times': Julia Allingham (Nowell) was Emily's older sister. General MacMahon (1808-1893) was a French aristocrat who fought in Algeria and the Crimea and did indeed lose to Prussia at the Battle of Sedan in 1870. He became President of the French Republic in 1875.

p. 267   American Civil War 1861-65. 'Uncle Wallie': Walter Hughes was killed in June 1916. His name is commemorated on Menin Gate memorial in Ypres.

Fall of Greece 6th April 1941.

Haile Selassie (1892-1975) Emperor of Ethiopia, exiled 1936. Returned 18th January 1941 and subsequently defeated occupying Italians with British and South African help. Re-entered Addis Ababa 5th May 1941.

'Parliament must sit in another room': the Palace of Westminster was severely damaged by bombing 10th / 11th May and the Commons Chamber was destroyed.

'Mr Ford's pig club': Pigs were fed with members' scraps and clubs were also allowed to purchase small rations. When the pig was slaughtered, half went to the government and half to the members. Margery was involved in this communal effort and used pig-keeping in her novel *Coroner's Pigeon* (1945).

p. 268   waterglass: sodium silicate.

'Where are you going to ...?': Rudyard Kipling, written for *A School History of England* (1911). Marg may have been the daughter of Mr Todd, killed on the *Thistle*. Her mother was housekeeper to Miss Bright in West Street, Tolleshunt D'Arcy.

'I know where he is': 'If you want to find the sergeant major' – soldier's song from WW1.

p. 270   'Your peace aims?': the Labour and Conservative parties had entered a coalition in 1940 and work was formally begun on post-war social reconstruction in June 1941. This led to the best-selling Beveridge Report, published in 1942.

p. 272   Christ's Hospital: school attended by P.Y.C as well as Joe Gregory and other of Margery's friends. A charity school with fees paid on a means-tested basis and a significant proportion of pupils educated free.

p. 275   Rudolf Hess (1894-1987): deputy German Fuehrer, flew to Scotland 10th May 1941 in an attempt to negotiate a separate peace with Britain. He was imprisoned for the rest of his life. His death was officially recorded as suicide but remains controversial.

Right: Mrs Moore and her school. *(Meg Bunting)*

Index of People and Places

Above: Tolleshunt D'Arcy War Memorial: Edward B. Chaplin, Donald R. Ford, Eric A. French, Julian H. Hortin, Alfred E. Keeble, John S. King, Edward J. Lock, Anthony D. Seabrook, Joseph Todd, Gerald E. Tatchell. *(Lesley Simpson)*